THE ADENAUER ERA

THE
ADENAUER

RICHARD HISCOCKS

Philadelphia / New York
J. B. Lippincott Company

ERA

THE LIPPINCOTT HISTORY SERIES

under the editorship of Robert F. Byrnes,
Indiana University

This book has been published in England under the title *Germany Revived.*

This rule holds good for the national community as it does for the life of an individual: what distress and suffering has destroyed is counterbalanced by the new forces, full of generative power and irresistible, which distress and suffering call into being.

—HERMANN ONCKEN

Preface

This book makes no pretence at being a systematic history of Western Germany under Adenauer. It is intended rather as a provisional appraisal of the Adenauer era, in which an attempt has been made to weigh up its positive and negative sides. I have sought to avoid any unnecessary overlap with my earlier volume, *Democracy in Western Germany* (Oxford University Press, 1957); and for this reason I have included little, for example, about the civil service and political education, both of which were subjects of importance during the first half of Adenauer's regime. I have not attempted, either, to deal with Adenauer's activities since he resigned in October 1963, because this phase of his career is not yet over.

During frequent visits to Germany since the war I have made many friends and have met and talked with a very large number of men and women who have influenced, in varying degrees, the process of revival with which these pages are mainly concerned. It would be impossible to mention them all, and invidious to make distinctions, but I wish to express my sincere thanks to all of them for the valuable help they have given me. To Dr.

Adenauer himself I am most grateful for his kindness in receiving me on two occasions and for the patience and courtesy with which he answered numerous questions. I have been particularly fortunate also in having had opportunities for long conversations with most of his closest political associates. More generally I should like to thank members of the staff of the organization known as *Internationes*: the British and Canadian ambassadors in Bonn and their staffs: the British Council representative in the German Federal Republic; and the librarians of the Bundestag and of the Federal Constitutional Court in Karlsruhe.

I am very grateful to all those who have helped in the task of preparing my manuscript for the press; in particular the following, who by their criticisms have saved me from many errors: Mr. T. H. M. Baker, Dr. J. C. G. Röhl, Dr. Hans Schuster, Dr. S. J. Wells, and Miss Elizabeth Wiskemann. For any errors that remain and for the opinions expressed I am, of course, entirely responsible.

In the bibliography I have confined myself to a short list of books that are likely to be of interest to the general reader and to a second list giving details of all other books and articles referred to in the text or footnotes.

Finally I should like to express my warm thanks to Sir Victor Gollancz and Mr. James MacGibbon for suggesting that I should write a book on the Adenauer Era.

R. H.

University of Sussex
December 1965

Contents

1
The Historical Setting

Only eighteen years after Hitler's defeat Western Germany had become a trusted member of the North Atlantic alliance and one of the most prosperous and economically powerful countries in the world. In May 1945, when the Nazi government signed its unconditional surrender, the German people were exhausted, disillusioned and bewildered. Their country was in a state of confusion and anarchy: its highly centralized totalitarian administration had collapsed; its cities were mostly damaged or destroyed; its communications had broken down; and its economy was largely out of action. By 1963 Western Germany, which in area is not much more than half the size of the Germany of 1937,[1] had foreign trade which in volume was second only to that of the United States; its railways, motorroads and airlines were excellent; its rebuilt cities included some of the best examples of modern town-planning; its population, which before the war was 42,999,000, had increased to 57,588,000;[2] its economy had absorbed over 13 million refugees and expellees and more than a million foreign workers; its armed forces amounted to more than 400,000 men and, after

[1] 247,978 square kilometers compared with 470,700 square kilometers in 1937.
[2] Including West Berlin.

the American forces, formed the largest military contribution to NATO.

For the first four of these eighteen years Germany was under Allied military government. During the remaining fourteen the head of the West German government was its chancellor, Dr. Konrad Adenauer. When Adenauer became chancellor in September 1949 he was seventy-three, and only a year younger than Bismarck at the time of his retirement. Five years earlier, in a Nazi prison, Adenauer's Gestapo gaoler had pleaded with him not to commit suicide on the ground that his life was over in any case. In the autumn of 1945 a British brigadier had dismissed him from his post as mayor of Cologne on a charge of incompetence.

Adenauer's progress towards the chancellorship was accompanied by a considerable amount of luck. But like the luck of other great men his good fortune was reinforced by determination and an ability to recognize opportunities when they arose. His dismissal from Cologne was a big stroke of luck in itself. Adenauer had been born in Cologne, he loved the city, and he had been its mayor with great success from 1917 to 1933. There is no reason to doubt that he would have been well content to spend the post-war years and the end of his working life in the arduous but rewarding task of rebuilding his home town which had suffered terrible destruction during the war. His abrupt exclusion from municipal politics by the British military governor opened up possibilities for still more important activity at a zonal and finally at a national level. Adenauer was not one of the original founders of the Christian Democratic Union (CDU), the party with which he was to become so closely identified. But at a meeting of its provisional zonal committee early in 1946 he became chairman by a piece of brash self-assertion. The meeting had been called by a Dr. Holzapfel. But Adenauer, seeing the chairman's seat vacant, sat down in it, saying that as the oldest person present he would consider himself, if no one objected, as chairman by seniority. He was shortly afterwards elected chairman of the party in the British zone with Dr. Holzapfel as his deputy. When the first elections to the West German Bundestag (parliament) took place in August 1949, it was widely believed that the Social Democratic Party (SPD) would win the largest number of seats. But actually the CDU obtained eight more than the SPD, and Adenauer was elected chancellor by a margin of one vote, which he has admitted was his own.

When Adenauer became chancellor his name was hardly known outside Germany. Even in his own country a public opinion poll conducted at the time revealed that not more than 8 per cent of the population had heard of him.

In spite of the fortuitous element in his success, Adenauer has given his name to an era. His regime lasted for several months longer than the Weimar Republic and for two years longer than Hitler's "Thousand Year Reich." Within four years of his taking office as chancellor he was referred to by Winston Churchill in the House of Commons as the wisest German statesman since Bismarck.

As a staunch supporter of the Western alliance and an inflexible opponent of communism, Adenauer naturally arouses widely different reactions in different countries and amongst exponents of conflicting political creeds. But amongst members of each political party in Western Germany and amongst citizens of Western democratic countries opinions about him also vary considerably. Even the nickname, the Old Man (Der Alte), by which he increasingly came to be known, might imply respect for a paternal and venerable figure or alternatively some impatience at having to tolerate indefinitely the authority of an increasingly opinionated veteran.

The Adenauer era cannot yet be seen in clear perspective while Adenauer himself is still alive, still playing an active part in German politics, and still kicking against the fact that he is no longer chancellor. But the attempt to estimate it involves trying to understand postwar Germany, and is therefore worth making. Its significance can best be judged in its broad historical setting.

In German history the half century which preceded the First World War was a period of brilliant military, diplomatic, and economic achievement. Within a few years and after three successful wars Bismarck united most of Germany under Prussian leadership and founded a new German empire with the King of Prussia as its Emperor and himself as its chancellor. During the next two decades, by a combination of diplomatic skill and moderation, he managed to consolidate his country's new position in spite of the resentment of a defeated France and the periodic fears and misgivings of Russia. Germany's economic progress was due rather to scientific and technical than to political developments, but it also got into its stride while Bismarck was chancellor. From being a predominantly rural country during the first half of the nineteenth century Germany became one of the greatest industrial nations of the world. Its output of coal rose from 30 million tons in 1871 to 190 million tons in 1913. Steel production increased from 0.9 million tons in 1886 to 13.1 million tons in 1910, when it exceeded British production by 72.7 per cent. The textile industry multiplied its production tenfold between 1878 and 1905, while the country's high standard of education gave it the leadership in the new chemical and electrical industries. During the quarter century starting in 1887 imports increased by 243.8 per cent and exports by 185.4 per cent. The increase in Germany's total volume of trade exceeded substantially the rate of increase both of Britain and of the United States.

But these great successes were accompanied by sinister developments and weaknesses in internal politics and national leadership. Bismarck unified Germany at the cost of defeating and sacrificing German liberalism. Soon after taking office he acted unconstitutionally and defied parliament against the protests of liberal politicians. Up to that time the liberals had been able to combine their national aspirations with their belief in political freedom and parliamentary government. Now they had to choose between the two. In the face of Bismarck's military and diplomatic triumphs and the long delayed unification of their country the majority of them submitted to his leadership. A National Liberal Party was formed, which condoned his unconstitutional actions and later supported his persecution of Catholics and Socialists. The German liberal movement never recovered from this betrayal. One of its most sinister aspects was that many of the intellectuals, including former leading champions of liberal policies, cast in their lot with the National Liberal Party.

Bismarck also, at a time when the whole trend in Europe was towards responsible government, steadily opposed the development of parliamentary democracy in Germany. He had been called to power during a deadlock between the King of Prussia and the assembly and had assured the King that he would rather perish with him "than forsake His Majesty in the contest with parliamentary government." He was astute enough to provide the new empire with a parliament (Reichstag) elected by secret ballot and universal suffrage. But this was little more than a deceptive gesture. The Imperial chancellor, or chief minister, was appointed by the Emperor and was responsible to him, not to parliament. Members of the Federal Council (Bundesrat), which combined the functions of second chamber and main executive organ, were not allowed to sit in the Reichstag. This meant that there was little inducement for able and ambitious politicians to enter the Reichstag, because it was not, as might have been expected, the normal channel to ministerial office. Ministers were more often chosen from the civil service than from the ranks of active politicians.

The system was clumsy and illogical. The Reichstag controlled expenditure and had the right to pass or reject laws.[3] Had it produced a leader of Bismarck's calibre, deadlock would have been inevitable. As it was, with Conservative and National Liberal support and by a mixture of bludgeoning and cajoling, the chancellor managed to work the constitution according to his will until he left office. When he fell in 1890, he had established a tradition of what one of his most distinguished critics, Theodor Mommsen, called "pseudo-constitutional absolutism," which was carried on by his less able and also less masterful successors. But the process of doing so almost exhausted Bismarck's ingenuity as well as his patience. He did not attempt to conceal the fact that he despised political parties and considered them unfit to govern an empire. He fought his political opponents with a ruthless lack of chivalry and described them, with a frank disdain for democratic propriety, as enemies of the state.

In 1918, when the Bismarckian constitutional system was on its last legs, Max Weber, referring to Bismarck's political legacy, wrote that he left behind a nation "without any kind of political education," . . . "without any kind of political will" . . . "a completely powerless parliament," whose powerlessness meant that it was at the same time "a parliament with deeply depressed intellectual standards." The state was run, he added, by professional civil servants and lacked the guidance and control of a politician—"Not of a political genius . . . not even of someone with considerable political ability, but of any politician at all."[4]

A third limitation in Bismarck's achievement related rather to his approach towards external relations than to his internal policy. Bismarck's political career coincided with an age of

[3] Bismarck, however, with National Liberal support introduced a system by which the army budget was voted for a period of seven years, so the Reichstag in practice had no year-to-year control of military expenditure.

[4] *Parlament und Regierung im Neugeordneten Deutschland*, Sections I and II, pp. 307, 308, 324.

intellectual ferment and unprecedented industrial and social development. The astonishing transformation and expansion of the German economy, which began during his chancellorship, can only be understood against a background of rapid progress in pure and applied science, the revolution in transport, and a world in which different countries were becoming increasingly conscious of their common interests and interdependence. Under these conditions Bismarck's strong emphasis on purely national considerations, though explicable in the light of his country's previous frustration, was untimely, inappropriate, and, from a long-term standpoint, unwise. Great Britain's economic heyday in the nineteenth century was supported by free trade and, on the whole, by a restrained and liberal foreign policy. Bismarck's diplomacy, with its concern for power politics and alliances, seemed to look backwards rather than forwards and to neglect consideration of the conditions which would best further the development of Germany's rapidly growing commercial interests. The English historian, G. P. Gooch, has written: "The presupposition of all profitable political and economic planning is a firm grasp of the unity of civilization. To the shaping of the human spirit for that supreme adventure of the human spirit he [Bismarck] contributed nothing."[5] The German historian, Franz Schnabel, wrote: "And the only standard by which peoples and civilizations can be measured and differentiated is whether a belief in a higher world order is alive within them. . . . He [Bismarck] had not the insight to see that in such a perplexing world there are tasks which extend far beyond the interests of the state."[6] A Scandinavian writer, Björnstjerne Björnson, has summed up this aspect of Bismarck thus briefly: "a chessplayer, who won every game, but meanwhile lost the future."[7]

[5] "Bismarck's Legacy" in Foreign Affairs, July 1952.
[6] "Das Problem Bismarcks" in Hochland, October 1949.
[7] Quoted by Josef Antz in "Bismarck und seine Wirkung auf das deutsche Volk," Frankfurter Hefte, January 1947.

Another unfortunate development which resulted from German unification was a further exaltation of the already self-confident and powerful Prussian military caste. It played an increasingly influential role in German society and politics at a time when scientific developments made militarism more and more dangerous. A company director would often take greater pride in being a lieutenant in the reserve than in his civilian position. Bismarck himself normally attended meetings of the Reichstag wearing the uniform of a Prussian general.

Prussia's military triumphs and the foundation of the empire gave rise to a great surge of self-confidence amongst the German ruling classes and Bismarck's numerous admirers. Frederick the Great and Bismarck had both set the example of divorcing ethical considerations from reasons of state, and the German government's policy came under the influence of a nationalism, which as a great German historian has pointed out, tended to become separated from morality and prepared the way for Hitlerism.[8] Leading intellectuals, generals, and members of the government fell victims to overconfident and insolent pride, which the ancient Greeks called *hubris*. Amongst them one of the most outstanding was the historian, Heinrich von Treitschke, who started his academic career as a fervent liberal, but in later years enlivened his lectures, which drew vast audiences, with severe criticisms of parliamentary government and arrogant national self-assertiveness. Austen Chamberlain, as a young man, attended Treitschke's lectures regularly and gave his impression of them in a letter written in 1887 and quoted in his memoirs:

Treitschke has opened to me a new side of the German character—a narrow-minded, proud, intolerant Prussian *chauvinism*. And the worst of it is that he is forming a school. If you continuously preach to the youth of a country that they stand on a

[8] Friedrich Meinecke, *Die deutsche Katastrophe*, pp. 41–42.

higher step of the creation to all other nations, they are only too ready to believe it. . . . But it's very dangerous. I fear my generation of Germans, and those a little younger will be far more high-handed and will presume far more on the victories of '66 and '70 than those who won them.[9]

Chamberlain unfortunately proved right. Treitschke had great influence on many Germans who held leading positions during the following crucial decades.

It is fair to point out, however, that during the whole period from the foundation of the empire until the fall of Hitler a comparatively small, perceptive, though not always articulate minority resisted the exaggerated nationalism and the autocratic tendencies of the age and maintained an ethical attitude towards political problems. On the evening of January 18, 1871, the day on which the empire was proclaimed at Versailles, a liberal-minded and idealistic south German prince, the Grand Duke Frederick of Baden, wrote a note in his diary that "this power [of the new empire] will henceforth only be used for good purposes, and that this must be the lesson, which our young German Empire brings home with it from amongst the historical memories of the Palace of Versailles."[10] Thirty-one years later Theodor Mommsen, who, as has been seen, was under no illusions as to the nature of Bismarck's internal policy, wrote to a friend that Bismarck had "broken the backbone of the nation"[11]—this at a time when Bismarck was the widely acclaimed hero of the great majority of his countrymen. In August 1918 Hans Delbrück, the famous historian, wrote:

[9] *Down the Years*, pp. 43–44.
[10] See Hermann Oncken, *Das Deutsche Reich und die Vorgeschichte des Weltkrieges*, Vol. I, p. 114.
[11] Letter to Lujo Brentano, January 3, 1902 (Kurt Rossman, *Wissenschaft, Ethik und Politik.*)

The world demands and has a right to demand that the German people should give it a guarantee that the pan-German spirit, the spirit of arrogance, of violence, of hostility to culture, of paganism is not the true German spirit.

Yet before we have crushed out pan-Germanism, its war aims and its blasphemous sermons about the German master nation . . . before then the hour cannot strike for peace negotiations.[12]

During his career as minister-president of Prussia and chancellor of the German Empire, Bismarck put into practice Ranke's theory of the primacy of foreign policy. Its inadequacy as a guide to action in the modern age was shown by the weakness of German leadership after Bismarck's dismissal and by the country's inability to solve its internal problems after the First World War. If too much attention is concentrated on foreign policy, there is a grave risk that unsatisfactory internal conditions will allow the control of foreign affairs to fall into the wrong hands. This happened twice in Germany, with the result that William II and Hitler led the country into two disastrous wars. If the constitutional system does not facilitate the emergence and employment of able political leaders, too much depends on the personal characteristics of the hereditary monarch and in a crisis such as arose in Germany at the end of the war, when the dynasty and the military leadership were both discredited, there are too few reserves to fall back upon.

Germany fared well enough under Bismarck on the basis of military strength, a rapidly expanding economy, and a policy of diplomatic restraint; but less well under William II with his swashbuckling diplomacy and his programme of naval expansion. The question of who was responsible for the First World War is highly complex and cannot be settled by the simple formula adopted by statesmen at Versailles. But William and his ministers bore a substantial share of blame for the 1914

[12] On August 18 and 29, 1918, in *Preussische Jahrbücher*, quoted by F. Meinecke, *op. cit.*, p. 50.

tragedy, though from the German point of view they were even more to blame for embarking on a conflict which ended in defeat. In the spring of 1918, within a few months of the empire's collapse, William declared that, if an English officer came to beg for peace, he would have to kneel before the Kaiser's standard, "because it would be a case of a victory for monarchy over democracy."[13] No incident illustrates with a more vivid irony how dangerous had been Bismarck's support of a hereditary monarchy untempered by parliamentary safeguards.

The loss of the First World War brought an end to the Hohenzollern dynasty, and in August 1919 the democratic Weimar constitution was proclaimed. As has often been pointed out, the constitution suffered from two serious initial disadvantages. In the first place, it was the result of military defeat, a defeat which was particularly difficult to bear, coming as it did after the great achievements and high hopes of the previous decades. This did not recommend it to the German people. Secondly, though it provided for a truly democratic form of parliamentary government with all the rights and duties such a system involves, it had not been fought for by those who were to put it into practice and enjoy its advantages. Free constitutions are usually the result of long and arduous constitutional struggles which themselves prepare and educate those taking part in them for the responsibilities that victory involves. In 1919 too few Germans were ready for democratic responsibilities. Too many of them were strongly prejudiced against a system of government which Bismarck and Treitschke had taught them to despise. There were two political parties that might normally have been expected to make the Weimar constitution work, the Liberals and the Social Democrats. But the Liberals had never recovered from the blow they had received half a century before, while the Social Democrats, who in 1914 were the largest Marxist party in the world, had been split

[13] Quoted by Fritz Fischer in *Griff nach der Weltmacht*, p. 837.

irrevocably over their attitude towards the war and had lost
several of their ablest leaders during the civil strife that followed the armistice. On the other hand, such influential elements in society as the civil service, the teaching profession,
and the army were predominantly hostile to the constitution.

Max Weber's criticisms of Bismarck's political legacy, which
have already been quoted, were written just over a year before
the constitution came into force and were particularly relevant
to the situation during the early years of the Weimar Republic
and to the problems which Germany's new political leaders had
to face. As Weber pointed out, when he wrote in the spring of
1918, they had had no real parliamentary experience, and the
few abnormal months since October 1918, when Ludendorff, in
the face of defeat, had handed over the government to the
constitutionally minded Prince Max of Baden, had been a quite
inadequate apprenticeship. Since Bismarck's resignation the
country had virtually been run by civil servants, or at least by
ministers who were officials in spirit. They considered themselves responsible, not to the Reichstag, but to the emperor and
to the state. The main burden of trying to make a success of the
democratic constitution fell on the moderate majority of the
Social Democrats and on the Catholic Centre Party. Yet it was
they whom Bismarck had treated as enemies of the state, and
the cleavage between them and the conservative official classes
was one of the main liabilities under which the republic
suffered.

A number of sincere democrats were naturally recruited into
the service of the state after 1918. But the great majority of
civil servants during the whole Weimar period were survivors of
the pre-war age or had at least been brought up in the old
Imperial tradition. Most of them were opposed in their hearts
not only to many of the twenty-one governments which followed one another during fourteen years of political instability
but to the whole republican system of government to which

their loyalty was due. They therefore caused difficulties, in innumerable ways, for Weimar's inexperienced parliamentary politicians.

The attitude of many judges especially was reprehensible and damaging to the regime. Numerous political murders were committed by enemies of the republic. The victims included the foreign minister, Walther Rathenau, and another minister, Matthias Erzberger, who had signed the armistice on Hindenburg's orders in 1918. The murderers in most cases were left unpunished or let off with absurdly light sentences, and reactions in conservative circles were often cynically tolerant or even approving. After the nationalist *putsch* in 1923, Ludendorff was acquitted against the clearest evidence, while Hitler, after receiving the minimum sentence for treason, was released after less than nine months in prison.

The record of academics and school teachers was little better. German intellectuals might have been expected to give a lead in reinterpreting German history in the light of recent events, and indeed a very small minority, to some extent, did so. But the great majority remained under the spell of Bismarck and the imperial tradition. They made no attempt to educate German youth to their responsibilities in a democratic society. On the contrary, they criticized and tended to dissociate themselves from the Weimar constitution.

The army had survived the war more satisfactorily than the empire and the dynasty which it had served. It had, at the last minute, skilfully saddled a civilian government with the odium of signing the armistice and coming to terms with the victors; its core of staff officers and military experts had remained virtually intact; and with the aid of the cleverly cultivated "stab-in-the-back" legend it convinced an increasing number of wishful thinkers that Germany's defeat had been due, not to the armed forces, but to revolutionaries and demoralized civilians on the home front. The volunteer force of 100,000, which Germany was allowed under the Treaty of Versailles, enabled General von Seeckt, the Chief of the Army Command, to build up a highly efficient professional army which could also serve as a nucleus for a much larger force at some later stage. Its officers were imbued with conservative and imperialist traditions and felt at best a perfunctory and grudging loyalty towards the new regime. They lived for the past and the future rather than for the present and, so far from defending the Weimar Republic during times of emergency, played a major part in bringing about its collapse. In 1920, when Wolfgang Kapp led a Right-wing *putsch*, General von Seeckt replied to the defence minister's request for help by saying that the national forces could not be asked to fire on their comrades, and retired to his home to see how things developed. It was left to trade unionists by a general strike to defeat Kapp's attempted coup. During the last months of the republic General von Schleicher, as defence minister and finally as chancellor, and General von Hammerstein, as Chief of the Army Command, used their influence to support Hitler's nomination as chancellor, though they misjudged the character of the man they were helping.[14] Eight months after coming into power Hitler said in a public speech: "We all know well that if, in the days of the Revolution, the Army had not stood on our side, then we should not be standing here to-day."[15]

On the death of Friedrick Ebert, the Socialist president of the republic, in 1925, the election as his successor of Field-Marshal von Hindenburg symbolized the strength of the traditionalist forces in German society. The majority turned to him as a reassuring substitute for the Emperor and he was re-elected in 1932, though by a different combination of voters, when he was eighty-four years old. During the greater part of his presidency Hindenburg was loyal to the constitution accord-

[14] J. W. Wheeler-Bennett, *The Nemesis of Power*, pp. 282–84.
[15] Quoted by Wheeler-Bennett, *op. cit.*, p. 285.

ing to his lights, but in his last years sentiment and old associations asserted themselves over his judgment, and he was too much influenced by his son, Oskar, by von Papen, and by the East German landowning class. Moreover, like other senior officers, he misjudged Hitler. Karl Dietrich Bracher, historian of the Weimar Republic, has pointed out that Hindenburg failed in all the main tasks he set himself: to win the First World War; to avoid the establishment of the republic; to defeat the republic's enemies; and finally to restrain Hitler. Yet the myth surrounding him grew steadily—symbol, Bracher adds ironically, of the German people's political discernment.[16]

However, Friedrich Meinecke was quite justified in saying to himself on January 30, 1933, after Hindenburg had called on Hitler to form a goverment, "That was not necessary," and of maintaining shortly after the Second World War that there had been an element of accident in Hitler's attainment of power.[17] The influence of Bismarck's legacy in internal politics, the strength of conservative, anti-republican forces in German society, and the German people's lack of parliamentary experience were responsible for the instability and weaknesses of the Weimar regime, and by 1932 the majority of the German people had come to favour some exceptional increase in the government's authority to solve the economic and political problems of the time. But the majority also were opposed to Hitler, and during the last six months before he attained power their number increased. In July, at the height of the economic crisis, the National Socialists obtained 37.3 per cent of the votes cast in the Reichstag elections, but in the elections that followed in November their votes dropped by two million, and their percentage fell to 33.1. That, in spite of this, Hitler became chancellor three months later was due to such fortuitous

---

[16] Die Auflösung der Weimarer Republik, p. 480.
[17] Die deutsche Katastrophe, p. 95.

reasons as the weakness and mistakes of Hindenburg, the inadequacy of von Papen and von Schleicher as statesmen, and the bad judgment of the nationalist Right, who, under the leadership of the industrialist press lord, Hugenberg, agreed to form a coalition with the Nazis.

When Adenauer became chancellor in 1949 the situation of Germany was very different from what it had been after the First World War. Quite apart from the substantial *de facto* loss of territory in the East and the division of the country into the Federal Republic and the Soviet zone, it was not only a system of government which had collapsed four years before but a state. When a totalitarian regime breaks down, it leaves by its very nature, at least temporarily, an administrative void. With the suicide of Hitler on April 30, 1945, and the imminence of unconditional surrender, the Nazi officials knew that their posts would incriminate them in Allied eyes, and in many cases, therefore, they had fled from the scene of their activities before the Allied armies arrived. As a result the whole Nazi administrative system had disintegrated. Military government had taken its place for a period of four years, and the political organization of the country had had to be built up again laboriously from the bottom under Allied supervision.

This time the war-guilt question was beyond dispute. There was no doubt whatever in the eyes of the world that the German government under Hitler's leadership had been responsible for the outbreak of war in 1939. No powerful reactionary elements were allowed to survive from the previous regime and make serious difficulties for the post-war governments. Although a heroic elite of army officers had provided some of the opposition leaders, the armed forces as a whole shared part at least of the discredit associated with the Nazi system. Every member of the forces had sworn an oath of allegiance to Hitler personally, the war itself had ended disastrously, and the general disillusionment with everything military had been increased by the nature of the weapons used in the last stages of the struggle; above all by the atom bomb. There were few regrets amongst the German people, therefore, when the armed forces were disbanded on Allied orders. The reputation of the civil service had suffered likewise. Its members also had taken a personal oath of allegiance to Hitler, and many of them had undoubtedly chosen the easier course of staying in office at the sacrifice of their personal convictions.

The German people as a whole were disenchanted and stunned. Those of them who were capable of a rational reaction to the national disaster repudiated Hitler and his system completely. Many of them realized also that Bismarck and the Right-wing nationalists bore part of the responsibility for what had happened. The new German government thus faced the formidable task of restoring Germany's position and reputation amongst the nations and giving the German people a new sense of purpose and direction after their degrading experiences during the Nazi period and after Hitler had been wholly and Bismarck partially discredited.

By the irony of fate Konrad Adenauer, the man on whom the main burden fell, was himself both a product of the pre-1914 era and a senior civil servant—that is, a member of the very class whose conservatism and inflexible loyalty to past traditions had been responsible to a substantial degree for Germany's unfortunate internal political development. However, if Adenauer had many of the characteristics of these two categories, he cannot be described as typical of either of them. For all his limitations he had the unusual mixture of human qualities which often accompanies greatness.

2
Adenauer's Achievement

(a) Germany after the War

Adenauer's achievement can best be gauged by contrasting Germany's internal situation and international standing in 1949 with either 1957, when he won his greatest electoral triumph and reached the highest point of his career, or 1963, when he resigned the chancellorship. In some respects his accomplishment mounted up progressively until the time when he left office. In others it reached its zenith in 1957 or thereabouts, and his last years, being marked by deterioration or a reversal of fortune, can appropriately be considered later in a more critical context.

The position of Germany in 1949 can only be understood in the light of developments during the previous four years.

German loss of manpower during the Second World War very seriously weakened the national life. Nearly 5¾ million soldiers and civilians were killed or presumed killed, not including over 1¼ million Germans orignally living in Eastern Europe or elsewhere abroad, who also lost their lives. In addition, in 1952, when most prisoners of war had returned home and conditions had settled down, 4.4 million Germans,[1] as a result of the war, were in receipt of maintenance grants from the state, of which just over 1½ million were disabled, and the remainder dependants.

The material damage suffered was correspondingly great. Twenty-two per cent of the dwellings in the area now covered by Western Germany were either completely destroyed or uninhabitable, while little more than half of them had escaped damage. Over 30 per cent of the country's industries had been either destroyed or damaged. Large areas of some of the main cities, for example Cologne and Hamburg, presented a picture of utter desolation. During the summer of 1945 one could stand near the centre of the great industrial city of Essen and see little but a wide expanse of rubble, with occasional desolate figures picking their way amongst the debris or emerging like rabbits from temporary underground dwellings in basements and cellars.

At the Potsdam conference in July and August 1945 it was decided that, pending the final peace settlement, the territories east of the Oder and western Neisse rivers, covering nearly a quarter of the total German territory in 1937, should be placed under Soviet and Polish administration. It was decided also that the German population remaining in them should be transferred to Germany. Before the war the territories had been the one area of Germany which had produced a substantial food surplus: they had sent each year over a million tons of grain, ½ million tons of potatoes, and ¼ million tons each of meat and sugar to the western parts of the country. The Potsdam decisions, therefore, added greatly to Germany's economic problem by removing a valuable source of food and adding considerably to the number of mouths to be fed. It was scarcely surprising that two years later the official food ration in industrial North

[1] This figure includes a small proportion of survivors from the First World War.

Rhine-Westphalia fell as low as 1,550 calories a day, and that the actual amount available was often very much lower, so that the British government introduced bread rationing, which it had not done during the war, in order to make grain available for the half-starving Germans for whom it was responsible.

In the immediate post-war years the breakdown in communications and the administrative confusion made it difficult to draw up reliable statistics. But it has been estimated that industrial production in 1946 was about a third of the 1936 level and in 1948 just over three fifths. The need to increase production was urgent for three special reasons: the country now had to import a high proportion of its foodstuffs and the imports had to be paid for; the restoration of the transport system and the enormous task of urban and industrial reconstruction required a correspondingly large supply of buildings and machinery; and jobs had to be found for the millions of refugees and expellees who were pouring into Germany from the East. Yet early in 1950 it was estimated that in order to employ one worker productively about $2,000 had to be invested.[2]

The human resources available for the task of national reconstruction had been severely and tragically depleted. In addition to the heavy war losses, some of Germany's ablest minds had been Jewish and had either emigrated during the thirties or become Hitler's victims in concentration camps. Many of the strongest and most sincere characters amongst the political opponents of National Socialism had been lost to Germany similarly. Furthermore, Hitler's ruthless measures against those who had any connection with the resistance movement, especially after July 20, 1944, had skimmed the cream off the opposition to his system and all that it stood for. Amongst the victims of the wholesale executions that took place during the last nine months of the war were senior officers, aristocrats,

[2] See M. Dönhoff, "Germany Puts Freedom Before Unity," in *Foreign Affairs*, April 1950.

socialists, spiritual leaders, diplomatists, trade unionists, and government officials; a group whose heroism is becoming better known in Germany and who deserve greater recognition in other countries.

With the collapse of the Nazi government in the spring of 1945 the responsibility for establishing law and order and rebuilding the administration fell on the Allied armies. As they swept across Germany from the west and from the east, they set up at first improvised and provisional forms of military government, which then gave way to better qualified and more carefully organized units. The next stage was to reconstruct under careful supervision a German administrative system. The process started at the municipal and county levels and proceeded upwards via the districts to the *Land* and, provisionally, to the zonal levels. It was a laborious and intricate undertaking. For example, Nazi influence on the legal system, education, and the press had been particularly strong. It was very difficult to find judges, teachers, and editors who could be trusted not to exert any harmful influence in the post-Hitler age. Yet courts of law, schools, and newspapers are institutions essential to the running of any well-ordered, democratic country. The Allies, therefore, tended to veer from overcaution to rashness based on expediency, with results that were not always satisfactory.

In June 1945 the Allies announced that, for the purposes of military occupation, Germany would be divided into four zones: an eastern zone under the Soviet Union, a northwestern zone under Great Britain, a southwestern zone under France, and a southern and central zone under the United States. Each zone was to be under the control of a commander-in-chief appointed by the Allied power responsible for it. The four commanders-in-chief together were to constitute a Control Council which was to deal with matters concerning Germany as a whole. Greater Berlin was to form a kind of island within the Soviet zone. It was to be occupied by forces from all four powers, each of which was to have its own sector of the city under a commandant. The four commandants were to constitute the Inter-Allied Governing Authority (Kommandatura), which was to direct jointly the administration of the Greater Berlin area under the general direction of the Control Council.

Each zone was divided up into *Länder*,[3] which correspond roughly to provinces or states. In the zones belonging to the three Western powers there were originally eleven *Länder*: Schleswig-Holstein, Hamburg, Lower Saxony, and North Rhine-Westphalia in the British zone; Rhineland-Palatinate, Baden, and Württemberg-Hohenzollern in the French zone; and Bavaria, Württemberg-Baden, and Hesse in the American zone, together with Bremen which formed an enclave in the British zone in order that the American occupation forces should have their own port. The union in 1952, after a referendum, of the three *Länder*, Baden, Württemberg-Hohenzollern, and Württemberg-Baden to form a new *Land*, Baden-Württemberg, reduced the total number of *Länder* to nine. The addition of the Saar in 1957 raised it to ten. If greater Berlin is counted as a *Land* the number again becomes eleven.[4]

In creating the *Länder* after the war the Allies were giving expression to the reaction against Hitler's overcentralization. The way had been prepared for their rather radical handling of the problem by Hitler's own ruthless treatment of Prussia,

[3] To translate the German word *Land* (plural *Länder*) by either "province" or "state" is misleading: the German word and its plural form will, therefore, be used throughout the book.

[4] The position of Greater Berlin is most complicated. Article 23 of the Basic Law includes it among the *Länder*. The Western Allies, anxious to preserve the status of Greater Berlin, suspended Article 23 and reduced the number and powers of Berlin's delegates to the Bundestag, who in the plenary sessions were not allowed to vote. In 1957 the Constitutional Court at Karlsruhe decided that Berlin was a *Land* of the Federal Republic and that the Basic Law was "valid in and for Berlin except to the extent that Three-Power measures, stemming from the occupation period and still maintained, limit its application."

Bavaria, and Lübeck.[5] The Allies were influenced by a mixture
of history and practical convenience. Historical tradition prevailed in their restoration of Bavaria, their promotion of the
former Prussian province, Schleswig-Holstein, to *Land* status,
and their recognition of the separate identity of Hamburg and
Bremen. In their treatment of the other *Länder* expediency was
the strongest motive. Although their decisions came in for criticism, they have on the whole been vindicated. In 1952, at the
request of the Bundstag, the federal government appointed a
strong committee under the chairmanship of the ex-chancellor,
Dr. Luther, to investigate the case for reorganizing *Land*
boundaries. The committee reported in 1955 and made no
clear recommendations for change. Three *Länder* came under
criticism, but in only one case, Rhineland-Palatinate, were a
number of different solutions suggested as possible, none of
which was subsequently adopted.

The division of Germany into zones was convenient during
the Allied occupation. But it was clearly intended to be no
more than a temporary arrangement. At Potsdam it had been
decided that during the occupation Germany should be treated
as a single economic unit, and provision had been made for the
establishment, under the Control Council, of central administrative departments, particularly in the financial and economic
fields. For two years after the war these plans were held up
owing to the persistent opposition of the French. They preferred that Germany should remain divided, and, not having
been represented at Potsdam, they did not consider themselves
bound by the agreements which had been made there.

However, Germany's critical economic position affected the
occupying powers in very different ways. The Russians and the
French had suffered under German invasion and the ruthless

[5] The Allies formally declared the abolition of Prussia in February
1947, but Hitler had already merged the Prussian government in the Reich
and reduced its provinces to mere administrative units.

treatment of Nazi officers and officials. Now that it was their turn to occupy German territory they were out to take their revenge. Their armies lived off the country, and they dismantled and took away whatever industrial equipment they wanted and could move. The American and British forces, on the other hand, provided their own rations, and the occupation cost their two countries about 700 million dollars a year. The United States and Great Britain therefore had a very real interest in Germany's economic recovery and wanted the country to be in a position to support itself as soon as possible.

During the summer of 1946 the British and American commanders-in-chief agreed on the economic union of their two zones, and the union came into effect on January 1, 1947. Appropriate administrative institutions for the so-called Bizone were subsequently set up, including a number of departments on the lines envisaged at Potsdam, an Executive Committee, comprising the directors of the departments, a Council of *Länder* made up of representatives from each *Land* government, and an Economic Council consisting of members elected by the parliaments of the *Länder*. The French declined to take part in any such development, while the Russians continued to favour the setting up of central administrative departments until the summer of 1947 and accused the British and American authorities of wrecking the Potsdam agreement.

By the spring of 1948 the cleavage between the Soviet Union and the West was complete. The proclamation in March 1947 of the Truman Doctrine by which America promised support to the victims of Communist aggression had been followed by the Soviet refusal of Marshall Aid and, on March 17, 1948, by the signature of the Brussels Treaty and the formation of Western Union. A few days later the Russian representative walked out of the Control Council for Germany, and the following month the Soviet blockade of Berlin began. The attempt to evolve an agreed Allied policy for the whole of Germany had failed. It was clear that the two sides had quite different conceptions of what they wished a united Germany to be.

The political challenge involved in the Berlin blockade and the economic opportunity presented by the Marshall offer made it urgently necessary that the administration in the three Western zones of Germany should be co-ordinated. The French agreed on this. So, on July 1, 1948, the three commanders-in-chief asked the heads of the eleven West German Länder to call a constituent assembly and draw up a democratic and federal constitution for Western Germany.

The reaction of the German statesmen was at first hesitant. They did not wish to do anything which might deepen the division of the country by giving a constitution to a part of it only. They emphasized that anything that was done must be strictly provisional in character—provisional, that is, until a constitution could be drawn up for the whole country. On the other hand, they were even more aware than the Allies of the advantages of co-ordinating economic activities, and the Berlin blockade, which had been countered by the impressive Allied airlift, brought home to them both the dangers of the European situation and the strength of American airpower. A compromise was therefore reached, great care being taken to avoid giving the impression that the system of government to be devised would be a definitive constitution. The constituent assembly was to be known as the "Parliamentary Council" and the provisional constitution as the "Basic Law."

The Parliamentary Council, which assembled on September 1 with Konrad Adenauer as its chairman, consisted of 65 members who were elected by the Land parliaments. Berlin sent five representatives, but they were present in an advisory capacity and did not vote. The Council completed its main task on May 8, 1949, when it gave its approval to the Basic Law. This, significantly, was within three days of the Soviet decision to lift the Berlin blockade and within five weeks of the signature of the North Atlantic Treaty. Shortly afterwards the Allied commanders-in-chief approved the law. They had exerted some influence on the Council's deliberations, particularly as regards the position of Greater Berlin and the relationship between the federal government and the *Länder*, France and the United States having revealed themselves as strong advocates of *Land* rights. But the Basic Law was in the main the product of the Council's own deliberations. According to a leading German constitutional lawyer the guiding principles laid down by the Allies for the Parliamentary Council corresponded closely to the political wishes of the German people.[6]

Before it ceased to exist, the Parliamentary Council made a further decision which has turned out to be of more importance than was generally anticipated at the time. Bonn was chosen as Western Germany's provisional capital by a small majority over the alternative suggestion, Frankfurt. For personal and political reasons Adenauer strongly favoured Bonn, because it was in his own part of Germany and in a Christian Democratic area, while Frankfurt was a socialist city in a predominantly socialist *Land*. The strongest rational and objective argument for Bonn, however, was put forward by those who held that Berlin alone could be Germany's permanent capital. The claims of a small provincial town like Bonn to be anything more than a purely provisional capital, they maintained, were so much weaker than those of a great commercial and banking centre like Frankfurt that it was much less likely to stand in the way of the ultimate recognition of Berlin. Nevertheless there have been serious political and cultural disadvantages for Western Germany in not having its seat of government situated in a really metropolitan centre.

Under the terms of the Basic Law elections for a West German Bundestag (Federal Assembly) were held the following August. The Christian Democratic Union and its Bavarian

[6] See Ernst Friesenhahn, *Grundgesetz und Besatzungsstatut*, p. 147.

counterpart, the Christian Social Union (CSU), together obtained 139 seats; the Social Democratic Party, 131, the liberal
Free Democratic Party (FDP), 52; and the conservative German Party, 17. Of the five other small parties, the extremes of
Right and Left, the neo-Nazi German Right party and the
Communists obtained 5 and 15 seats respectively. Professor
Theodor Heuss, chairman of the FDP, was elected federal president, and Dr. Konrad Adenauer, the leader of the largest
party, was chosen as federal chancellor by the smallest possible
margin. Adenauer proceeded to form a coalition government
with the Free Democrats and the German Party.

On September 21 the United States, Great Britain, and
France formally recognized the establishment of the Federal
Republic of Germany. The Soviet Union replied on October 7
by announcing the formation of the "German Democratic Republic" in the Soviet zone. Both governments claimed to provide a basis for the government of united Germany. But the
West German chancellery and the three Western Allies at once
declared that the new Soviet creation, as it was not based on
free elections, was authorized to represent neither all of Germany nor even East Germany.

At the same time as the Federal Republic was recognized,
the Occupation Statute, a new instrument defining the relationship between the three occupying powers and the federal government, also went into force. In it the Allied governments gave
their assurance that they desired and intended that the German
people should enjoy the maximum self-government consistent
with the continuance of the occupation. They went on to define
the powers which would be reserved to the Allied authorities so
long as the occupation lasted. These included disarmament and
demilitarization, reparations, industrial controls in the Ruhr,
foreign affairs and foreign trade, displaced persons and refugees, and the protection of Allied forces and their dependants.
The Allies also declared that military government had come to

an end: in future the military functions of the occupation would be exercised by the commanders-in-chief, while political control was to be in the hands of three high commissioners, whose staffs would be restricted to a minimum and who would together form an Allied High Commission.

When Adenauer took over the government in his country few could have foreseen the developments that were to occur during the succeeding decade. Much had changed since September 1944, when Roosevelt and Churchill had discussed the Morgenthau Plan for pastoralizing Germany, and since the summer of 1945, when the nonfraternization rule had forbidden normal human relations between the German people and the occupying troops. The Allies, especially the United States, were giving active support to German economic revival, and they promised the German people a large and growing share of political control over their own affairs. On the other hand, the provisional constitution and the new government enjoyed little credit either at home or abroad. The Parliamentary Council had produced the Basic Law to order within a few months, but the new state had no real historical roots and few apparent links with the nation's past. In the eyes of the world Germany was still besmirched with the memories of Nazi atrocities, the full horrors of which had only become widely known since the war ended. It was still a dependent and pariah state which was not allowed to rearm nor maintain normal diplomatic relations with other countries.

After Germany's defeat in 1918 Adenauer, as mayor of Cologne, had declared: "Times of political catastrophe provide particularly good opportunities to create something new." If he was hopeful in the summer of 1949, his optimism must have been based on confidence in his own ability, stamina, and sense of purpose.

(b) Diplomatic Recognition and the Western Alliance

Although Adenauer under the Occupation Statute was not responsible for the conduct of German foreign affairs, his first important task as chancellor was in fact a diplomatic task, the establishment of good relations with the Allied high commissioners. Success in this task would depend partly on his own tact and other personal qualities, but it was above all necessary to convince the high commissioners that his concept of Germany's relations with the Allies and other foreign countries was one which they could approve. He had therefore to think out the principles of German foreign policy as if he were actually responsible for it. It was in his response to this challenge that Adenauer showed himself to be a master, and foreign affairs remained his dominant interest throughout his chancellorship.

His two main objectives were: first, to regain for Germany the confidence of the Allies and convince them that the majority of the German people were not as bad as they were commonly believed to be, and, secondly, to win for Germany a place in the Western alliance as the best defence against possible Soviet aggression. Adenauer's hostility to communism, which was natural in a man with his background and Catholic convictions was reinforced by his knowledge of what his fellow countrymen were experiencing in the Soviet zone. His faith in the security offered by the Western alliance was strengthened by the recent demonstration of American airpower during the Berlin airlift. In his first declaration of policy in the Bundestag he stated his position as follows: "Our only path to freedom is by seeking, in agreement with the Allied High Commissioners, to regain our liberties and enlarge the scope of our authority step by step."

In one respect Adenauer was singularly ill-qualified to handle foreign relations. He could speak no foreign languages. Apart from taking holidays in Switzerland before the war, he had, up to this time, never been abroad, and he had little understanding of foreign problems and foreign attitudes to life, especially in the Anglo-Saxon world. He was, and still remains in some ways, a typical provincial, with the restricted outlook of a man who has spent most of his working life in one city.

Yet Adenauer was remarkably successful in impressing the high commissioners not only with his concept of Germany's international position but with his personal qualities as a partner in negotiations. He combined a quiet acceptance of the consequences of defeat and a stubborn firmness, when his country's vital interests were at stake, with the persistent pursuit of clearly defined objectives. The Allied authorities liked dealing with him, because he was reliable and they knew where they were with him. His level-headed, unemotional approach, his willingness to incur public criticism, his habit of stating the issues frankly and then facing them without evasion, all inspired confidence. Unlike many of his fellow countrymen he was very sensitive to foreign points of view on subjects about which he was negotiating. In a speech made in Cologne during February 1919, on the subject of Rhenish federalism, he expressed opinions on which he consistently acted thirty years later:

We must always try to understand the train of thought of our opponents. In considering all questions of foreign policy one only reaches a sensible conclusion if one thinks about them from the other man's point of view and asks oneself: how would you act if you were now in the position of France, England, or America?

The first important result of Adenauer's negotiations with the Allies was the Petersberg Agreements of November 1949, named after the hotel near Bonn where they were drawn up.

The negotiations preceding them were tough. Both sides fought hard over details. Adenauer's task was the more difficult, as he had to evolve a working basis on which to clarify his ill-defined relationship with the high commissioners. But he made up for the weakness of his position by a combination of firmness and patience, and, when the discussions ended, the mutual respect of the two sides had increased.

From the German point of view the agreements involved a step forward towards the restoration of sovereignty and a clear recognition that Western Germany was fit to take its place in the European and the international communities. The Bonn government undertook to maintain the demilitarization of federal territory, to eradicate all traces of Nazism from German life, and to co-operate with the Allies in the Military Security Board, set up by the High Commission, and as a member of the International Authority for the Ruhr. In return the Allies agreed to curtail the dismantling of German industrial plant for reparations, to stop dismantling in Berlin altogether, to relax restrictions on shipbuilding, and to allow the federal government to initiate the gradual re-establishment of consular and commercial relations with other countries. In addition both parties declared that their primary objective was "the incorporation of the Federal Republic as a peaceful member of the European community" and that "to this end German association with the countries of Western Europe in all fields should be diligently pursued." They expressed their desire that the Federal Republic should be promptly admitted to the Council of Europe as an associate member and agreed "to promote the participation of Germany in all those international organizations through which German experience and support can contribute to the general welfare."

In retrospect it can be seen that the Petersberg Agreements provided an excellent foundation on which Adenauer could develop successfully his plans for Germany's future, and it was a remarkable achievement on his part to have laid such a foundation within little over two months of becoming chancellor. In spite of this he came in for severe criticism from the Socialist opposition, when he defended the agreements before the Bundestag. It was on this occasion that the SPD leader, Dr. Schumacher, called him, "Federal Chancellor of the Allies." Germany at that time would have made very slow progress indeed, had the federal chancellor not established good relations with the Allies. Schumacher's remark, in the heat of debate, was justified neither by the nature of Adenauer's relations with the high commissioners nor by the very considerable benefits that the agreements brought for Germany.

The attitude of the Allied governments and their representatives contributed considerably to the good relationship with the new West German government. They had learned much from the mistakes made after the First World War, and the menacing attitude of the Soviet Union, which had led to the foundation of NATO, provided additional reasons for not alienating Germany. It was greatly to Germany's advantage that the strongest and most influential of the Western Allies was also the country in which anti-German resentment was weakest and which had greatest confidence in the German people. Adenauer himself was deeply impressed by the fact that from 1946–49 some 16 million "Care" packets were sent across the Atlantic to Germany at the time of its greatest need.

Two decisions taken by Adenauer in 1952 increased the confidence felt in the Federal Republic and in his leadership by the Western powers and in the world at large.

The first related to the settlement of Germany's public and private foreign debts, most of which went back to pre-war days, though some to the early years of the Allied occupation. Adenauer was advised by banking authorities that the sums proposed were beyond the country's capacity to pay. But he preferred to take the advice of Herr Hermann Abs, director and later chairman of the Deutsche Bank, to whom he had entrusted the negotiations in London. Abs took a statesmanlike view of the problem and was fully aware of its political implications. Adenauer himself was solely interested in the political aspects. Though he had the capacity to make a sound common-sense appraisal of the financial possibilities, he normally took up a detached, rather disdainful attitude to purely financial arguments, and this often brought him into conflict with his finance ministers. It was finally agreed that Germany's total foreign indebtedness amounted to approximately 14 milliard marks, and the agreement for their settlement was signed in London in February 1953. The acceptance of this liability, at a time when its economic recovery was not very far advanced, greatly strengthened the Federal Republic's claim to be the legitimate successor of pre-war German governments and to be a reliable financial and trading partner.

Adenauer's second decision was to make some compensation to Israel for the sufferings of the Jews under Hitler. In his negotiations with the representatives of Israel in this connection he showed up at his best. *The Economist* once rashly described him as "the conscience of Germany."[7] During this phase of his career the description was justified. He considered the whole question to be a moral rather than a political one. On the German side, he took the initiative and had no difficulty in carrying the majority of his fellow countrymen with him. But for Israel the problem was more difficult. Many Jews did not like the idea of their representatives having any direct dealings with the German government, and in these circumstances Adenauer showed the greatest tact and understanding. Israel had originally asked for $1,000 million from the Federal Republic and $500 million from the "German Democratic Republic." The sum finally agreed to by Adenauer, again in disregard of expert financial advice, was not far short of the

[7] On January 1, 1955.

amount requested from Western Germany. Israel was to be paid $715 million in goods spread over a number of years, and $107 million was to be made available to Jewish world relief organizations in token compensation for unclaimed Jewish assets in Germany. The settlement was approved by the Bundestag with a large majority in March 1953, the whole house standing for a minute in silence at the suggestion of its president.

During 1951, on the foundations laid at the Petersberg, the Federal Republic made further considerable progress on the road to sovereignty and full diplomatic recognition. In March the first formal revision of the Occupation Statute was announced. Western Germany was allowed to have its own foreign ministry, and Adenauer himself became the first foreign minister. The previous year German consuls-general had been appointed in the three Allied capitals, and from now on the Federal Republic was given increasing freedom to appoint diplomatic and consular representatives abroad and receive foreign diplomats in Bonn. Within two years it had diplomatic and consular relations with forty nations. India took the lead in ending the state of war with Germany at the beginning of 1951, and was followed in July by Great Britain, other nations of the Commonwealth, and France, and in October by the United States.

In April the Allies lifted restrictions on shipbuilding and several important branches of industrial production. At the end of the year the limitations on coal production were abolished, and it was agreed that the international control of the Ruhr should end.

At the conclusion of a conference in Washington in September the Allied foreign ministers issued a declaration relating to Germany. They defined their objectives as "the inclusion of a democratic Germany in a European community on the basis of equal status" and the complete reorganization of German-

Allied relations amongst other things through the supersession of the Occupation Statute by treaty arrangements and through the co-operation of the Federal Republic in the defence of the West.

In May 1951 Western Germany was admitted to full membership of the Council of Europe. There was no question of its becoming a member of the United Nations, because the Soviet Union would undoubtedly have made membership for Eastern Germany a precondition of its approval. But, in accordance with the terms of the Petersberg Agreements, West German representatives began to attend meetings of a number of international organizations, first as observers and later as representatives of a full member state. By the end of 1952 the Federal Republic was a member of the Food and Agricultural Organization, the World Health Organization, the International Labour Organization, the World Bank, the International Monetary Fund, and UNESCO, and she had acceded to the General Agreement on Tariffs and Trade.

Throughout the whole period from his assumption of the chancellorship until the spring of 1955 Adenauer was highly successful in his avowed aim of winning the confidence of the Allies. The questions of German rearmament and European integration will be dealt with fully at a later stage. But some reference to them is necessary for an understanding of Adenauer's progress towards his primary diplomatic objective during these years. His attitude towards both problems did much to win him the trust and admiration of the Allied governments. The outbreak of the Korean War in June 1950 made clear the danger that the conflict between the communist camp and the West might spread to Europe and caused Allied statesmen to realize that Germany would be required to take part in the Western defence system. In face of considerable opposition within Germany, Adenauer at once responded positively to the change in the Allied attitude. Yet, during the difficult negotiations of the next four years to decide what Germany's role should be, Adenauer behaved with exemplary patience, tact, and courage and never aroused suspicion by anticipating Allied decisions. As regards European integration he responded immediately and very warmly to Robert Schuman's plan for a European Coal and Steel Community and was the strongest and most steadfast supporter of a European solution for every major problem that arose, whether economic, military, or political.

The West German government also, under Adenauer's calm and rational leadership, rose above the morbid tendency shown by a good many Germans at this time towards touchiness and self-justification. As a result no doubt in most cases of their memories of implication in Nazi misdeeds and of an unresolved sense of guilt, these people criticized Allied mistakes in relation to Hitler and the Soviet Union before and after the war and failed to acknowledge the imagination and generosity shown by Western statesmen towards post-war Germany. Adenauer, on the other hand, with his own anti-Nazi record, accepted the fact of his country's defeat, recognized that the Hitler regime had committed great crimes against humanity, and considered it appropriate to emphasize the magnanimity and other merits of Western statesmanship.

The Bonn government used its influence to foster contacts and improve relations between the German people and the peoples of the Western alliance. The numerous schemes for educational and cultural exchanges put forward by the Allies were on the German side primarily the concern of the *Land* or local governments, unless they owed their origin to private persons or professional groups. But the federal government gave its moral and in some cases its practical support to all such activity. Adenauer himself became a frequent traveller to the countries of the Western alliance. During the four years from 1952 to 1955 he went to England three times, France nine times, Italy twice, and the United States three times, his visit to the States in April 1953 being the first official visit of the head of a German government to that country. In spite of his previous lack of experience in foreign countries he proved a good ambassador.

From all his actions and from all his public statements Adenauer left no doubt whatever that he strongly favoured the closest association of Germany with the Western alliance. In an interview given to the press during the summer of 1954[8] he was asked if it were true that after 1945, as after the First World War, Germany had a chance of acting as a mediator between East and West with the aim of producing a balance of power in Europe. After pointing out that the aid of the Western Allies was essential to Germany after the war, Adenauer went on to say that neither Germany nor the rest of the world could in any way be judged according to the conditions prevailing say in 1926. In the age of the hydrogen bomb, with Soviet troops stationed in the middle of Germany, the idea that Germany might feel called upon to play a mediatory role between East and West, with the intention, according to its need or mood, of attaching itself to one side or the other, was absurd, in fact suicidal.

Towards the end of 1950, as the most innocuous solution of the problem of German rearmament, the French Prime Minister had suggested the creation of an integrated European army which would include German contingents. This had led in February 1952 to an agreement being reached on a draft treaty for setting up the European Defence Community (EDC) and to the signature of the treaty on May 27 of the same year by France, Italy, the Federal Republic, and the Benelux countries. The previous day the three Western Allies and the Federal Republic had signed agreements at Bonn which are sometimes known as the Treaty of Germany. They were to come into force

[8] *Rheinische Merkur,* July 9, 1954.

at the same time as the EDC Treaty, which had still to be ratified. Their purpose was to bring an end to the Allied High Commission and the Occupation Statute and to integrate Western Germany "on a basis of equality within the European community." The Federal Republic was to have full authority over its internal and external affairs except for certain rights which were retained by the Allies. These included conditions relating to the stationing of armed forces in the country and the right to conduct negotiations regarding reunification, Berlin, and a final peace settlement. They were of importance not only to the Allies but to the Federal Republic, which was in no position to negotiate alone successfully with the Soviet Union on such vital matters.

The agreements reflected the trust felt by the Western powers in the new West German regime. Though they were not intended to take effect before the EDC Treaty went into force, during the long period of waiting for the treaty to be ratified the Allied authorities acted increasingly as if they were already effective.

After delays due to SPD opposition and an intricate constitutional position the Federal Republic finally ratified the EDC Treaty in March 1954. The following August, however, the treaty was rejected by the French Assembly, in the very country where the plan for an integrated European army had first been put forward. This was the worst setback suffered by the Western alliance since the formation of NATO. Mr. Anthony Eden, who was then British Foreign Secretary, made a rapid tour of European capitals in an attempt to save the situation. Conferences were held in London and Paris during September and October, and an alternative plan was agreed upon. The Brussels Treaty of 1948 was to be extended to include the German Federal Republic and Italy and was to become known as Western European Union; the Federal Republic was to become a member of NATO; and the Bonn agreements of May 1952, subject to certain minor alterations, were to come into force.

These arrangements, known as the Paris treaties, were ratified in February 1955 by the Federal Republic and in March by France. They went into effect on May 5. The Western occupation of Germany came to an end; the Allied high commissioners became ambassadors; subject only to the reservations agreed upon in May 1952, the Federal Republic attained full sovereignty; and it became a member of the Western alliance.

Professor Walter Hallstein, who was the federal chancellor's closest associate in foreign affairs from 1952 to 1955, once said that, although Adenauer was not at all susceptible to emotions, he had never seen him more moved than when, for the first time, he took his seat in the NATO Council.[9] This is understandable. In May 1955, within six years of becoming chancellor, he had attained his main objectives: the restoration of sovereignty, diplomatic recognition, and a place in the Western alliance. The right to rearm had not been one of his primary aims. But the fact that the Federal Republic was given this too was a convincing proof of Allied confidence. The Weimar Republic had never been allowed any modification of the disarmament clauses of the Treaty of Versailles: the first *de facto* concessions had been made to Hitler after he had taken the law into his own hands. The contrast between Allied policies after the First and Second World Wars was an indication that the Allies had learned from past mistakes, but it was also a testimony to Adenauer's statesmanship.

On May 31, 1954, Lord Vansittart, the veteran British diplomatist, wrote in a letter to *The Times*: "My lifelong antipathy to Germany is known—yet for once in all the blue moons of existence I acknowledge a German government and tendency which might perhaps be turned to the account of Christian

[9] To the writer in an interview in July 1964.

civilization." It has been seen that German and British historians have agreed that a serious limitation in Bismarck's statesmanship was his failure to recognize the significance of the universal element in man's political progress. A few months before he resigned the chancellorship, Adenauer wrote about NATO:

Its military organization, therefore, is not an end in itself. It is based on a close unity of the states on both sides of the Atlantic who share the same basic views on the meaning of life and the mission of men throughout the world. This strong link must be intensified in all fields.

It was in this broad view of his purpose as a statesman that Adenauer rose above Bismarck's level. In the sense also that he aroused less resentment than did Bismarck against his country and its aspirations amongst other nations his achievement was greater than his predecessor's and is likely to be more permanent.

(c) Social and Political Stability

Adenauer's diplomatic success greatly increased his popularity and strengthened his political position. A defeated, lonely, but fundamentally self-respecting people, who had gone through the experience of the Nazi era, wanted nothing so much as recognition and acceptance. It was just these advantages that the restoration of sovereignty and membership of NATO brought to them. But Adenauer himself, though primarily interested in Germany's external relations, did not neglect the most urgent aspects of internal policy. His shrewd understanding and skilful handling of the country's social problems further enhanced his personal prestige and the strength of his government's position.

In the circumstances of post-war Germany Adenauer's age, his past experience, and his personality were in themselves considerable assets. The German people were not hankering after a policy which looked to the past. The majority of them knew that National Socialism had been evil; they realized that the Weimar Republic had been a failure; and an increasing number of them were becoming aware that there must have been something wrong with the old imperialist order, which had, after less than half a century, led Germany into a disastrous war and then paved the way for Hitler. Yet they felt lost and uprooted. They wanted stability, and they wanted to link up again with the elements that were good in the national traditions. Adenauer, in many respects, incorporated in his person his countrymen's aspirations. He had stood up to Hitler; he had declined political office under Weimar; he had never been a soldier; he rejected nationalism as a political ideal; and he was anti-Prussian. On the other hand, he personified many of the virtues of the old Germany. From comparatively humble middle-class origins he had, through a combination of ambition, industry, and a deep sense of duty, made a highly successful career in municipal administration. He had deep religious convictions, his family life was exemplary, and he revealed an attractive, old-world urbanity in his personal bearing. Moreover, when he became chancellor, he had spent more than half his life in pre-1914 Germany and had in consequence a certain reassuring detachment from the events of the previous thirty-five years, which had overwhelmed or deeply shaken many of the younger men who had survived them.

Adenauer, therefore, contributed to German social stability through his personal qualities. Many actions taken by his government served the same end. During his first declaration of policy before the Bundestag in September 1949 he said: "The guiding star of all our work will be the endeavour to alleviate need and achieve social justice." In September 1963, a few weeks before he resigned the chancellorship, his SPD opponent, Herbert Wehner, confirmed the validity of this statement by referring to him as "a man who had brought about the combination of conservatism and striving after social security, which is so characteristic of his party."[10] One of Adenauer's closest collaborators, himself a specialist in foreign affairs, has expressed the opinion, though not everyone would agree with it, that the new social order in Germany has brought about a stability and measure of reconciliation of conflicting interests which perhaps represent Adenauer's greatest achievement.[11]

During the post-war years Western Germany was in a state of economic and social disorder and instability. Millions of people were dispossessed and homeless as a result of war damage; millions more were refugees or expellees from the East; demobilized servicemen and repatriated prisoners of war were seeking jobs and accommodation; released inmates of concentration camps and other victims of Nazi persecution were waiting to be re-absorbed by society; while the industrial dislocation and the shortage of food caused widespread hardship and suffering. The first emergency measures to deal with the situation were taken by the Allied military governments. But after the foundation of the federal government a great deal remained to be done, and Adenauer's government became very conscious of the inequality of losses and misfortune that had fallen upon the German people.

A series of measures were therefore passed with a view to evening out the hardships suffered. A Law for the Equalization of Burdens was approved in 1952. By taxing all forms of property, that had been spared by the war, up to 50 per cent of their total value, the law made available a sum of over three milliard marks yearly for paying compensation to refugees and all those

[10] In *Tatsachen-Argumente* 1963, No. 71, October 1963, p. 3.
[11] Herr Herbert Blankenhorn in an interview with the writer in August 1964.

who had suffered losses as a result of expulsion from their homes or war damage. The compensation was to be paid in instalments over a period of thirty years. The following year two further measures were passed: one with the purpose of sharing out fairly the burdens falling on the different *Länder* as a result of the compensation programme, and the other, the Expellees and Refugees Law, which set out to make uniform the various laws of the *Länder* on the subject, to place refugees from the Soviet zone on an equal footing with those from other areas, and to facilitate resettlement on the land of refugee farmers.

In 1951 two more specialized laws were passed dealing with the rights of former members of the civil service. The first was in fulfilment of Article 131 of the Basic Law, which provided that federal legislation should regulate the legal status and pension rights of persons, including refugees, who in May 1945 were employed in the public service, had left it "for reasons other than those arising from civil service regulations or collective agreement rules, and have not until now been employed, or are employed in positions not corresponding to their former ones." These categories included many refugees, officials from branches of the administration that had been abolished, and over 50,000 who had been dismissed owing to their Nazi associations. The law provided for the reinstatement in office, or the restoration of pension rights, of all former officials, except those who had been disqualified under the denazification procedure, of which there were little over a thousand, who owed their original appointment to their close Nazi connections, or whose only appointment had been in the Gestapo. Public authorities were obliged to fill 20 per cent of their posts with unemployed former officials, from amongst refugees or those whose posts had been abolished. Former members of the armed services, who had joined up before May 1935, were also entitled to pensions.

This measure was due partly to a reaction against Allied denazification procedure. It surprised by its generosity many of those who benefited from it and had the effect of restoring to office, often to important office, men who had been associated with some of the worst aspects of the Nazi system, sometimes at the expense of candidates who were politically beyond reproach and victims of Nazi persecution. It can be defended, within limits, partly as a natural reaction to Allied mistakes, and partly because it tended to reconcile to a moderate regime elements which might otherwise have reinforced extremists groups, a tendency which Adenauer always sought to further.

A second law, passed at the same time, set out to make amends to the victims of National Socialism. It covered former civil servants, apprentices for the civil service, university teachers, and professional soldiers. People in these categories were given the right to reinstatement or a pension at the rank they could be presumed to have reached had they not been dismissed. The dependants of victims who had died also received benefits.

The desire to promote social stability was the motive behind other governmental actions which were not mainly concerned with the consequences of the war. By many legislative and administrative means the government aimed at furthering social equality and contentment. For example, in various fields of social insurance the same benefits would be received by different insured persons, although the contributions paid, owing to inequalities in income, had not been equal. The father of a large family might, in some cases, pay the same premium as a single person, when his claims were likely to be much higher. Pension contributions would be reckoned according to wage rates, but children's allowances and payments to surviving dependants could cause the sums paid out to vary considerably.

Moved by a characteristic mixture of human and electoral considerations, Adenauer himself took an active interest in the problem of wages, prices, and the stabilization of currency. The most important piece of social legislation during his chancellorship was the law passed early in the election year of 1957 to ensure that the pensions earned by workers and employees would retain their value in terms of purchasing power. Pension rates were thus to be determined, not in accordance with the actual contributions paid during the pensioner's working life, but in accordance with their value adjusted to the wage and price rates at the time of retirement. They were subsequently to be adjusted annually to keep pace with developments in productivity, wages, and prices.

The main crisis in relations between Adenauer's government and the trades unions also ended in a settlement which promoted social harmony. The principle of co-management had been introduced into the German coal and steel industries early in 1947 by the British occupation authorities. At the time there was wide agreement, in which the CDU joined, that some degree of democratic control over industry was desirable. The SPD and the German trades unions were disillusioned with the results of nationalization in socialist Britain as well as under communism, and they adopted co-management as their programme for industry, because it seemed to provide the best chance of realizing true economic democracy. After the formation of the Federal Republic it became necessary to replace the Allied legislation by a federal law. However, the weight of influence in the CDU was moving towards the Right, and the government was reluctant to continue co-management. So the trades unions then took the matter up. The miners and metalworkers organized a referendum; 94 per cent voted for co-management; and a strike was threatened for February 1, 1951, unless the government took action. Shortly before the strike was due to begin Adenauer met Hans Böckler, the chairman of the Trade Union Federation, and agreed to a procedure which ended in the introduction of the necessary legislation.

This result was due partly to good personal relations between Adenauer and Böckler, who was a statesmanlike and moderate leader and who had given valuable support to Adenauer on a previous important occasion. But the settlement was due also to Adenauer's liking for the kind of compromise that co-management involved: it was preferable to nationalization, it gave the workers some say in running the industries in which they were employed, especially as regards working conditions and social problems, and it contributed to the harmony of industrial relations.

Some years later another method was developed by which German industrial workers were given a stake in the enterprises in which they worked. In the Hamburg Programme of the CDU, drawn up in 1953, it was stated that one of the problems of economic and social policy which the Party had to solve was how to encourage "the acquisition of personal property by a large section of the population." This idea was developed in the government's declaration of policy after the 1957 election, in which the possession of property by a greater proportion of the population became part of the government's political programme.

The government's intention was put into practice on a large scale in 1959. The state-owned Prussian Mining and Smelting Company (*Preussag*) had decided on a capital expansion programme. Advantage was taken of this opportunity to offer new shares in the company to private investors from the lower and middle income groups at a price substantially below the estimated price had the shares been offered in the open market. Although the number of shares that could be bought under these conditions by the individual subscriber was strictly limited, the amount offered at a total nominal value of 30 million marks was greatly oversubscribed, and the government decided to make available another 53 million marks' worth of the company's state-owned capital to would-be subscribers.

In 1961 a plan for the partial denationalization of the Volkswagen works, which had been put forward by Dr. Erhard shortly before the 1957 elections, went into effect. Shares amounting to 60 per cent of the company's capital were offered to the general public; in the first instance, to those in the lower and middle income groups. The price of issue was very favourable, as was shown by the fact that the market price subsequently rose to more than three times the original rate. A "social discount" was allowed to purchasers: 10 per cent to single persons with taxable incomes not exceeding 8,000 marks a year; 20 per cent to married couples with incomes up to 16,000 marks a year; and an additional 5 per cent to families with three or more children. Purchases were again limited, the maximum for single persons being shares of the nominal value of 500 marks, but the limit was doubled in the case of employees of the Volkswagen company.

During the government's declaration of policy in November 1961 Professor Erhard, who as vice-chancellor was speaking on behalf of Adenauer, pointed out that the number of shareholders in the country had quadrupled since 1957, that it then stood at two million, and that the government intended to continue the successful policy which had led to the broader distribution of capital.

The initiative for this whole development came from the CDU and the CSU, and Adenauer himself strongly supported it. He was inclined to favour all measures which reconciled the conflicting interests of capital and labour, and his political wisdom was revealed in the result. Western Germany since the Second World War has become more than ever before a nation of industrial workers, and yet this social change has not been accompanied by an increase in socialist strength. Rather, the attention paid to social justice and the more widespread distribution of property and wealth have led to greater social stability, broadening and strengthening the foundations of an economic order based on competition and free enterprise.

The federal elections of 1953 and 1957 showed very clearly what the German people thought of Adenauer's policies, both in internal and external affairs.

In 1953 the CDU/CSU won 244 seats compared with the SPD's 151; the FDP obtained 48; the new Refugee Party, 27; and the German Party, 15. There were three specially significant aspects of this result. For the first time in German history after free elections one party gained a clear majority in the federal parliament. Secondly, no extreme party of Left or Right won a single seat. Thirdly, out of about fourteen parties which put up candidates only six were successful in winning seats: there was thus a healthy trend towards a two-party system and no sign of a repetition of the Weimar tendency towards proliferation. The German people clearly supported a policy based on European co-operation and association with the Western alliance. One of the most effective posters employed in the election campaign used the slogan about Adenauer: "He has re-established links with the free world."

The elections of 1957 brought an even more remarkable victory. Adenauer's clear majority was increased to forty-three, and the number of successful parties was reduced to four. It was not an accident that this result was achieved in the first federal elections to be held after Western Germany had become a sovereign state. The German people were thankful for the recognition the chancellor had won for their country and appreciated the sense of stability and security his government had given them. This time the most successful election slogan had been: "No experiments." The choice of Bonn as the meeting place for the NATO Council four months before also contributed to the result.

More than anything else the two elections were plebiscites in favour of Adenauer. It was his name and his portrait that were the chief vote catchers. The CDU acknowledged the fact by exploiting his personality to the full in all the *Land* election campaigns as well. Not only had Adenauer pursued policies which appealed to the electorate. He had the invaluable ability to simplify the complex issues of foreign policy and make voters feel that they understood them and his views on them. Moreover, he managed somehow to win the confidence both of the newly enfranchised and perplexed younger generation and of the voters already on the lists, amongst whom, as a result of the war, there was an unusually high proportion of women and people over forty-five years old.

(d) Economic Recovery

Western Germany's economic recovery influenced those other aspects of the country's progress for which Adenauer was mainly responsible: social and political stability and acceptance into the Western alliance. Yet the influence worked both ways. Stable political conditions and absence of serious industrial conflict contributed greatly to economic revival, and Germany's rising international reputation naturally favoured the development of her foreign trade. Adenauer, therefore, though not the moving spirit behind his country's economic progress, provided the essential framework within which it took place.

Although he had no specialist knowledge of financial and economic matters, he exercised in two ways an important influence on these sides of the national life. In the first place, he made a habit of interesting himself in those aspects of the economy which were politically important, whether from a domestic or a diplomatic point of view. In internal politics wages, prices, and anything affecting living standards might obviously have an influence on the government's popularity and electoral prospects. In external affairs, he was concerned about economic problems which had some bearing on the development of the European Coal and Steel Community or the Common Market. Secondly, he brought to the consideration of important economic questions a balanced, broadly human, and common-sense point of view, which often had the salutary effect of counterbalancing the rigid professional standpoints of his ministers of finance and economic affairs. As was his custom in most branches of politics, he took the precaution of arming himself with the best available expert advice and in so doing by no means confined himself to ministers and other official advisers.

Some of the foundations of economic recovery had already been laid before the establishment of the Federal Republic in 1949. It was a strange and ironic fact that the destruction of German industries by Allied bombing and the subsequent Allied dismantling programme worked out in the end in favour of the country's economy. The Germans were obliged to replace the equipment that had been destroyed or removed, and they did so naturally by the most modern and efficient equipment available, often from the United States. The Marshall Plan also, which was announced in 1947 and went into effect the following year, brought Germany economic aid from the United States, worth in all nearly one and a half milliard dollars, just at the time when such assistance was most urgently required. Professor Erhard has written of it: "This magnanimous support deserves above all to be assessed from the point of view of its moral effect. It gave German people the feeling that they were no longer written off by the rest of the world but that they also could again take part in the progress of the free world. Its economic and financial significance was, moreover, no less."[12] Lastly, the Allied currency reform of June 1948 played a vital part in preparing the way for economic progress: it brought an

[12] In *Wohlstand für Alle*, p. 335.

end to a period of uncertainty and widespread black-market activities and restored confidence in the mark; by reducing cash holdings and credit balances to one tenth of their former value it greatly increased the incentive to earn and save; and by fixing the exchange rate so that the mark was undervalued during the early years of recovery it helped German exports.

West German recovery was based on the policy of *soziale Marktwirtschaft* which literally means "social market economy" but can be better translated as "free enterprise tempered by social conscience." The policy can best be understood in the light of the personality of its initiator, Professor Ludwig Erhard, and in relation to the two very different schools of thought that influenced him.

Erhard was a specialist in industrial economics. He had become director of the Economic Council in the Bizone in 1948, and the following year Adenauer appointed him Federal Minister for Economic Affairs. Although he had orginally stood closer to the FDP and it was that party which had proposed him for the bizonal post, he joined the CDU before the 1949 election. He believed ardently in the virtues of free competition and of giving full play to the market mechanism, and his belief was influenced by his knowledge of the German character. He knew well that the industry of his fellow countrymen fitted them specially to take advantage of economic freedom and that after twelve years of totalitarian controls followed by several years of military government they would appreciate the opportunity of doing so. He was as much opposed to restrictions arising from cartelization as to those resulting from trade-union action. On the other hand, there was a warm human side to Erhard as an economist, as a politician, and as a man. He was fully convinced that a market economy must develop for the good of society as a whole and not merely for the benefit of hardheaded and enterprising individuals.

The policy of social market economy, therefore, combined

concern for social justice and stability with giving scope to individual industry and initiative. As, however, the current tendency, in any case was to place more emphasis on the social obligations of the state than upon the need for free enterprise, Erhard was perhaps inclined in his statements to give more attention to the second aspect. The following extracts from an article published in January 1950 and a speech delivered in February 1961 are characteristic:[13]

My economic policy is determined by confidence in the power of personality and by the fact that I consider human freedom to be the highest value in every community.

It is indispensable that every class in our society, in fact, every single citizen should be conscious of the fact he should not inveigh against the "capitalists" and not make the state alone responsible for his social existence, but that it is his duty to co-operate in the shaping of his own and our common future.

The emphasis on free enterprise in the policy of social market economy was due mainly to liberal influence. It was significant that Erhard himself had a good deal of sympathy with the FDP and that the FDP participated in Adenauer's governments during nine of its fourteen years' existence. In spite of the party's comparatively small size, it exerted, throughout the whole period, a disproportionate influence on the attitudes of Germans of all parties towards economic affairs. The *social* aspect of Erhard's policy reflected the general trend in the Western world towards the welfare state, and within the Federal Republic it had two chief protagonists, the SPD and the Left wing of the CDU. The SPD, as the main opposition party, exercised a steady influence on the government to make concessions in the direction of social justice. Within the CDU a similar influence was exerted by the Catholic trade unionists, led by Karl Arnold, the influential minister-president of North Rhine-

---

[13] L. Erhard, *Deutsche Wirtschaftspolitik*, pp. 121 and 551.

Westphalia, and Jakob Kaiser, who was at first CDU chairman in the Soviet zone and later Federal Minister for All-German Affairs. This group inspired the social and economic programme of the CDU in the British zone, the so-called *Ahlener Programme*, which was drawn up in 1947. The programme was critical of capitalism, advocated a system of controls and cooperation in industry, and supported the principle of co-management. Although the party as a whole subsequently moved towards the Right, the group, which formed itself into "social committees," continued to exert considerable influence, which Adenauer was disposed to accept, because it harmonized with his own views on social stability.

West German economic recovery has been frequently described as "the German miracle." The expression has remained in fashion for so long for two reasons. What happened was a very remarkable achievement, and the word "miracle" does full justice to the astonished reaction of foreigners. As far as Germans were concerned, it provided somewhat melodramatic satisfaction to a people whose morale was in need of a boost. For this reason responsible Germans, such as Erhard and President Heuss, have taken exception to it. On one occasion President Heuss, after indicating his dislike of the expression, quoted the saying, "A miracle is the favourite child of faith."[14]

So far from being supernatural, German economic recovery is neither inexplicable nor even hard to explain. In addition to the foundations laid before the summer of 1949, which have already been described, there were three basic reasons for the country's rapid economic expansion.

The first was a mixture of the psychological and the severely practical. A proud and industrious people with many fine qualities had been defeated and humiliated. They had a burning desire to make good and to show by their actions what they were really worth: the great majority of them were prepared to

---

[14] In an informal discussion in 1955 at which the writer was present.

work very hard to achieve this objective. In the early post-war years their readiness was often reinforced by the fact that they had lost most if not all of their possessions. In order to pay for simple necessities in furniture or clothing, very long hours were worked willingly, because they meant overtime and higher rates of pay, and the habits then acquired persisted after the need for them had really passed. As late as 1955 and 1956 many men were working on an average sixty to seventy hours a week by their own choice, and volunteers to do double shifts were common amongst dock workers. In 1948 one enterprising statistician worked out that under existing conditions a German could expect to obtain a new shirt every eighteen years, a new pair of socks every twenty-nine years, and a new suit every ninety-eight years. Whether or not the calculation was accurate is immaterial. The very act of making it revealed a sensitivity to their situation, which provides a clue to the attitude of many Germans at the time.

The second reason was the high rate of investment throughout the post-war years. In 1950 the West German investment ratio was already very high compared with that in other countries and from then until about 1958 it rose still further. In 1960 total capital expenditure "at current prices was over three times, and at 1954 prices over two and a half times greater than it had been in 1950."[15] From 1950 to 1960 total fixed investment at home absorbed 21.9 per cent of the gross national product in Western Germany compared with 16.6 per cent in the United Kingdom.[16] These results could be achieved owing to German industry's willingness to plough back profits into the enterprises that produced them and owing to the desire of the German people to save. From 1950 to 1960 private consumption amounted to only 59 per cent of the gross na-

[15] Hans Fecher and Alois Oberhauser, Economic Development of Western Germany, p. 45.
[16] R. G. Opie, Western Germany's Economic Miracle, p. 6.

tional product in the Federal Republic compared with 65 per cent in the United Kingdom.[17]

Thirdly, there was a very large and quite exceptional increase in the labour supply. By 1963, as has been seen, the Federal Republic had absorbed over 14 million refugees, expellees, and foreign workers. The great majority of refugees arrived during the immediate post-war years and were at first a serious burden on the economy. But up to August 1961 there was a fairly steady flow of immigrants from the Soviet zone, and the foreign workers only started to come in on a large scale in 1960, when there was a demand for them. This state of affairs greatly facilitated the expansion of industry, though until about 1960 it was not accompanied by a condition of full employment with the consequent pressure on wage rates.[18] Furthermore, the additional workers who became available had two great advantages. They were more mobile than labour usually is. Having either lost their homes or left them voluntarily, they were, on the whole, prepared to go where the demand was greatest. Also the refugees included many skilled workers, especially those who had come from Silesia, the Sudetenland, and the Soviet zone. A considerable number of them had the skills necessary to set up valuable industries on their own; for example, the lensmakers from the Zeiss works in the Soviet zone and the glassworkers from Gablonz in Czechoslovakia.

German recovery was thus due to favourable conditions which were partly fortuitous, partly the result of effort, and partly the consequence of wise decisions. During the fourteen years of the Adenauer era the country's economy was transformed.

Between the foundation of the Federal Republic and the end

[17] *Ibid.*, p. 8.

[18] There were more than a million registered unemployed up to 1955, and more than half a million up to 1959, though there were also many vacant posts waiting to be filled.

of 1962 over 6.8 million dwellings were built, and the average number and size of the rooms in each of them increased. In road-building Western Germany stood next after the United States and Canada. The amount spent on federal main roads rose from 480 million marks in 1955 to 2,387 million in 1962. The number of motor vehicles in use increased in round numbers from 1.4 million in 1949 to 9.5 million in 1962. German airlines (*Lufthansa*), which were refounded in 1955, carried 229,670 passengers in 1956 and 1,860,000 in 1962.[19]

The German genius, since the Second World War, has found its fullest expression no longer in the cultural or military fields but in industry and salesmanship. The production of rolled steel goods rose from 6,339 thousand tons in 1949 to 20,990 thousand in 1963,[20] and in 1961 the Federal Republic was third among the world's steel-producing countries, excelled only by the United States and the Soviet Union. The number of passenger cars produced increased from 104,055 in 1949 to 2,186,000 in 1963.[21] Before Adenauer's resignation Western Germany was second only to the United States in engineering and electro-technical exports and was third, after the United Kingdom and Japan, in the world list of shipbuilding countries. Her merchant fleet rose from 300,000 tons in 1949 to 5,203,-000 tons at the beginning of 1963.[22]

To look at the country's progress in broader terms, the index of total net industrial production, taking the 1950 figure as equivalent to 100, rose by 1963 to 283,[23] while industrial production per working hour more than doubled between 1950 and 1962.[24] These results were not accompanied by an undue

<hr>

[19] The figures in this paragraph are taken from *Regierung Adenauer 1949–1963*.

[20] *Statistisches Jahrbuch für die Bundesrepublik Deutschland, 1964.*

[21] *Ibid.*

[22] *Regierung Adenauer 1949–1963.*

[23] *Statistisches Jahrbuch für die Bundesrepublik Deutschland, 1964.*

[24] *Regierung Adenauer 1949–1963.*

rise in the cost of living. The German people, having lived through inflations after the two world wars, were very anxious to avoid a repetition of the experience. Erhard endeavoured to prevent any rise in wages that was not justified by an increase in productivity and summed up his attitude by writing: "Inflation does not come upon us like a curse or a tragic stroke of fate: it is always brought about by an irresponsible or even a criminal policy."[25] With 1950 again as a basis the cost of living index rose by 1959 to only 121 compared with 147 in the United Kingdom and 167 in France.[26] At the same time the industrial worker's average gross weekly earning rose from 58.21 marks in 1950 to 149.74 marks in 1962.[27] As a result, on the one hand, the amount of private savings increased considerably, while, on the other hand, private consumption per head rose by 58 per cent between 1953 and 1960, compared with an average of 24 per cent in all OEEC countries and only 25 per cent in the United Kingdom.[28] In more specific terms between 1950 and 1960 the number of private cars increased about eightfold,[29] and from 1952 to 1960 the amounts of brandy and cigarettes consumed were doubled and trebled respectively.[30]

If the increase in the labour supply made possible the exceptional rate and scale of German recovery, the fact that so many additional workers could be absorbed was also the best proof of the economy's strength. According to official statistics, between 1950 and 1962 the number of employed persons rose from 13,827,000 to 21,097,000, while the number of unemployed

[25] *Wohlstand Für Alle*, p. 271.
[26] *Ibid.*, pp. 345–46.
[27] H. H. Götz, *Weil Alle Besser Leben Wollen*, p. 262.
[28] R. G. Opie, *Western Germany's Economic Miracle*, p. 5.
[29] N. J. G. Pounds, *The Economic Pattern in Modern Germany*, p. 108.
[30] Hans Fecher and Alois Oberhauser, *Economic Development of Western Germany*, p. 46.

fell from 1,580,000 to 142,000.[31] The figure for the unemployed in 1962 was made up largely of those temporarily out of work, including refugees in transit camps, and was much lower than the number of vacant posts. In fact, it was so low that for some months in 1961 and 1962 the contributions for unemployment insurance were suspended altogether, and later the rate was reduced. Early in 1950 a well-known German journalist pointed out that the 9 million German refugees that had entered the Federal Republic up to that time exceeded the net emigration from Germany to North America during the whole period from 1908 to 1949 and this at a time when Germany had lost her main food surplus area in the East.[32]

Agriculture was not able to keep pace with the expansion rate of West German industry. The task facing German farmers after the war was formidable. Their farms were suffering from devastation, loss of livestock, inadequate equipment, and lack of labour. The millions of refugees made the loss of food supplies from the eastern territories much more acute. With government assistance the farmers' achievement was substantial. During 1948–49, the first year after the currency reform, the consumption of food per head of population was about a third below the pre-war level. By 1955–56 it had reached the pre-war level, and in 1961–62 it was about 13 per cent above the average for the immediate pre-war years. During the period from 1948 to 1962 the proportion of food consumed, which was produced at home, averaged about 70 per cent, although the needs of the Federal Republic were about 30 per cent greater than those of the same area before the war. Nevertheless the relative contribution of agriculture to the gross national product decreased.

[31] Publications of the Federal Ministry for Labour and Social Affairs and of the Federal Statistical Office, quoted in *Regierung Adenauer 1949–1963*, p. 697.
[32] Marion Dönhoff, *Germany Puts Freedom Before Unity*.

There were several basic and intractable reasons for this. The great majority of the larger German farms, which could be most easily mechanized and modernized, were in the lost eastern territories. The Federal Republic in its agriculture is predominantly a land of peasant farmers. The average size of agricultural holdings, not counting those of less than half a hectare, is about 8.3 hectares (20.5 acres). The total number of tractors increased from less than 100,000 in 1949 to over a million in 1963, but, as more than a quarter of the farms were under 2 hectares in area, and over a half did not exceed 5 hectares, it is not surprising that in 1955 about four fifths of the farms did not own or have a part share in a tractor. Another serious problem for German agriculture was a more general phenomenon, the flight from the land. The varied possibilities and the regular hours offered by industrial employment made it difficult for many young people in the country to resist the attractions of town life. The agricultural population in the territory now occupied by the Federal Republic numbered 7 million in 1939, or 17.9 per cent of the total: by 1960 it was estimated as having shrunk to 5.6 million, or 10.5 per cent of the larger total. At the same time this trend has been accompanied by another that is also damaging to agriculture, a shift of certain types of industry from the town to the country. During the Adenauer era the character of the German countryside has been changing. Small factories have sprung up in many villages, especially in Baden-Württemberg, though in other parts of the country as well. As a result of these two tendencies, it was estimated in 1960–61 that of the total number of people permanently employed on the land only about a tenth were farm labourers, the rest being the owners of the farms or members of their families.[33]

Under these conditions from a world point of view German

[33] The figures in this paragraph and the last are mostly taken from *Regierung Adenauer 1949–1963*.

farming could not compete with the large-scale farming of the United States, Canada, and other countries. Within the European Economic Community (EEC), as regards production per hectare, the Federal Republic stands below Holland, Belgium, and Luxemburg, but above France and Italy. But France and Italy both have much larger areas under cultivation. Western Germany is the only country in the EEC which does not export more than it imports in the case of a single important agricultural product. Amongst Common Market countries it is the chief importer of agricultural produce.

The federal government has been aware of the need to strengthen the position of agriculture. It has passed laws and drawn up so-called "Green Plans" for the purpose of guaranteeing markets for farm produce at suitable prices, consolidating scattered holdings, joining together small, uneconomic farms, modernizing buildings, and facilitating other methods to increase productivity. Some of these measures have conflicted with Erhard's views on free enterprise, but Adenauer, with his well-developed social sense and his desire to satisfy the rural electorate, complained that Erhard did not always see the political implication of economic policy, and he used his own authority to put the measures through. They have inevitably led to difficulties in Western Germany's relations with the Common Market.

The result of German economic expansion most noticeable to the world as a whole, and to Germans themselves the most gratifying, was the country's astonishing achievement in external trade. The first indication of what might happen was given during the fifteen months that followed the foundation of the Federal Republic. Between October 1949 and December 1950 West German exports trebled. But imports increased so quickly also that the trading balance remained passive. Between 1950 and 1963, however, a transformation took place which could scarcely have been foreseen by anyone. The value of Western

Germany's imports rose from 11.4 milliard marks to 52.3 milliard, and its share of world imports from 4.6 per cent to 9.2 per cent. During the same period its exports increased from 8.4 milliard marks to 58.3 milliard, and its share of world exports from 3.6 per cent to 11 per cent.[34] In 1963 the Federal Republic had the same percentage of world imports as the United Kingdom but had become the world's second exporting country, second only to the United States. Its trade balance changed from a deficit of 300 million marks in 1950 to a surplus of 5,300 million in 1959. Its reserves in gold and convertible currencies increased by $6,000 million between the end of 1952 and the end of 1960. In March 1961 the federal government decided, some said belatedly, to revalue the mark upwards by 4.75 per cent.

As the Federal Republic's economic recovery had contributed to its acceptance into the Western alliance, so its growing industrial strength after 1955 increased its diplomatic influence. Its achievement made a special impression on the United States, which came increasingly to respect Western Germany's value as an ally. It added greatly to the self-confidence of West German statesmen and diplomatic representatives, and it enhanced the country's potential role in the trial of strength between communism and the Western democracies, particularly in relation to underdeveloped countries. The Federal Republic's powerful economic position made it easier for it to take up a magnanimous and forward-looking attitude towards most international questions, in contrast to the regressive national self-assertiveness of de Gaulle with his unresolved complexes. According to Prince Hohenlohe, the Austrian ambassador to Germany, Kaiser William II in June 1918 spoke disparagingly of the Anglo-Saxon philosophy of life, which he described as an idolatrous attitude towards money.[35] There is a good deal of

[34] *Statistisches Jahrbuch für die Bundesrepublik Deutschland, 1964.*
[35] See Fritz Fischer, *Griff nach der Weltmacht*, p. 838.

irony in the fact that the Kaiser's own country, after being defeated twice by the Anglo-Saxon democracies, was to owe the recovery of its diplomatic prestige to a large extent to its material success. In fact, in spite of William II's sanctimonious talk on the same occasion about "justice, freedom, honour, and morality" as typically German characteristics, Germany had even during his own reign owed a great deal to its industrial achievements.

(e) European Integration and the European Community

Adenauer, as has been seen, was an untypical product of the pre-1914 era. He was born in 1876, just in the middle of Bismarck's twenty-eight years in office, and he was already thirty-eight years old when the First World War broke out. He also had many of the characteristics associated with Germans of his generation. He was hard-working, self-disciplined, conservative by temperament, respectful of authority, and loyal to his country. Yet the Second Empire was the age of triumphant nationalism in German history, and its foundation marked the triumph of the Prussian spirit in German political life. Adenauer was never a narrow or a passionate nationalist, and he was well aware of the part played by the nationalists in preparing the way for Hitler. As a Catholic from what may be called the heartland of Europe he disliked the Prussians, whose influence he considered to be at best Protestant and at worst pagan. In a sense he belonged as a man to the Second Empire and as a political thinker and a statesman to the twentieth century.

Adenauer was determined to wipe out the disgrace of the Nazi era. He realized that Hitler's regime had parodied in a grim way the overdone nationalism of the Second Empire. He therefore set out to replace nationalism by a new European ideal. "The age of the nation state belongs to the past, a past full of jealousy and steeped in blood,"[36] he wrote. German youth, he believed, must be given the ideal of working for Europe. His conception of Europe, however, was different from that which came to be adopted by the younger generation in Germany and other countries. Twentieth-century youth, looking to the future, was rationally convinced in increasing numbers that nationalism was inadequate as an ideal and that political integration was necessary, at least on a regional, and if possible on a world basis. Adenauer's Europeanism, on the other hand, was rooted in the past.

The clue to his European attitude lies in his being a Catholic and a Rhinelander. As a Catholic he was deeply concerned to save Europe's great Christian heritage from the results of an exaggerated and discredited nationalism and from the new threat presented by Soviet communism. Roman Catholicism has always contained a cosmopolitan element and it was not, therefore, surprising that two of Adenauer's closest associates in the European integration movement were the Catholic Christian Democrats, Robert Schuman, the French foreign minister, and Alcide De Gasperi, prime minister of Italy. The intellectual pioneer of European integration, Count Coudenhove-Kalergi, suggested towards the end of 1952 in an article entitled, *Europe without Europeans*, that this triumvirate had been so successful as the architects of European federation, that there was a danger that Europe might unite before the mass of Europeans had developed sufficient European loyalty.[37] It was equally important that Adenauer was a Rhinelander, and it was not wholly accidental that his first State Secretary for Foreign Affairs, Professor Hallstein, also came from the Rhineland. The Cologne-Aachen area, with which the Adenauer family was associated,

---

[36] In an article, "Unsere beiden Völker," published in *Die Zeit*, June 26, 1952.
[37] *Rheinische Merkur*, November 14, 1952.

produced one of the lowest proportions of Nazi votes in all Germany during the last elections before Hitler came into power. Adenauer was proud of this, and of the traditions of his homeland. Ernst Reuter, the great Socialist mayor of Berlin, once said that the main difference between Adenauer and himself was that the chancellor came from the Rhineland, while he himself was a Prussian. As a Rhinelander Adenauer had, in some ways, closer affinity with Paris than with Berlin and Eastern Germany of which he always had a certain dislike and suspicion. So in his conception of European integration it was natural that the Franco-German alliance should occupy a special place.

In March 1950 he gave two press interviews in which he spoke of the need for Franco-German co-operation, even suggesting that it should lead ultimately to political union. Just two months later Robert Schuman put forward his proposals for the common control of French and German coal and steel production. The following April Adenauer went to Paris to sign the Schuman Plan treaty. On arrival at Orly airport, he pointed out that it was his first official visit abroad as chancellor and then said: "It is with deliberate intention that my first official visit is to the French capital. I wish in this way to demonstrate that I consider Franco-German relations to be the central question in the solution of the European problem."[38] The next year he published a number of newspaper articles in which he reverted to the same subject. In June 1952, for example, after mentioning that "the ballast" of misunderstandings and errors between the French and German peoples must not be carried from generation to generation, he wrote:

We can no longer afford to continue this feud, because we stand today before the historical necessity of bringing about a union of all those peoples, who like us are endeavouring to

[38] Quoted by P. Weymar, *Konrad Adenauer*, p. 606.

preserve Western values and the principles of freedom which they imply.[39]

As things turned out, the Schuman Plan and the other plans for European integration in special fields were all confined to the six countries: Western Germany, France, Italy, and the Benelux group, Belgium, Holland, and Luxemburg. Some of Adenauer's fellow countrymen were interested primarily in German reunification and the related East European problem. Others believed that an integrated Western Europe must include Great Britain and the Scandinavian peoples. But Adenauer, the Rhinelander with a sense of history, was substantially content with a Carolingian conception of an integrated Western Europe, made up of the Six, at least as a beginning. The countries involved were also predominantly Catholic. To those who maintained that the conception was too limited, the chancellor could reply that this nucleus had almost the same number of inhabitants as the United States; that its total production of goods and services was only about 15 per cent lower than that of the Soviet Union; and that its volume of trade was far in excess of the amount handled by the Soviet Union, and even greater than that of the United States. It formed, therefore, a very satisfactory basis for an integrated Europe.

Adenauer's attitude to Europe was that of a traditionalist. From the German point of view, he repudiated the exaggerated and harmful nationalism associated with his country's recent history, but he was a staunch patriot. He believed in the traditional German virtues and the great contribution that Germany could still make to Europe and to the world. But he considered that under existing conditions its best chance of exerting its influence would be within the framework of an integrated Europe in which it would undoubtedly play a leading role. From the European point of view, he was proud of the great role the

[39] "Unsere beiden Völker," *Die Zeit,* June 26, 1952.

continent had played in the development of Christian civilization, and he deeply regretted two suicidal world wars, because
their results had so seriously reduced Europe's relative authority. For him European integration was essential, if the continent was again to assert the political, cultural, and economic
influence in the world that was her due. On March 19, 1953,
during the Bundestag debate on the third reading of the treaty,
which was to set up the European Defence Community, Adenauer said:

These West European countries are no longer in such a position that each can defend itself on its own, they are no longer
in such a position that each can save European culture by itself.
These aims, which are common to all of us, can only be attained, if West European countries join together, politically,
economically, and culturally, and if above all they also render
any further warlike contests amongst themselves impossible.

Adenauer's belief in the European idea, therefore, was that
of a proud but disappointed European, not that of a typical
twentieth-century citizen of the world. For this reason he was
most interested in political integration, for it alone would prevent the recurrence of wars which had done so much harm in
the past. He wanted Western Europe to be so closely integrated
politically that, in future, statesmen in his own or the associated
states would not be in a position to make dangerous political or
military decisions to further the supposed interests of their own
countries. It was left to Erhard and others to expound from the
German point of view the way in which integration could be
furthered by such economic means as free trade and the free
convertibility of currencies. Adenauer himself, in his realistic
way, welcomed and took up proposals for the establishment of
such institutions as the European Coal and Steel Community
(ECSC), the European Defence Community (EDC), the European Economic Community (EEC), and the European

Atomic Energy Community (Euratom), because they were likely to further his own main purpose. But that purpose remained closer political association.

A statement on European integration made in November 1954 by Herr Hermann Abs, to whom Adenauer often turned for advice, perhaps throws more light on the chancellor's own attitude than any single statement he himself made:

There is a deep-rooted conviction throughout all the parties active in the Federal Republic that the era of nationalism has passed its culmination point, and that the parts of Europe which are still free should make a special effort to achieve greater political unity than ever before. On the other hand, an appreciation of the federal structure of the Continent, in other words, the preservation of national characteristics and interests, continues to be clearly discernible among Germans who, after all, are in the habit of jealously defending their own tribal characteristics in argument with one another. . . . One thing is certain: no nation can claim to have outdone the Germans in nationalist exaggerations during the past forty years or so. In terms of centuries, however, I believe that the notion of the national state is not so deep-rooted in my own country as for example, in France. That country's greatness would seem to have been in a higher degree founded upon the existence of a powerful state under a central leadership . . . up to the beginning of the nineteenth century the Germans clung to the idea —admittedly worn thin with the years—of a Holy Roman Empire. This concept was certainly not in line with the notion of a national state; nor can it always and solely be construed as an expression of German imperialism. Incidentally, it is quite possible that the Germans are finding it easier to become accustomed to the presence of supra-national contacts because, living as they do on the very boundary of the Soviet sphere of power, they are being taught in a particularly painful manner to realize how inadequate are the possibilities for self-assertion today for the comparatively small national states composing Central and Western Europe. Nor do the Germans appreciate that the introduction of a supra-national authority involves parting with sovereignty rights. Having for a number of years not enjoyed sovereignty, it is easier for them to part with it than those countries which retain it in full.[40]

The Petersberg Agreements paved the way for the acceptance of the Federal Republic into the European community. But, when they were signed, the Allied high commissioners could not have foreseen the part Adenauer was to play in the development of the community. One month before, on October 20, 1949, the Federal Republic had become a member of the Organization for European Economic Co-operation (OEEC), the body which had been given the specific task of planning the Marshall Aid programme at the European end. At the time of the Petersberg negotiations, however, the one institution that existed with broad objectives and the avowed purpose of furthering European integration was the Council of Europe. Its statute had been signed the previous May and twelve countries had already become members: the Benelux group, Denmark, France, Greece, Ireland, Italy, Norway, Sweden, Turkey, and the United Kingdom. In September during its first session the Council's Assembly had decided that "the aim and goal of the Council of Europe" was "the creation of a European political authority with limited functions but real powers." For Western Germany, therefore, membership of the Council would mean an important step towards recognition in the Western world and a channel through which its chancellor could pursue his European aims. So Adenauer had good reason to be gratified with the Allied high commissioners' desire that the Federal Republic should become an associate member. The associate membership was taken up in July 1950, and full membership followed ten months later.

The Council of Europe has some valuable achievements to

[40] From "Germany and the London and Paris Agreements," an address given at Chatham House on November 18, 1945; published in *International Affairs*, April 1955.

its credit, in particular as a forum for the expression of European points of view. But it has failed in its aim of creating a European political authority with real powers, owing to differences of opinion amongst its members. Adenauer's interest in it has therefore declined.

His immediate and favourable reaction to the Schuman Plan in May 1950 can be explained on two main grounds. In the first place, as he pointed out in a press conference at the time, the plan contained "not just general phrases but concrete and precise proposals."[41] Secondly, he saw at once its important political implications. The iron ore of Lorraine and the coal of the Saar had become two of the chief bones of contention between France and Germany since the industrial revolution had made its impact on the two countries. Germany's growing industrial strength and France's fear of it had accentuated the traditional rivalry between them. Adenauer believed that, if their heavy industries came under a common authority, war between them would scarcely be possible. During the Bundestag debate on the Schuman Plan in July 1951 he said:

I believe that for the first time in the history of the last few centuries countries intend of their own free will and without any compulsion to give up part of their sovereignty, in order to transfer this sovereignty to a supra-national body. That is, it seems to me—and I want to emphasize this particularly—an event of significance in world history, an event which means the end of nationalism in all these countries.

Schuman's original proposals related specifically to France and Western Germany, but they were to include any European countries that were willing to participate. They culminated in a treaty for the establishment of the European Coal and Steel Community comprising France, Western Germany, Italy, and the Benelux countries. The Federal Republic, early in 1952,

[41] P. Weymar, *op. cit.*, p. 517.

was the first country to complete ratification of the treaty. After it had done so, Jean Monnet, who in the background had been the real architect of the community and became first president of its High Authority, telegraphed to Adenauer: "Europe is born, long live Europe." The American high commissioner, McCloy, speaking for himself and his French and British colleagues, told Adenauer that they were all very happy he had taken up Schuman's idea so promptly.

Adenauer responded with equal readiness to the proposals for the creation of an integrated European army and the establishment of a European Defence Community, though they met with much greater opposition both in the Federal Republic and in France. He himself had little or nothing of the traditional German pride in military power and efficiency. He once said rather plaintively, and with justification, that it was a paradox of history that the task of reintroducing soldiers into Germany should have fallen to him. But he was very conscious of the communist threat and very anxious that Germany should co-operate fully with the Western powers in the emergency created by the Korean War. Moreover EDC, in which the general staff was to be organized internationally, seemed the framework within which German rearmament could take place with the least possible military or political danger. After the chancellor had carried on a long and successful struggle to ratify the EDC Treaty, it was turned down, as has been seen, by France. This gave Adenauer the biggest shock and disappointment of his career as chancellor. His normal equanimity gave way, and a British diplomatist who met him at the time had the impression that he was shattered. It was not until Eden arrived with his plans for an alternative solution, that he visibly revived.

When the Council of Ministers of the ECSC met for the first time in September 1952, Adenauer took the chair. The meeting decided to draw up a draft treaty for the establishment of a European Political Community. This idea fitted in with Adenauer's conception of European integration. The Political Community might dovetail in with and pull together the Coal and Steel Community and the proposed Defence Community. An *ad hoc* committee was set up to prepare the draft treaty, and it completed its report early in 1953. It proposed that the Political Community, a supra-national organization, should assume the powers of the ECSC and the EDC and any other powers which the governments of the six member states wished to transfer to it. It was to have a bicameral parliament to which its Council of Ministers should be responsible.

Consideration of the draft treaty by the governments concerned was repeatedly postponed, as successive French cabinets hesitated to risk presenting it for parliamentary approval. In the end, with the rejection of EDC, the draft treaty was dropped too. In one respect Coudenhove-Kalergi was proved right: in the European movement the statesmen were ahead of popular feeling, though the fact had revealed itself before rather than after federation had been achieved.

Western European Union and West German membership of NATO were perhaps a second-best solution to the problem of how Germany could safely be brought into the Western defence system. NATO implied some limitation of each nation's control over its armed forces. But the system adopted avoided the renunciation of sovereignty which EDC and the Political Community would have involved, and which might well have proved the irrevocable step on the road to full integration. Furthermore, the idea of a European army with common uniforms and common equipment made a much greater appeal to the imaginations of the new generation of Germans, who were prepared to put European loyalty before the dangerous nationalism of the past.

Adenauer, however, after six years of strenuous effort, was well content with what had been achieved by May 1955: his country's sovereignty had been restored; the Federal Republic had been recognized as a respected member of the Western community; and the bold experiment of a European Coal and Steel Community was proving a success. He gave his full support to the further steps towards integration that were taken during the next two or three years. But they were primarily economic in character, and he did not personally play such an outstanding role in the next phase of development as he had played during the first vital years.

Two events had occurred before May 1955 which prepared the way for further progress towards integration. In November 1954 Jean Monnet, as a reaction to the French government's opposition to supra-national institutions, gave notice of his intended resignation from the presidency of the ECSC High Authority and announced that he intended to devote himself as a private citizen to the cause of European federation. His resignation took effect in June 1955, and the stimulating influence of this great practical idealist's new activities soon began to make itself felt. Early in 1955 also the Benelux governments made it clear that they considered the time ripe for further steps in the direction of economic integration. As a result representatives of the six ECSC countries met at Messina in June and discussed a memorandum submitted by the Benelux countries. The conference finally approved a resolution in which it was agreed that the time for a new phase in constructing Europe had arrived, especially in the economic sphere, that it was necessary to continue the creation of a United Europe through the expansion of joint institutions and the creation of a common market, and that atomic development for peaceful purposes should be jointly organized.

After the Messina proposals had been the subject of careful study and negotiation, two treaties were eventually signed at Rome, on March 25, 1957, by the Six. One created a European Economic Community, the main purposes of which were to establish a Common Market by abolishing customs quotas and restrictions between the members, and to consolidate the separate external tariffs into a single tariff system in relation to the outside world. The Economic Community, according to the preamble, was also intended as a step towards political unification. The second treaty provided for the setting up of a European Atomic Energy Community for the purpose of co-ordinating nuclear research and power projects. The two treaties laid down that two of the institutions of ECSC, the Assembly and the Court of Justice, should have their powers extended and redefined in order to serve EEC and Euratom as well. It was a tribute to the part played by Adenauer in European integration that his close associate, Professor Hallstein, who had represented him at Messina, was appointed the first president of EEC's main executive body, known as the Commission.

In December 1960 a convention was signed in Paris replacing OEEC by the Organization for Economic Co-operation and Development (OECD.) It took effect the following September. The change had two main purposes. First, it extended the basic function of OEEC, which was to organize economic co-operation between its members, to include the provision of assistance to less developed, or so-called developing, countries. Secondly, it added the United States and Canada as full members to the OEEC's membership of eighteen states. In the convention the signatories recognized that the economic recovery and progress of Europe had opened fresh perspectives for applying "the new tradition of co-operation," which had evolved among them, to "new tasks and broader objectives." One of their main aims was "to contribute to sound economic expansion in member as well as non-member countries in the process of economic development."[42]

For some years Western Germany had been showing an increasing interest in the developing countries. In 1953 official funds were made available to send German experts overseas,

[42] See Preamble and Article I of the OECD Convention.

and three years later the first officially sponsored technical trainees from developing countries started coming to Germany. By 1963 they were arriving at the rate of more than 1,000 a year. According to OECD figures in 1957, 1958, and 1959 the Federal Republic contributed more than any other country to developing countries through multilateral agencies, while in 1962 its total contribution from public and private sources through multilateral agencies or on a bilateral basis exceeded 2.5 milliard marks, or £226 million, which came near to the British figure of £241 million.[43] German official statistics give the total amount of aid to developing countries in all forms during the twelve years from 1950 to 1962 as over 20 milliard marks.[44] In 1960 an Inter-ministerial Committee for Development Assistance was created to co-ordinate aid policy, and the following year after the federal elections a Ministry for Economic Co-operation was set up, with the task of handling the government's aid programme. A Development Service was also established, on the lines of the British Voluntary Service Overseas and the American Peace Corps, to encourage qualified young Germans to work in developing countries for limited periods, and the number of volunteers was soon comparable to that in the British Service.

Erhard was a consistent and persuasive supporter of aid to developing countries. He gave it high priority in Western, and especially German, policy on three grounds: moral obligation, political wisdom, and economic good sense. It was a moral duty, because the *per capita* income in the Federal Republic was over 900 dollars a year, while over a milliard people in the world had an income of less than 100 dollars. Moreover, it was owing to American aid that Germany had been able embark on her own recovery programme. It was politically wise, because it

[43] See the article by John White, "West German Aid to Developing Countries" in *International Affairs*, January 1965.
[44] *Regierung Adenauer* 1949–1963, p. 425.

was the necessary complement of the Western defence effort: the developing countries must be helped to liberate themselves from poverty and need within the framework of a free economic and social order and not be driven to resort to communist coercion. Finally, it was economically sound, partly because good relations with the developing countries were in themselves desirable and Germany was relatively free from the colonial taint, and partly because highly developed industrial states could not expect to enjoy a comfortable and undisturbed existence indefinitely, if the contrast between their standard of living and that of the have-not states grew greater rather than less. The Social Democrats also were strong advocates of a generous aid programme, for reasons which were much the same as Erhard's.

Adenauer personally was not much interested in the developing countries. The idea of devoting large sums to remote and little known countries for the sake of long-term results was a new one, typical of the twentieth century, which at his age he could hardly be expected to make his own. In this matter the narrow, provincial side of his character asserted itself. But under his government Western Germany had become a powerful industrial state and a leading member of the West European community. Its commercial position brought with it responsibilities which it could scarcely renounce, and, when OEEC gave way to a body with a universal rather than a continental horizon, the Federal Republic was faced with a correspondingly greater challenge.

One facet of Franco-German relations revealed in a striking way the strength of Adenauer's European convictions. Soon after the war the Saar, which had at first formed part of the French zone, was joined economically to France and placed under a French high commissioner. In 1950 a number of conventions were signed between the French government and the Saar prime minister by which, pending the conclusion of a peace treaty with Germany, the autonomy of the Saar was recognized and its coal mines were leased to France. Adenauer protested against these bilateral negotiations without reference to Germany, and in April 1952 the Bundestag passed a resolution declaring that the Saar was German territory and that its fate could not be decided without German approval. For several years the Saar was a serious cause of discord between France and Germany. Then, with the formation of the Coal and Steel Community, relations in general improved, and Adenauer made great efforts to reach a settlement over the Saar. During 1953 and 1954 attempts were made to find a solution within the framework of the proposed European Political Community, and, when this project fell through, a statute was agreed on, in October 1954, for the internationalization of the Saar under the supervision of Western European Union. The statute had to be approved by a plebiscite in the Saar, but it was generally assumed that it would go into effect. At this stage Adenauer came in for some severe criticism in Germany. When the statute came before the Bundestag, four members of his cabinet did not vote with the government, and, when the chancellor tried to influence the plebiscite in favour of the statute, the criticism became justifiably stronger. In the end the Saar voters rejected the plan to internationalize their territory, and in 1957 it became a *Land* of the Federal Republic.

As things turned out Adenauer's moderation paved the way for the return of the Saar to Germany and achieved this result at the expense of a minimum friction with France. But his actions made clear that he was prepared to forego territory for the sake of reconciliation with Germany's hereditary rival and that the internationalization of the territory, in his opinion, made the sacrifice acceptable.

Adenauer's achievement for European integration is all the more impressive, when the opposition of the Social Democrats is taken into account. The SPD attitude was due mainly to their first post-war leader, Dr. Kurt Schumacher, whose personality was so strong that it continued to exert an influence on party policy for several years after his death in 1952.

Schumacher differed greatly from Adenauer both in his background and in his political views, and the two men were bitter and relentless rivals before and after the vital 1949 election, which gave Adenauer the chancellorship. The opposition leader was a West Prussian from beyond the Oder-Neisse line. He had served as a young officer in the First World War, been wounded many times, and lost an arm. His opposition to Hitler had been courageous and uncompromising, and he had refused to take refuge abroad. As a result he spent ten years in Nazi concentration camps and emerged just before the end of the war such a physical wreck that he had to have a leg amputated in 1949.

It was natural that Schumacher should have a conception of foreign affairs very different from Adenauer's. His concern for the lost eastern territories was deeper and more personal. His own record under the Nazis was such that he saw no reason to be apologetic or on the defensive in his relations with the Allies, and in taking up a strongly critical attitude towards them he forgot that his fellow countrymen as a whole did not share his own blameless past. Finally, he was determined to avoid a repetition of the situation under the Weimar Republic, when the Right-wing parties monopolized the appeal to national sentiment: under Schumacher's leadership the SPD's attitude was more narrowly nationalist than that of Adenauer's CDU. Retrospectively the policy towards European integration, which arose out of these basic attitudes, can be seen to have been misguided and wrong, but it was based on sincere if too subjective convictions.

Too much importance need not be attached to Schumacher's insult to Adenauer during the acrimonious debate on the

Petersberg Agreements.[45] But it arose out of a failure to appreciate the advantages the chancellor had just won for Germany. Subsequently Schumacher opposed German membership of the Council of Europe and vigorously attacked both the Schuman Plan and the proposals for a European Defence Community. His consistently negative attitude appears to have been due partly to the predominantly Catholic and capitalist character of the Six and partly to a belief that the various schemes for European integration would prolong Germany's inferior position as a defeated power. He suspected a deliberate Allied, particularly a French attempt to prevent the Federal Republic attaining equality of status, and he failed entirely to see that in supporting the schemes Germany incidentally was working its passage back to full recognition within the Western community. While criticizing the Schuman Plan he said: "Much of what is to-day called 'European' is in reality only 'Allied.'" With regard to the EDC treaty, he went even further with the statement: "Whoever approves this treaty ceases to be a German." It is at least arguable also that, had the SPD not delayed ratification by taking the matter to the Federal Constitutional Court, the French might have ratified the treaty before opposition within France had had time to develop.

After Schumacher's death in August 1952 the SPD took no part in the work of drawing up a draft treaty for the establishment of a European Political Community. His successor, Herr Erich Ollenhauer, even opposed the Paris treaties and the Federal Republic's membership of NATO. But the logic of events was beginning to make itself felt. The federal elections of 1953 had been a clear endorsement of Adenauer's European policy. In 1957, the next election year, the SPD voted in favour of the Common Market Treaty.

During the Bundestag debate on the Schuman Plan, in January 1952, Adenauer said that he envied the Anglo-Saxons, be-

[45] See p. 31.

cause in England and the United States the opposition and government went hand in hand in the most important questions of foreign policy. Though the personal obstacles to a bipartisan foreign policy were caused as much by Adenauer's as by Schumacher's attitude, the steady and often unreasonable opposition of the SPD greatly increased the difficulties of his diplomatic task. There were, however, a number of alleviating circumstances.

Though the Trade Union Federation was nonpolitical in character, its sympathies were naturally more with the Left than with the Right. Nevertheless on a number of occasions it took a different line from the SPD and gave valuable support to Adenauer. It showed a general sympathy with his policy of European integration, and over the Petersberg Agreements and the Schuman Plan came down openly in his favour. Again three of the oustanding personalities in the SPD, Ernst Reuter, Max Brauer, and Wilhelm Kaisen, mayors respectively of Berlin, Hamburg, and Bremen, disagreed strongly with the party's official foreign policy, as laid down by Schumacher. They all believed that the SPD's purely negative reaction to Adenauer's policy was wrong. Kaisen and Brauer thought that the Social Democrats themselves should make West European integration an urgent aim, while Reuter, who was mayor of Berlin from the time of the blockade until his death in September 1953, not only pressed for the formation of NATO in 1949 but subsequently advocated the inclusion of Western Germany in the North Atlantic alliance. As a reaction to the electoral defeat in 1953, a group of young Social Democrats in Berlin drew up fifteen theses for the renewal of the party. They suggested as chairman of the executive committee, Kaisen, Brauer, or George Zinn, the moderate and independent-minded Minister-President of Hesse, and opened their thesis on foreign policy with the crushingly frank statement: "The foreign policy of the

party up to the present has proved unintelligible to the electorate."

The culmination of the SPD's self-criticism in the field of
foreign policy came in the summer of 1960. On June 30 Herbert Wehner, who had by then become the key figure in the
formulation and revision of the party's policy, made a speech in
the Bundestag which he clearly intended to pave the way for a
bipartisan approach to foreign affairs. He virtually declared
that the government's diplomatic achievements would in future
form the basis for the SPD's standpoint on external relations.
"Divided Germany," he said, "cannot tolerate Christian Democrats and Social Democrats who are incurably at loggerheads
with one another." "The German Social Democratic Party
bases its policy on the assumption that the European and Atlantic treaty system, to which the Federal Republic belongs, is
the foundation and framework for all efforts in the field of
German foreign and reunification policy." Some Social Democrats thought that Wehner should have referred in his speech to
Adenauer's missed opportunities in relation to reunification.
But it had evidently become the party's policy not to revive past
controversies.

The movement for European integration owes a great deal to
the imagination and oratory of Winston Churchill and to the
creative ideas and initiative of such eminent French Europeans
as Herriot, Briand, and Monnet. But Churchill's lead was not
followed up by successive British governments, including his
own, and Mendès-France and de Gaulle between them have
done much to offset the French contribution to the movement.
Adenauer himself has not a creative intellect, and during his
last years as chancellor he undid some of his previous constructive work. But the fact remains that in the six years from
1949 to 1955 no statesman made a greater practical contribution to integration, and the contribution was all the more im-

portant coming as it did from the ruler of a country with a strong nationalist tradition.

Without Adenauer the actual progress that has been made towards West European federation since the war is unthinkable. At the time of his resignation from the chancellorship Paul-Henri Spaak, the leading Belgian champion of federation, wrote of Adenauer:

Without him there could have been no Coal and Steel Community, no Common Market, and no Euratom. . . . Without him the dream of a united Europe could not have become a reality.[46]

Perhaps as important as his diplomatic achievements will prove to be his influence on the attitude of West Germans towards Europe, especially the attitude of German youth. When he left office, the idea that Germany could ever again be at war with her West European neighbours had disappeared. This was not solely due to him: it was the result of influences and forces more powerful than the work of any individual. But the fact that many young Germans could travel frequently in France or Italy almost without a sense of being in a foreign country can be attributed largely to his influence and example. Although his own European loyalty was rooted in the past, he carried with him a new generation that drew its inspiration from the future.

[46] See *Der Spiegel* of Oct. 9, 1963.

3
The Political System

The Basic Law of 1949 has illustrated the truth of the statement that there is nothing so permanent as the provisional. With some minor amendments it remained in force throughout the fourteen years of the Adenauer era, and it will probably continue to be the Federal Republic's "provisional constitution" until some major and unforeseeable change in the international situation leads to a solution of the whole problem of divided Germany.

In drawing up the law, members of the Parliamentary Council were deeply impressed by the failure of Weimar democracy. They were most anxious to prevent a repetition of the experience during Germany's second experiment in parliamentary government, and they set out to avoid the main weaknesses of the Weimar constitution. Of these there had been two: a president with too much power and a chancellor with too little.

By misusing his prerogative President Hindenburg had paved the way for Hitler. For nearly two years, between 1930 and 1932, he had allowed Dr. Brüning to make free use of presidential decrees, a procedure only constitutionally justified in an emergency involving a "serious disturbance or endangerment of public order and security." This action was at least partially justified so long as Brüning was trying sincerely to protect the republican constitution against extremists on the Right and on the Left. But Hindenburg had then appointed in succession as chancellors, von Papen and von Schleicher, to whom he had given similar powers and who were both quite incapable of coping with the situation within the spirit of the constitution. Finally, he had called on Hitler to form a government and had acquiesced two months later in his virtual suspension of the constitution.[1]

Under the Basic Law, therefore, the reserve powers of the president were considerably reduced. If there is a deadlock in the Bundestag, emergency legislation can be resorted to, but it requires the support of the second chamber, the Bundesrat (Federal Council), and the emergency is limited to six months. The president can only appoint a chancellor who has been elected by the Bundestag, normally by a majority of its members.[2] In two specific situations he has the power to dissolve the Bundestag, but in each of them the Bundestag can avoid a dissolution by electing a chancellor with a clear majority. Federal ministers are appointed and dismissed by the federal president but "upon the proposal of the federal chancellor."[3]

Under the Weimar constitution the president was elected by popular vote, and this system had led in 1932 to the re-election of the senile Hindenburg and to Hitler, his runner-up, obtaining over 13 million votes. It was considered by the Parliamentary Council that indirect election would be a better system of choosing a president, and at the suggestion of Professor Heuss the Basic Law provided that the president should be elected by an *ad hoc* body, known as the Federal Convention, consisting of the members of the Bundestag and an equal number of members elected by the legislatures of the *Länder*. Such a body

---

[1] By the Enabling Act of March 1933.
[2] There is one situation in which the person elected need only receive "the largest number of votes": see Basic Law, Article 63, paragraph 4.
[3] Article 64.

ought to be better qualified than the whole electorate to judge whether a candidate for the presidency has the qualities of wisdom and dignity required by the holder of such an office.

A strong chancellor was needed in order to avoid a repetition of the Weimar Republic's record of having a new government on an average every eight months, a record of instability little better than that of France under the Third Republic. The Basic Law strengthened the chancellor's position in four ways.

First, there was the ingenious device known as the "constructive vote of no-confidence," the most important innovation in the law relating to the chancellorship. Article 67 lays down that "the Bundestag can express its lack of confidence in the federal chancellor only by electing a successor by the majority of its members and by requesting the federal president to dismiss the federal chancellor." This precludes the possibility of the government being weakened or embarrassed by irresponsible votes of no-confidence carried by fortuitous and temporary combinations of opponents. To bring about the fall of a government its critics must not only form a majority of the Bundestag but they must also be able to agree on a successor to the chancellor. The idea actually originated with the SPD, but it was supported both by the SPD and CDU members of the Parliamentary Council, partly no doubt because each party expected to win the first federal election and form a government. Secondly, Article 68 provides that, if the chancellor is not given a vote of confidence by a majority of Bundestag members, when he asks for one, he can request the president to dissolve the Bundestag. Thirdly, according to Article 65, the chancellor "determines, and is responsible for, the guiding principles of policy"; and fourthly, in appointing and dismissing federal ministers, the president, as has been seen, acts on the chancellor's proposal.

The chancellor's position was still further strengthened at the time of Western Germany's rearmament. Under the Weimar Republic the Supreme Command of the armed forces was in the hands of the president and was not therefore subject to parliamentary control. In March 1956 the Basic Law was amended to provide that the commander-in-chief of the armed forces should be the federal defence minister in time of peace and the federal chancellor in time of war.

The provisions of the Basic Law could not determine the exact lines along which the offices of president and chancellor would develop. There was a measure of flexibility in the interpretations which could be placed on certain of its key articles, and a good deal of scope was left to the statesmen who were to hold the offices, especially to the two first holders. Heuss and Adenauer, in fact, exercised a decisive influence, and the extent of the influence each had on the office that he held becomes very clear, if the student of German politics allows himself to speculate on what would have happened, had their positions been reversed; had Adenauer been the first president and Heuss the first chancellor of the Federal Republic.

Heuss set the tone for the presidential office in a way that won such general acceptance and admiration that it is likely to influence his successors for many decades. It was a tone which reflected his own personality and the combination of qualities that he brought to the office. Whereas the two presidents under the Weimar Republic had been Ebert, the leader of the strong Social Democratic Party, and head of the post-war provisional government, and Hindenburg, a field-marshal and symbol of the old imperial order. Heuss was chairman of a small political party and his only previous political office had been as Minister of Culture for Württemberg-Baden for a short period after the Second World War. He owed his election primarily to his personal qualifications to be a democratic president.

He was a man of broad humanity and wide cultural interests. Before the war he had been an author, a journalist, a professor of political science, and a member of the Reichstag. Just as

Adenauer was a reassuring link with the past as a public servant with the traditional German virtues, so Heuss seemed to reestablish in his person continuity with Germany's best cultural traditions. His conception of the presidency was not primarily political. As Head of State he set an example, unusual in German history, by combining a sense of political responsibility with the highest ethical standards, a well-balanced interest in the human, intellectual, and artistic aspects of the state's life, and a rather whimsical sense of humour. In so far as he concerned himself with political matters, he did so in much the same detached and strictly impartial way as the British constitutional monarchy. After his election he resigned his membership of the Free Democratic Party, and he took care never to act in a way that would impair his capacity to represent the state as a whole. The federal president, he said, "must not take part in the practical decisions of day-to-day politics, but he is permitted to help in improving the atmosphere."[4] The combination of dignity, modesty, and cultivated intelligence that he brought to his representational duties in foreign countries and to his meetings with foreign representatives, contributed greatly to improving Western Germany's foreign relations. In view of the very satisfactory developments in Franco-German relations during his term of office, it is significant that he said unofficially that his main interest in foreign affairs was to bring an end to the traditional hostility between Germany and France.[5]

Heuss was a liberal in the best sense of the word. He combined patriotism and pride in his country's past with a willingness to face frankly the implications of Nazi crimes. He once made a moving speech on the site of Belsen concentration camp, and he took part regularly in the commemorations of the heroic but unsuccessful plot against Hitler on July 20, 1944.

[4] H. Welchert, *Theodor Heuss*, pp. 212–3.
[5] During the same informal discussion, attended by the writer, referred to on p. 53.

His speech on the tenth anniversary of this event contained the characteristic sentence: "The testament is still effective, but our obligations have not yet been fulfilled."

Most important of all, Heuss, through his actions and his speeches, exercised a strong democratic influence at a time when the country's leaders were either not interested in the tender plant of German democratic life or were too occupied with political tasks and rivalries to give it sufficient attention. When he finally gave up office in 1959, a number of commentators emphasized the value of his work as an educator. He educated his fellow countrymen in democracy in the best possible way: by personal example. He was accessible, simple and unassuming in manner, and, in marked contrast to Hindenburg, who completely lacked the common touch, he enjoyed meeting people in all walks of life and attending functions and gatherings, however small, of which he could see the political, social, or cultural importance. On the evening of September 12, 1959, the last day of his presidency, he gave a radio address to the German people. In its concluding passage he appropriately summed up in the following words the message that his life during the previous ten years had conveyed:

I hope that my fellow countrymen will gather from these parting words, which are accompanied by gratitude for all the affection they have shown me, that I myself was never subject to control and, in face of changing circumstances and the changing tasks which have confronted me, whether personal or public in character, have never allowed myself to be robbed of my inner freedom. For that freedom and its potentialities are the most precious gift which God has given to man and which human dignity requires that man should interpret as a challenge.

In 1954, at the end of Heuss's first five-year term as president, the German people's respect for him and their appreciation for his services were reflected in his re-election by the

Federal Convention with an overwhelming majority. Towards the end of his second term it was proposed that the Basic Law should be amended, in order that he might be re-elected for a third term. But Heuss characteristically would not agree to this suggestion.

After Adenauer had failed to persuade Erhard to stand for the presidency and after the unfortunate episode of his own candidature, which will be dealt with later, Dr. Heinrich Lübke, who had been Minister of Agriculture since 1953, was chosen as CDU/CSU candidate, and defeated his SPD rival, Professor Carlo Schmid. Lübke owed his election to the government's decision to treat the presidential election on party lines, and to the strong position of the CDU/CSU at the time. But it was a retrograde step, compared with the selection of Heuss in 1949, both for the prestige of the presidential office and from the point of view of German democratic development. The advantages of having a truly national figure as president would have been considerable. It should have been possible for the parties to agree on some distinguished nonpolitical person, or alternatively many members of the CDU might have been prepared to support Wilhelm Kaisen of Bremen, if the SPD had had the wisdom to put his name forward.

Lübke had shown himself to be a sound politician, and he had unostentatious virtues. But he was scarcely of presidential calibre. He sensibly endeavoured to follow in his predecessor's footsteps, but it was difficult for him, as a purely party nominee, to maintain the same detachment and impartiality,[6] and, without Heuss's intellectual and cultural qualities, to continue his nonpolitical conception of the office. Lübke's past experience, as well as his limitations, have therefore caused him to show rather more political initiative than Heuss. On at least two occasions he hesitated to approve Adenauer's proposals for

[6] This has not applied since his re-election in 1964, but Lübke's second term as president lies outside the scope of this book.

ministerial appointments and in one case even asked the advice
of the president of the Constitutional Court, although the interpretation of the relevant article of the Basic Law was scarcely a
legal matter. After the 1961 election he used his influence,
during the long drawn out inter-party negotiations, in favour of
a coalition which would include the Social Democrats, though
without success. In foreign affairs also he had ideas of his own
which he did not refrain from expressing. During de Gaulle's
state visit to Germany in 1962 he deliberately corrected the
impression made on the visitor by Adenauer's enthusiastic
manner through the more formal tone of his reception, and he
told de Gaulle that the German people were in favour of an
integrated Europe greater than the Community of Six, which
would include the United Kingdom.

Although Lübke was of smaller stature than Heuss, and the
presidency lost some of its interest and distinction during his
tenure of it, he maintained, so far as he could, the tradition
established by his predecessor and did not actually undo the
work that he had done. The office of president as envisaged in
the Basic Law and developed in practice by Heuss and Lübke,
so far from being a threat to democratic government as it
turned out to be under Weimar, became one of the strongest
influences making for a democratic interpretation of the provisional constitution.

Adenauer's influence on the chancellorship was at least as
great as Heuss's on the presidency. If the framers of the Basic
Law did their best to strengthen the office on paper, its first
incumbent, by his interpretation of it in practice, gave it an
authority which few people could have anticipated that it would
possess. In fact, having become chancellor by the skin of his
teeth, Adenauer took such full advantage of the powers given
him by certain articles of the law to determine policy and virtually appoint and dismiss his ministers, that the additional security provided by the article dealing with the "constructive

vote of no-confidence," though a source of strength in the background, was in practice not needed.

There were two main reasons why Adenauer came to exercise so much power as chancellor. In the first place, he deliberately set out to build up his authority. He had been chairman of the Parliamentary Council, which had been very conscious of the weaknesses of Weimar, and he was determined to avoid a repetition of the fiasco of Weimar instability. At the same time the tasks facing him were so formidable and his own party's majority over the Social Democrats was so small that he was determined to do everything possible to strengthen his position, both by attention to the electorate and by cultivating the possibilities of his office. Secondly, he was authoritarian by temperament and from past experience. He was the typical senior civil servant with a deep sense of loyalty to the state and no experience of responsibility to parliament. As mayor of Cologne he had developed the paternal attitude of the efficient and dutiful Prussian burgomaster, who, though elected by the city council, was a permanent official, and it was an attitude difficult to shake off at the age of seventy-three.

Two other circumstances throw light on Adenauer's conception of the chancellorship. The provisional constitution was federal in character. The governments of the Länder were already in existence, when the Federal Republic was founded, and most of the heads of these governments were men of strong character. There was a widespread belief that the powers of the federal government were not in some respects adequate, and Dr. Eugen Gerstenmaier, later president of the Bundestag (or Speaker), went so far as to say that the system was only made workable by Adenauer's strong personality.[7] Again, during his first few years in office he was not in the normal position of a prime minister responsible only to parliament and public opinion. The Occupation Statute was still in force, and he was

[7] In a conversation with the writer in March 1956.

subject in many fields to Allied authority. It was therefore na-tural, indeed inevitable, that, in matters in which the high commissioners had the ultimate authority, he should get the best terms he could in negotiation with them and then submit them to the cabinet and the Bundestag, virtually as *faits accomplis*, for formal approval. It was not a strictly democratic procedure, and it accentuated Adenauer's inherently autocratic tendencies. But true democracy cannot be practised under mili-tary occupation.

Adenauer's interpretation of the chancellorship was reflected in his attitude to the cabinet, to the Bundestag, and to his party and its coalition partners.

The section of the Basic Law most relevant to the cabinet is Article 65. After stating that the chancellor "determines, and is responsible for, the guiding principles of policy," it goes on to say that "within the limits of these guiding principles, each federal minister conducts the business of the federal govern-ment in accordance with the rules of procedure adopted by it and approved by the federal president."

Two phrases in the article leave room for different interpre-tations. Does the chancellor determine the guiding principles of policy according to his personal opinions, or bearing in mind that according to Article 63 he is elected by the Bundestag and according to Article 20 the Federal Republic is a democratic state? Should he, in fact, exercise his authority with a sense of responsibility to parliament? Again how far is a federal minis-ter's departmental responsibility limited by the chancellor's determination of the guiding principles of policy? In May 1951 the Rules of Procedure of the federal government were issued and the paragraphs relevant to Article 67 ran as follows:

The federal chancellor determines the guiding principles of internal and external policy. These are binding on federal minis-ters and are to be put into practice by them in their departments independently and on their own responsibility. In cases of doubt the federal chancellor's decision must be sought.

The federal chancellor has the right and the duty to see that the general principles are put into practice.

The chancellor and his staff no doubt had the decisive say in drawing up the rules of procedure, which amounted to further steps towards strengthening the chancellor's authority. In the light of the two paragraphs quoted, the independence and personal responsibility of a minister in his department might, if Adenauer so wished, amount to very little.

The British Cabinet is generally considered to be inconveniently large when it reaches twenty. The West German Cabinet has usually contained about the same number of ministers as the British, but it has, on the whole, been a larger body, because it is normally attended also by the heads of the President's Office, the Chancellor's Office, and the Federal Press Office, and by the chancellor's personal secretary. Ministers, in addition, may be represented at cabinet meetings by the state secretaries—that is, the senior civil servants in their ministries, and can even be accompanied by them.

Adenauer's cabinets contained some very able men, but on the whole the standard was not high. One main reason was that he was not usually able to choose his ministers according to their qualifications for their posts but had rather to consider the need for a balanced representation of various interests and categories. For example, it was necessary to ensure a fair distribution of places between Catholics and Protestants, the different Länder, the parties making up the government coalition, and various groups within the CDU itself. On several occasions new ministries were set up, for example, those for Bundesrat and Länder Affairs, Family and Youth Affairs, and Economic Co-operation, mainly in order to create posts for people who had to be fitted in somehow. Nevertheless it was also true that Adenauer, like other rulers with his autocratic temperament, did not wish to have around him many men of outstanding intelligence and independent character. He was quite content that the majority of his ministers should be compliant and hard-working mediocrities. As chancellor he did not aim at being the skilful captain of a brilliant team so much as the respected director of an efficient administration, and he could rely on the civil service to ensure a reasonable standard of efficiency in government.

Under these conditions it was not difficult for Adenauer to interpret Article 65 as he wished. In foreign affairs, his main interest, he always had the decisive say, even after he had handed over the ministry to Herr von Brentano in 1955. The foreign minister, in fact, had considerably less influence in the government than the state secretary in charge of the Chancellor's Office. But even in other departments he was not always content to lay down guiding principles of policy. He did not hesitate to take the initiative, if he considered a matter important, and he did not always consult beforehand the minister most closely concerned. On a number of occasions ministers first heard through the newspapers of decisions by the chancellor on matters which were within their own competence.

Cabinet meetings were prepared very carefully by the chancellor's staff, and chaired with great skill by Adenauer from the point of view of attaining his objectives with the least possible difficulty. The cabinet was too large a body for fruitful discussion, and almost all important questions that came before it had been thrashed out and decided beforehand.[8] The majority of those present belonged to the type of obedient, nonpolitical official described by Max Weber, and few dared to say very much. Adenauer could usually foresee who was likely to cause difficulties. He was strict in deciding what matters should be

[8] The writer was told this by two members of the cabinet independently, both of whom were close associates of Adenauer.

discussed and often defeated opposition by sheer timing. For example, he would allow the discussion of a comparatively trivial matter to go on for a long time and then, when everyone was exhausted and wanting to go home, take a snap vote on an important point over which he had feared trouble. His confidence as chairman must have been greatly strengthened by the provisions of the Basic Law which gave him ultimate, if somewhat loosely defined responsibility for decisions on policy. As Theodor Eschenburg, the distinguished German political scientist, has put it: "If the federal chancellor is outvoted, he must, symbolically speaking, withdraw from the cabinet meeting to his study and make a decision again on his own, which is then the final decision."[9]

The Bundestag presented little challenge to Adenauer's authoritarian conception of his office. He had no more difficulty in controlling it than he had in managing the cabinet. Article 38 of the Basic Law did lay down that members of the Bundestag "are not bound by orders and instructions and are subject only to their conscience." But this was a pious aspiration reiterating an ideal expressed in previous German constitutions and did not fit in with the general trend of the age in the direction of stronger party organization and discipline. The framers of the Basic Law, under the influence of Weimar, were so concerned with strengthening the executive that it does not seem to have occurred to them that it might be parliament that needed their sympathetic attention. The debates in the plenary sessions were mostly perfunctory and dull, the government and opposition standpoints and the main list of speakers having been decided upon in advance by meetings of the parliamentary parties. The attitudes of the majority of members were determined by expediency rather than by principle or personal conviction. There were two main reasons for this: first, the absence of a vigorous

[9] Quoted by T. Ellwein in *Das Regierungssystem der Bundesrepublik Deutschland*, p. 164.

German parliamentary tradition, and secondly the fact that 40 or 50 per cent of them owed their positions on the electoral lists, and thus their chances of re-election, to the party executives.[10] Most members were professional politicians and were dependent for their livelihood wholly or mainly on their salaries and allowances and, in some cases, on the emoluments of other political offices as well. Advancement of members was the reward less for sheer ability and originality of mind than for obedience and the conscientious fulfilment of the duties required of them. In these circumstances the Bundestag very rarely offered any serious obstacle to the fulfilment of the chancellor's policies, and it was not until 1955 that, on an important issue, it challenged his autocratic methods on a major issue with success.

The Bundestag for Adenauer was not a great democratic forum from which he drew strength as the elected leader of the people's representatives: he was not interested in encouraging lively parliamentary debates as an aspect of political life that was valuable in itself. But he attended the plenary sessions regularly, treated the assembly with a somewhat patriarchal respect, and used it as an appropriate setting for reporting on his achievements and making important declarations of policy. After the emotional oratory of which Germans recently had had all too much experience, his clear and rational style of speaking and his quiet, dignified manner set an excellent tone for Germany's new parliament. His age, his authority, and his growing success much impressed the rank and file of members and helped to make the Bundestag, with its safe and increasing government majority, a pliant instrument of government.

As regards Adenauer's relations with his party, it has been said of the CDU that under Adenauer it was transformed from

[10] For the 1949 election it was 40 per cent, but this was raised to 50 per cent before the 1953 election.

the government party into the party of the government.[11] This rather subtle distinction brings out that it was not the party itself which laid down the policy to be carried out by its chosen leader but rather the leader who imposed his policy on the party. Adenauer could achieve this result for two reasons. In the first place, he knew clearly what he wanted and revealed a genius for simplifying the complex issues of politics and making them clear and acceptable to the rank and file of his followers. Secondly, he imposed a rigid discipline on the CDU, which was facilitated not only by his control over the party's electoral lists and by the considerable patronage that party leadership brings with it but by his great skill in handling people.

Adenauer naturally had to be more circumspect in dealing with his coalition partners. But here again he was in a strong position as regards the leaders to whom he gave office, and, by choosing very carefully the recipients of his favours, he was able to control their parties through them with a good deal of success. It was an indication both of his ability as a manager and of the attractions of office for German politicians that, when differences arose within the coalition parties, he was usually able to retain the allegiance of the ministers he had picked from them, even at the cost of disrupting the parties concerned. On the whole, until the federal election of 1961, Adenauer's influence with the CDU and its partners was such that their support strengthened his authority.

Adenauer's authoritarian conception of his office and his success in realizing it in practice led to his method of government being described as "chancellor-democracy." The expression implies a modification of pure democracy in the direction of one-man government and implies also therefore that the method was open to criticism from a democratic point of view. This aspect of chancellor-democracy will be dealt with in detail at a later stage. But, at the time when it was evolved, the

[11] R. Altmann, *Das Erbe Adenauers*, p. 40.

system had great merits for two reasons. During the early post-war years the German people were in no mood to engage in a fight for democratic freedom. Hitler had indeed deprived them of their liberties. But his regime had also led to material de-struction, lack of food, economic dislocation, and loss of confi-dence, not to mention its effects on Germany's international status. These were the problems which occupied their attention. They wanted a statesman with a strong hand to lead them out of their difficulties, and most of them therefore welcomed with relief and gratitude Adenauer's decisive leadership. This one great advantage of chancellor-democracy was well summed up from the SPD side in the autumn of 1963, when Herbert Wehner described Adenauer's regime as follows:

> I would regard his time in power as a period when forces were concentrated, concentrated for a new effort, after the German system of government had broken asunder during the twelve years of Hitler's rule and the few years which preceded it.[12]

Its second great advantage was, from the long-term point of view, still more important. In retrospect Weimar democracy was discredited, because it had been unstable and ineffective, in contrast to the strength and efficiency of the Bismarckian sys-tem and the Prussian monarchy at its best. If Germany's new experiment in democracy, therefore, was to be successful and to win popular support, it was essential that the government set up under the Basic Law should be strong and effective. Chan-cellor-democracy diverged from the spirit and practice of au-thentic Western democracy by making concessions to the Ger-man traditions of efficiency and undisputed authority and has thus done much to reconcile the German people to a political system which is constitutional and parliamentary in form. In

[12] In an interview published in Der Spiegel of September 25, 1963.

spite of his authoritarian interpretation of his rights as chancellor, Adenauer did not violate the letter of the Basic Law, and he has therefore left to future generations of his countrymen a basis on which they can work out, as they may wish, a more democratic interpretation of the provisions and spirit of the constitution.

In addition to the presidential prerogative and the vulnerable position of the chancellor, there was a third weakness in the Weimar Republic which contributed a great deal to its failure but with which the framers of the Basic Law, in spite of their anxiety about the Weimar precedent, concerned themselves little; due probably to its having revealed itself in practice rather than having been inherent in the provisions of the constitution. This weakness was the way in which the party system developed. The method of election by proportional representation encouraged, in the first place, the formation of many parties. But, instead of their tending to consolidate for reasons of expediency, as the years went by, governmental instability was matched by a correspondingly dangerous proliferation of parties. The process of splintering grew progressively worse, until in the 1930 elections as many as ten parties polled more than a million votes each, and in the end there were no less than thirty-six parties and groups competing for Reichstag seats. The Basic Law might have guarded against a repetition of this situation by providing for a system of majority voting in single-member constituencies, but in fact it left the details of the electoral system to be regulated by a federal law. The provision in Article 38 relating to members and their consciences did nothing to help party organization and discipline.

Adenauer, however, was very conscious of this additional weakness of the Weimar Republic. He was well aware of the need for an over-all strategy towards the party problem, and no one had a greater influence on the steady trend towards a two-party system in the Federal Republic. The number of successful parties dropped from nine in the federal election of 1949, if the CDU/CSU is counted as one party, to six in 1955, four in 1957, and three in 1961.

His first major decision on the general party problem was made after the 1949 election. At the time there was a substantial body of opinion in favour of what is known in Germany as the "great coalition"—that is, the coalition between the two main parties, the CDU/CSU and the SPD. There were strong arguments for establishing a united front in relation to the occupying powers and as the best basis for working towards reunification. The policy, on the whole, was favoured both by the heads of governments in the Länder and by the trade-union leaders. In most Länder coalition governments had been formed to tackle the formidable tasks of reconstruction in the immediate post-war years, and in a number of cases great coalitions had been set up with success. Adenauer himself decided against a great coalition for several reasons. There is no doubt that he disliked the idea of working with the socialists, and, after fighting the election on the programme of social market economy, it would have been difficult for the CDU to pursue a common economic policy with the Social Democrats. But he gave as another reason that he believed in the value of a strong parliamentary opposition and that, if the CDU and the SPD formed a government together, it would encourage the growth of opposition on the two extremes of Right and Left. Whatever the main reasons for Adenauer's decision may have been, there is little doubt that it has turned out for the best from the point of view of West German democratic development. In internal politics the emergence of two strong and moderate parliamentary parties has been one of the most satisfactory aspects of the post-war period.

Of the two extremist dangers in West German politics the threat from the Right was much more serious than the threat from the Left. So many citizens of the Federal Republic had

had experience of communism in practice that it was most unlikely that a substantial number of them would fall victims to its theoretical attractions. A high proportion of demobilized troops had spent some time on the Eastern front; the great majority of refugees had had some experience either of communist armies or of Communist methods of government; while almost every family in Western Germany either had relatives or friends in the Soviet zone and had heard through them or through the reports of refugees about living conditions under communism. On the other hand, there were two large elements of the population that were natural sources from which membership of extremist Right-wing parties might be drawn: former members of the Nazi party and refugees. There has never been any really serious danger of a neo-Nazi revival in post-war Germany. Disillusionment about Hitler and disgust at the revelations of Nazi atrocities have been too strong. But among former party members there was a small minority of incurables, and those who had been the victims of denazification were sometimes sufficiently embittered to succumb to the propaganda of extreme nationalist groups which drew their inspiration rather from the old imperialist traditions than from memories of Hitler. Refugees also tended to be extreme nationalists and naturally felt much more strongly about the question of reunification than those who had been born and brought up in Western Germany.

Adenauer was well aware of the dangers inherent in the situation. His government challenged the constitutionality of two parties before the Federal Constitutional Court, in accordance with the provision of the Basic Law which prohibited associations directed against the constitutional order. These two were the Communist Party, which won fifteen seats in the federal election of 1949, and the blatantly neo-Nazi Socialist Reich Party, which was founded in the autumn of 1949. The court banned the Socialist Reich Party in October 1952, and the Communist Party, after nearly five years delay, in August 1956. The Communists won no Bundestag seats in the 1953 election, and it was arguable that a small Communist Party working in the open was likely to be less harmful to the constitutional order than a banned party working underground. But a court of law, having been asked for a legal ruling, could not settle the matter according to the criterion of political advantage.

A much more serious threat arose from the possibility of a constitutional but strongly nationalist party being built up from the large number of discontented refugees and ex-Nazis. Such a party could have jeopardized the fulfilment of Adenauer's European aspirations, his external policy based on the Western alliance, and his internal policy of stability founded on social justice. From motives of political expediency he met this threat with an attitude of moderation and tolerance towards men with whom he sometimes had little or no personal sympathy. He acted on the principle that it was better to absorb dangerous elements into the basically democratic CDU by the use of lenience and kindness than to provoke them into intransigence by the severe and open criticism that they often deserved.

Adenauer's methods can be best illustrated by his handling of the Refugee Party and the German Party. Early in 1950 a group of refugees in Schleswig-Holstein under the chairmanship of Herr Waldemar Kraft, founded a party which they called the Union of Expellees and Dispossessed (Refugee Party, for short). Schleswig-Holstein had a higher proportion of refugees in its population than any other part of the country, at one time amounting to two-fifths. In the subsequent *Land* elections the party polled nearly a quarter of the total votes cast. Later an organization was founded at the federal level with Herr Kraft as chairman and Professor Theodor Oberländer as one of his deputies. Herr Kraft himself had been a member of Hitler's SS and had been interned for two years after the war. Professor

Oberländer had held high academic and administrative posts under the Nazis and in circumstances which subsequently made him the target of very strong criticism. Herr Kraft welcomed former Nazis into the party, though he did emphasize that they must be *former* and repentant Nazis.

Ultimately the party had 180,000 paying members, which was the largest membership of any Germany party in proportion to its electoral support. In the 1953 election it obtained twenty-seven Bundestag seats. Adenauer invited it to join the government coalition, and Herr Kraft and Professor Oberländer both entered the cabinet, Oberländer as Minister for Refugees.

The Refugee Party avowedly represented the interests of a special section of the population, and it exerted strong pressure on the federal and *Land* governments to improve the lot of the refugees. Its real purpose was to render itself unnecessary, and in this it was quickly successful. The Civil Service Law of 1951 and the Law for the Equalization of Burdens of 1952 both benefited the refugees greatly. An effort was made with little success to give the party new life by associating it especially with the reunification movement and adding the words "All-German Union" before the already clumsy title. In June 1955 there was a serious internal dispute which led to Kraft, Oberländer, and six other members of the Bundestag leaving the party. The two ministers very properly offered their resignations. But Adenauer characteristically persuaded them to stay on in his government, and the eight seceders all finally joined the CDU. In the 1957 federal election the party won no seats at all.

The German Party was a small Right-wing party with a Hanoverian background and its centre of gravity in Lower Saxony. In 1949 it obtained seventeen seats in the Bundestag and maintained its representation at about this level with the help of the CDU in 1953 and 1957. Its programme was based on a curious mixture of rather emotional conservatism and modern and enlightened policies, such as European integration and the abolition of the death penalty. Adenauer bound its leaders effectively to his allegiance by appointing two of them to his first cabinet, a higher proportion than the party merited on numerical grounds. Of the two Dr. Seebohm who became Minister of Transport and has retained the office ever since, was one of the most controversial figures in Adenauer's successive governments. Having been brought up in the Sudetenland, he has made himself the spokesman of the extreme nationalist and revisionist elements in the German and Refugee Parties and has, from time to time, made statements which have not only been a flat contradiction to the chancellor's own convictions and the government's declared policy but have sometimes also been meaningless in themselves. For example, in the spring of 1956 he spoke of "winning back the Sudeten German territory from Czechoslovakia in peace and freedom."[13] Dr. Seebohm proved himself a hard-working, efficient, and very well-informed Minister of Transport. For this reason and in order to propitiate those whom he represented, Adenauer tolerated his indiscretions. During the summer of 1960 nine members of the German Party in the Bundestag, including the two ministers, joined the CDU/CSU. A few months later the remnants of the party joined the survivors of the Refugee Party, in a kind of death-bed marriage, to form the "All-German Party." The new party won no seats in the 1961 federal election.

Yet in Adenauer's strategic plan for dealing with the party problem his main objective and his most important achievement related to his own party. He set out to create in the CDU a strong and comprehensive party, with wide popular support, which would provide a firm parliamentary basis for his government's authority. He did so with such success that the SPD decided, after a good deal of hesitation, to copy his tactics and even adopt some of his policies.

[13] See *Deutsche Zeitung und Wirtschafts Zeitung*, May 26, 1956.

German political parties have, by tradition, been ideological parties, as opposed to Anglo-Saxon parties whose programmes have been drawn up rather to achieve practical political purposes. Members of the German parties have been brought together by the bond of common convictions and philosophies of life. For example, of the precursors to the two main post-war parties, the Centre Party had been essentially Catholic, while the Social Democrats had been Marxists.

The CDU broke with this tradition by the very fact of its foundation. The Centre Party had been theoretically a Christian organization open to Protestants, but in practice it became predominantly Catholic. Common persecution under Hitler and the common danger from communism brought Catholics and Protestants together to form the Christian Democratic Union, whose joint origin is reflected in its name. At the same time progressive Left-wing trade unionists, who believed in radical social reform and some measure of state control, joined together with more conservative elements which opposed socialist tendencies and supported free enterprise. This alliance, as has been seen, was reflected in the economic policy of social market economy.

These two compromises set a pragmatic tone for the CDU which Adenauer accepted and cultivated. He referred repeatedly to the Christian character of the party. But the proportion of Protestants in it rose to 40 per cent during the first few years of its existence, and he made quite clear to leaders of the Catholic Church that it was he not they who would determine the party's attitude on every question. There was some irony in the fact that so sincere a Catholic as Adenauer should have done much to banish the remnants of clericalism from German political life. His attitude towards ex-Nazis and revisionists within the party was similar to his attitude to the same elements in the Refugee and German Parties. He was not prepared, he said, to take action against simple followers of the Nazi Party and to drive them into the arms of Right-wing radicalism.[14] The CDU thus became a kind of rallying point at which all opponents of socialism were welcomed without much likelihood of their being asked embarrassing questions. Adenauer frowned upon any public discussion of party ideology for the good reason that he preferred that the many different opinions held by members should be kept beneath the surface.

The discipline, in fact, which Adenauer imposed upon the CDU was not accompanied by doctrinal rigidity. The party organization was relatively loose; the party bureaucracy was not comparable in size to that of the SPD; and party membership was only about half the SPD's. The CDU organizations in the *Länder* were allowed a large measure of freedom, and its youth organization prided itself on its free and frank discussions. What Adenauer did demand was that CDU members of the Bundestag and party officials should support his policy as chancellor. For him the government's current programme was virtually party doctrine. The wide and increasing support which the electors gave Adenauer and the CDU from 1949 to 1957 was due partly to their approval of his policies and partly to their appreciation of his undogmatic party leadership.

Adenauer's success in building up a popular and comprehensive party by flexible and pragmatic methods exerted a decisive influence on the SPD. When Wehner in 1963 spoke of the chancellor's achievements in concentrating forces, he went on to say that this had led to a concentration of the Social Democrats, "as regards, namely, their political ideas."[15] The SPD's task in fact was to transform itself from a party representing a class to a party representing the nation as a whole.

The SPD was Germany's oldest political party. It alone of the major parties in the Federal Republic retained its name

[14] See K. Adenauer, "Germany and the Problems of Our Time" in *International Affairs*, April 1952.

[15] See p. 97.

from the Bismarckian era. It had an honourable record of resistance to National Socialism, and it alone of the parties represented in the Reichstag had had the courage to vote against the
notorious Enabling Act of March 1933, by which Hitler had
virtually suspended the Weimar constitution. It had reason,
therefore, to be proud of its past, and when it resumed normal
political activities after 1945 it was suffering from a somewhat
stultifying inner conservatism. As a party of *émigrés* or underground workers it had not had the opportunities for new and
constructive thinking on socialism which had been going on, for
example, in Britain and Scandinavia.

As leader of the SPD, Schumacher was responsible for several considerable achievements. In the first place, his own
heroic record, his deep socialist convictions, and his strong
personality provided a valuable rallying point for the party
under the difficult conditions of the post-war years. Secondly, he
was largely responsible for the decision that Social Democrats
in the Western zones should not ally with the Communists, as
their fellow socialists had done in the Soviet zone: this deprived
the Communists of a firm foothold in the Federal Republic and
ensured that the SPD would side with the West. Thirdly, he laid
some at least of the intellectual foundations for the party's
reform. On a number of occasions Wehner quoted his statement: "It makes no difference whether a man has become a
Social Democrat through the Marxist method of economic
analysis, for philosophical or ethical reasons, or in the spirit of
the Sermon on the Mount."

On the other hand, Schumacher was so taken up with his
interest as a nationalist in foreign affairs, so occupied with his
bitter and too negative opposition to Adenauer's government,
and so weakened by his physical infirmities and illness that he
could give little attention to the reform of the party organization or the modernization of its programme. The day-to-day

running of the SPD was therefore left to men of a different calibre.

As a result the party suffered from two serious weaknesses even while Schumacher was still its leader. It was managed by a rigid bureaucracy, or machine, made up of paid officials, most of whom owed their positions to long years of loyal service and who had too much security of tenure. One expert adviser at the party headquarters in Bonn admitted in a moment of cynical frankness that he had a lifelong job, provided that "he did not succumb to the temptation to steal a silver spoon."[16] Such people were content to let the machine run in the way to which they were accustomed; they tended to suffer from the power complex characteristic of petty officials; and they were not much interested in new ideas. So the second weakness of the system was a self-satisfied adherence to traditional party doctrine. Schumacher was like the commander of an army that already existed, but which had little power of attracting young recruits.

The quality of the SPD officials was, for several reasons, inadequate for the big tasks with which they were faced. The party had lost some of its finest men as victims of National Socialism; for example, Julius Leber, who had been executed after July 20, 1944, and who as far back as 1933 had made a penetrating criticism of the old-fashioned ideas, the rigidity, and the indecision of the SPD bureaucracy. Party members, who had left Germany during the Hitler period, returned after the war to take up responsible positions in the hierarchy, bringing with them the embittered attitudes of men who had been living in the isolated, unreal world of émigré politicians. Nevertheless they and a group of mostly undistinguished bureaucrats established a strong hold over the national executive in Bonn and resented the claims of stronger and more independent personalities in the *Länder* and in federal politics to play a role in

[16] See K. P. Schulz, *Sorge um die Deutsche Linke*, p. 90.

the higher councils of the party. Thus men like Reuter, Kaisen, Brauer, Willy Brandt, Carlo Schmid, and Fritz Erler either exercised little influence on SPD national policy or had to wait too long before they could make their influence felt.

With the striking CDU gains in the federal elections of 1953 and 1957, it became increasingly clear that the traditional socialist domestic policies, with their Marxist and antireligious flavour, and Schumacher's new nationalist emphasis in foreign affairs would never produce a swing of the pendulum in the SPD's favour. As prosperity increased, German workers no longer thought of themselves as the proletariat and victims of class oppression. The German people, as a whole, became progressively bored and impatient with the party's opposition to almost every aspect of the government's policy, even when its policy seemed to make very good sense, as in the cases of European integration, NATO membership, and Erhard's economic programme.

When Schumacher died in 1952 his real heir was the party bureaucracy, although its head, Herr Erich Ollenhauer, succeeded him as chairman of the party. In spite of some admirable qualities Ollenhauer was an arch-mediocrity. On the crucial issue of the party's future he was content to be a benevolent mediator between the traditionalists and the reformers. Thus valuable time was wasted and ground was unnecessarily lost before the leadership agreed on a programme of modernization. But eventually the reformers won, and the Godesberg Programme of 1959 resulted, [17] owing mainly to the persistent efforts of its chief architect, Herbert Wehner, and of the able, clear-headed, and well-informed Fritz Erler, whose chief disadvantage, so far as party advancement was concerned, was that his intellect was much keener and his outlook broader than most members of the SPD bureaucracy.

[17] So called, because it was submitted to a special conference of the SPD at Bad Godesberg in November 1959.

The Godesberg Programme amounted to a sweeping victory for the modernizers and presented the party's programme to the German people in a new and much more acceptable light than any in which it had previously appeared. As Adenauer himself put it, with the new programme "Herr Wehner made it possible for the SPD to gain access to certain sections of society which had hitherto associated the name SPD with something terrible."[18] It was approved by the surprisingly large majority of 324 votes to 16.

Its general character can be gathered from three short quotations. On the opening page democratic socialism is described as "rooted in Europe in the Christian ethic, humanism, and classical philosophy." The Social Democratic Party of Germany is called "the party of intellectual and spiritual freedom." Towards the end of the programme the party's achievement is summed up in the words: "The Social Democratic Party has been transformed from a party of the working class into a national party."

The following are some of the more important detailed provisions:

The Social Democratic Party accepts the free market wherever competition really exists. But where markets have come under the control of individuals or groups, a variety of measures may be necessary to preserve economic freedom.

Competition so far as possible—planning so far as necessary![19]

Where a healthy balance of economic power cannot be ensured by other means, public ownership is expedient and necessary.

All payments of a social character made by the state, including pensions to wounded soldiers and to dependants of those who have fallen, are to be adjusted continuously to the rising wage rates.

[18] In an interview with the writer in June 1964.
[19] This last slogan had been coined by Karl Schiller several years earlier.

The Social Democratic Party of Germany believes in defending the free, democratic social order. It accepts the need for national defence.

The Social Democratic Party demands the outlawing by international law of mass means of destruction throughout the world.

The section of the programme dealing with religion was of special importance. Nothing had done more to hinder the development of the SPD into a national party than its traditional association with the antireligious element in Marxism. The association alone explained the preponderance of the CDU in the highly industrialized but Catholic *Land*, North Rhine-Westphalia. The most important provisions relating to religion run as follows:

Only a mutual tolerance, which respects those of other beliefs and opinions as fellow men of equal dignity, offers a sound foundation for living together fruitfully from a human and a political point of view.

Socialism is no substitute for religion. The Social Democratic Party respects the Churches and religious communities, their special mission and their independence. . . .

It is always ready for co-operation with the Churches and religious communities under conditions of free partnership. It welcomes the fact that men, out of a sense of religious obligation recognize their duty to behave with a sense of responsibility towards society.

As regards external affairs the programme contains a chapter on the International Community which emphasizes the party's interest in peace, international co-operation, and the need for co-operation amongst European states in economic matters and defence. A paragraph also expresses deep concern for the needs of developing countries and recognizes their claims to generous and disinterested help. But it was left to Herbert Wehner, in his Bundestag speech of June 1960, to give full expression to the SPD's changed outlook on foreign affairs, and his announcement was all the more impressive, coming as it did from one whose chief handicap to advancement within the party had been his former record as a communist. Some regrets were felt that both the programme and Wehner's speech approached world problems from a basically German point of view and that something of the old burning consciousness of international tasks, that was part of the Social Democratic tradition, was now missing.

The small minority, who opposed the Godesberg Programme, hoped that it would be possible to modify it in a reactionary sense after the 1961 federal election. The reform had certainly originated with the party's intellectual leaders rather than with the rank and file of the functionaries, and it was inevitable that it should take some time before the party as a whole could get accustomed to the new policy. But the 1961 election gave the SPD twenty-one additional seats in the Bundestag compared with the loss of twenty-eight seats by the CDU/CSU and the obliteration of their coalition partner, the German Party. So it was considered a relative victory and a clear justification of the new programme.

Whereas during the first decade of Adenauer's government the SPD was accused of unreasonable and indiscriminate opposition, after 1959, and, still more after 1961, it was reproached with scarcely offering any opposition at all. Its leaders were increasingly convinced of the desirability, by one means or another, of attaining power and of proving that the party was fit to take part in government at the federal as well as at the *Land* level. Their restraint, therefore, was due as much to the possibility of forming a great coalition as to the desire to underline the moderate nature of their new course. Certainly the Godesberg Programme had brought the policies of the two main parties much closer together and had paved the way for such a development. During the summer of 1964 a joke was being passed round in Bonn to the effect that anyone who could not accept the full CDU programme would be excluded from the SPD.

The attitudes of the two parties, however, still remain sufficiently different, especially their conceptions of democratic practice and social policy. In the course of the ups and downs of party politics it is perhaps not a bad thing for German democracy that a period of bitter animosity should be succeeded by a period of rather exaggerated reconciliation.

In influencing the SPD to emulate his tactics and adopt some of his policies, Adenauer increased the chance of the CDU being overtaken by its rival in a federal election. But he excluded the possibility of Germany being ruled by a government diametrically different from his own, and after 1959 he could scarcely repeat what he said during the 1957 election campaign, that a victory for the Social Democrats would mean Germany's ruin. His efforts to avoid the weaknesses of party politics under the Weimar Republic had remarkable success, and the clearest indication of it was the existence before he left office of two strong and yet moderate parties, each of them loyal to a democratic constitution and each capable of governing the country.

Adenauer's political achievements were the result of an impressive combination of qualities, and perhaps the most appropriate moment to consider these qualities in more detail is between a description of his positive accomplishments in external and internal policy and a more critical treatment of his record as a statesman.

His character is reminiscent, in its composition, of a painting by Rembrandt or Velasquez. There is a striking simplicity about the main outline, so that the observer feels that he has grasped the artist's purpose and the nature of the subject almost at the first glance. But, on examining the work more closely, he discovers a great variety of unexpected and complex details which the artist has blended into a deceptively simple whole but which nevertheless adds to the painting's attractiveness and quality. The comparison cannot be carried too far. A great picture by either of the two masters will, from an aesthetic point of view, be wholly acceptable and satisfying, whereas the mixture of simplicity and complexity in Adenauer's character is not so much satisfactory from a moral or a human point of view as intellectually fascinating.

Just as Adenauer had the ability to simplify political issues, to concentrate on essentials, and to pursue his main objectives with great singleness of purpose, so he possessed certain outstanding personal qualities which gave to his character a tangible quality that made it possible for the German people and for foreigners to form a clear conception of what he was and what he stood for. Apart from his autocratic disposition, which has been emphasized already, four of his most characteristic qualities were his courage, his stamina, his deep convictions, and his highly developed political sense.

His courage, which was both physical and moral, revealed itself in a variety of ways. In 1917, just before he became mayor of Cologne, he was involved in a severe accident, when his car ran into a tram. He emerged from the wreckage streaming with blood, with his nose and cheekbones broken, his lip torn, several teeth knocked out, his lower jaw crushed, and deep cuts in his head. He walked erect to the hospital, and it was not until the surgeon had stitched him up without an anaesthetic—owing to his loss of blood—that he became unconscious.[20] As a result of this experience his appearance was greatly changed, and his features acquired artificially the look which is to some people suggestive of a Mongolian or Red Indian extraction. After Hitler came into power Adenauer re-

[20] P. Weymar gives a full account of the accident in *Konrad Adenauer* pp. 58–60.

fused to allow the swastika flag to be flown from Cologne city hall. When Hitler himself arrived in Cologne, after addressing an election meeting in West Germany, he did not greet him personally but sent his deputy to the airport instead, on the ground that the Führer had come as a party leader and not in his capacity as chancellor. Later he insisted on Nazi flags being removed from a Cologne bridge, because they had been put up without his authority. It is not surprising that he was soon afterwards dismissed. During the Nazi period he spent months as a fugitive, he was imprisoned three times, and he only narrowly escaped with his life. His moral courage was clearly revealed during his early years as chancellor, when, under difficult parliamentary conditions and dependent as he was on his coalition partners, he boldly pursued policies that he believed to be right, including rearmament within the Western alliance, which at first aroused considerable opposition.

Adenauer's stamina was proved by the fact that, having first attained power at the age of seventy-three, he became during the following fourteen years the greatest German statesman of the century. And for four of these years he was foreign minister as well as chancellor. His stamina was based on most unusual physical powers and mental tenacity. In his late eighties he could hear well, did not usually wear glasses, and was neither bald nor grey, though his hair had become rather faded. Even in 1964, after he had ceased to be chancellor, both his political opponents and his friends agreed that he was physically, as well as mentally, fully alert. His mental resilience was shown by his vigorous reaction to being dismissed from the mayoralty of Cologne in 1945. Like Churchill he worked extremely hard but conserved his powers systematically, as a general rule taking short periods of rest in the afternoon and evening and allowing himself long regular holidays in the Black Forest or Italy. His powers of endurance and his fighting spirit showed up particularly in election campaigns. His most successful election was fought in 1957 when he was eighty-one. A few days before the campaign opened he was in bed ill. But, once it had started, he set the tone for his whole party by the tireless energy and earnestness with which he played his own leading part. His tenacity of purpose was well summed up by one of his closest associates, Dr. Heinrich Krone, in the remark: "On the day after a successful election he discussed the next one."[21]

Adenauer was a man of deep convictions, especially about religion, communism, and the future of Europe. During the early months of the Nazi regime, when he was in great danger, he characteristically took refuge in a monastery and remained there for nearly a year. He once wrote, no doubt with complete sincerity: "Who would deny that there is no genuine freedom in a true democracy, unless it is tied to the eternally valid principles of Christian ethics?"[22] He is said to have impressed upon his younger colleagues that one should never despair of oneself. Certainly he acted on this precept. These characteristics accounted largely for the firmness and consistency of his policy and for his success in giving to his followers and to many of the more politically minded young Germans a new ideological purpose to replace the discredited nationalism of the past. They also provided a clue to his remarkable tranquillity of manner, a most formidable quality in a statesman, when combined, as it was in his case, with great determination and astuteness.

Finally, Adenauer had a strong political instinct which developed with his experience as mayor of Cologne, party chairman, and chancellor, and he applied it with consummate skill both at the tactical and strategic levels. His strategic successes were reflected in his main achievements in internal and external

[21] Made during an interview with the writer in June 1964.

[22] In his own epilogue to E. Alexander's *Adenauer and the New Germany*.

affairs and can be appreciated by anyone who has followed the broad lines of his policy. But the tactical successes were attained, so to speak, beneath the surface that was presented to the public and were part of the extremely complex process of managing parties, men, and public opinion, which is difficult under any parliamentary system but was especially intricate in a country with little democratic experience and no helpful democratic traditions.

Those who observed him in action are agreed that Adenauer had an almost uncanny feeling for power. With less intellectual gifts than several other members of his government he had a remarkable capacity for exploiting every opportunity, every element in a given situation, to further the simple and well-chosen aims he had set himself. He understood the strong and weak points of most of the men with whom he worked, whether they were Allied high commissioners, cabinet ministers, party officials, rank-and-file politicians, or representatives of interest groups. He usually disliked and tended to despise journalists and radio publicists, but he had a very shrewd idea as to how to manage them and as to when it was advisable to appeal to public opinion. For example, after a prolonged difference of opinion with his finance minister as to whether or not to economize as a matter of principle, Adenauer, who was against the economy, yielded and immediately called a press conference to inform the public that his government was out to economize.[23] His sense of timing was not confined to the management of Cabinet meetings. After the 1961 election, when his personal stock was at a low ebb and his party had lost its clear majority, members of the Bundestag began to discuss how Adenauer could best be kept out of office. He at once called a press conference for nine o'clock the following morning and announced that he was going to form a new cabinet. On another occasion, when his state-secretary reported some opposition in

[23] The minister in question informed the writer of this incident.

the parliamentary party of the CDU/CSU, he quietly fixed a meeting at the members' normal lunch time, partly as a punishment and partly to discourage the dissidents from discussion. Nearly every social contact that he made, however casual and disarming his manner might be, had some purpose behind it. During a visit to England he had breakfast with one of his ablest expert advisers and began quite informally to criticize the British on orthodox lines. The adviser, who knew England much better than did Adenauer, defended them as well as he could, and his arguments were used by the chancellor in a public speech the same evening.

However, behind these well-marked and clearly recognizable qualities of character lay a highly complex, subtle, and contradictory personality. Its contradictory aspect has been summed up by Golo Mann in a sentence in which he was referring to both Adenauer and Bismarck: "In the great affairs of state both showed themselves capable of consistency, honesty, candour, and fidelity, and both showed themselves capable of the exact opposite of these qualities."[24]

At decisive moments throughout his career Adenauer revealed an ambition and self-confidence which amounted sometimes to arrogant self-assertion. He obtained his first appointment in the Cologne city administration by pressing his own claims against those of a candidate who seemed likely to be given the post. There was a strong element of arrogance in the method by which in 1946 he became chairman of the CDU in the British zone, and in the whole episode of his candidature for the federal presidency in 1959, which will be considered in detail later, he displayed a self-assertiveness and egotism which were thoroughly distasteful. The way in which he clung to office during his last years as chancellor was a pathetic example of self-centredness and bad judgment. Yet he combined these

[24] See his article, entitled "Bismarck and Adenauer," in *Encounter*, April 1964.

weaknesses with a gentleness, a courtesy, and an unassuming charm of manner in private conversation and even in some of the more personal aspects of his political life. A state-secretary, who was his close associate and adviser for ten years, has related that after every interview during the whole period, even when there had been differences of opinion between them, Adenauer never failed to accompany him to the door of his office and shake hands, as he left.

In his personal relations in politics he could be hard and ruthless. He publicly criticized two such important members of his cabinet as Professor Erhard and Herr Schäffer, his Minister of Finance. He repaid with ingratitude two of the ablest and most loyal supporters of his foreign policy; Herr von Brentano, whom he dropped as foreign minister in 1961, and Herr Kiesinger, who, having been given no federal ministry, finally left Bonn in 1958 to become minister-president of Baden-Württemberg. Yet kindliness and sensitivity were revealed in his family life, in his appreciation of painting and music, and in his love of flowers, especially roses, which provided him with his main hobby for many years.

As a political leader he was authoritarian in his methods and often opinionated in his views. But these qualities were offset by others which reduced the irritation and other disadvantages resulting from his autocratic manner and acted as a lubricant to the process of government. Although the amount of effective discussion that took place in the cabinet was strictly limited, Adenauer did have regular discussions with his closest advisers which were usually attended by his State-Secretary, Hans Globke, Heinrich Krone, for six years chairman of the CDU parliamentary party, and by the chancellor's old friend, the banker, Robert Pferdmenges.[25] These meetings in no sense constituted a "brains trust," except insofar as Pferdmenges was a financial expert, but rather an intimate group of kindred spirits

[25] Pferdmenges died in 1962.

or disciples. They did, however, ensure that Adenauer's decisions had been subject at least to sympathetic criticism before they were presented to the cabinet and the public. At them the chancellor welcomed the frank expression of opinions and listened to them carefully, often postponing a final decision on some point until they had all had time to reconsider it.[26] Indeed his capacity to listen was one of his most valuable qualities. In committees, in the cabinet, and at meetings of the CDU parliamentary party, it was his technique to let people have their say, on the principle that, if a man has had a hearing, he is half satisfied already: he would then sum up the discussion with well-weighed moderation, but in the sense that he wanted, and usually obtained unanimous approval. One of Adenauer's most effective weapons was a dry and laconic sense of humour. Opposition was often disarmed completely by a good joke, which, combined with the chancellor's age and venerable presence, would win him the amused support of the majority and make the opponent's case seem rather trivial. On one occasion Herr Franz-Josef Strauss, one of the strongest and most intelligent personalities in West German politics, went with other members of the CDU/CSU to see the chancellor about a matter on which they disagreed with him. After some time Strauss said impatiently: "Herr Chancellor, we have not come here to say 'Yes' and 'Amen' to all that you say." " 'Amen' is not necessary," replied Adenauer, " 'Yes' will be quite sufficient."

One further contrast may be mentioned in conclusion. As a politician he displayed a cynical realism and sometimes an unscrupulousness, which prompted the remark of a member of the FDP that he had read Machiavelli in an edition produced by Ignatius Loyola. Soon after the Second World War he told an acquaintance that politics was a dirty game and that he was too old for it. But, having decided to play the game, he appears to

[26] This account is based mostly on information given to the writer by Dr. Krone and Dr. Globke.

have found little difficulty in accepting its unpleasant side, and he repeatedly expressed himself in scornful terms about the human race. A characteristic remark of his was that God had not created men very satisfactorily: had they been more intelligent, they would have understood the way things should be done, and, had they been less intelligent, they would have been easier to govern. One of his most unscrupulous actions occurred during the 1953 election campaign. The SPD had laid much emphasis on the CDU's dependence on industry for funds and just before the elections produced a lot of information on the subject. Adenauer replied by alleging that two SPD officials had obtained communist subsidies for election purposes from the Soviet zone. Legal action followed, and after the election, when the damage had been done, he had to withdraw his statement and apologize. When the matter came up for discussion in the Bundestag, Adenauer made the astonishingly cynical statement: "I am indeed permitted to take part and speak in a party contest as chairman of the CDU. If my participation has cost you (the SPD) several million votes, then I am very glad about it."[27] Yet his cynicism and unscrupulousness were accompanied by an inner serenity and steadfastness in adversity, which sprang undoubtedly from his genuine but curious and rather too pliant form of Christianity. His own acceptance of the contradiction is revealed in his remark quoted by Paul Weymar in his biography of Adenauer: "The political profession is not exactly beneficial for a Christian. It is as if one holds a stick in water: owing to the refraction of the light rays by the water the stick always appears to be distorted."

The contrasts in Adenauer's personality were matched by contrasts in his political record. In spite of his substantial achievement for German democracy, as a democratic leader he had one great shortcoming, which overshadowed and, in the

[27] T. Eschenburg, *Herrschaft der Verbande?*, pp. 70–1.

opinion of some, outweighed his positive contribution. He failed to educate the German people for their democratic responsibilities. In fact, he did not seem to appreciate the need for trying to do so.

At the end of the First World War, in an article entitled "The Future Structure of the German State," Max Weber wrote: "The technical aspects of government are unfortunately not without importance, but they, of course, are politically not the most important. Much more decisive for Germany's future is the question whether the great body of citizens will cultivate a new political spirit which will give them more self-assurance and greater readiness to accept responsibility." For a number of reasons the question was still more important after the Second World War. Germany's predicament was much worse. National Socialism had proved the danger of not finding an effective substitute for the old empire. Democracy had been discredited by the failure of Weimar and by Nazi propaganda. And some of the country's boldest, most responsible, and far-sighted potential leaders had lost their lives in the resistance movement. The conspirators of July 1944, for example, were, on the whole, altruists with a strong sense of civic duty and often with deep religious convictions.

However, the problem of how to cultivate a greater sense of democratic responsibility was formidable. Nostalgia for the past was no longer the difficulty it had been after 1918. But the younger generation had been brought up under a totalitarian system and had been taught to despise democracy, while too many of their parents, who had grown up under Weimar or the old Empire, had been implicated one way or another in the Nazi regime and were not therefore either willing or suited to act as democratic preceptors. It was thus a case when the task of teaching the principles of free and responsible government could only be carried out effectively by the nation's political leaders, elected under the terms of the provisional constitution, and aided by an *élite* of journalists, publicists, and teachers, who had survived the Hitler era comparatively unscathed. In these circumstances, according to the criterion of Max Weber, it was most unfortunate that the Federal Republic's first chancellor, who set the tone of political life during its first years, was a man whose fundamental standpoint towards politics had already been formed and settled before 1914. His attitude was that of the loyal, dutiful, and efficient civil servant, whom Weber, in modern terms, would have considered a technocrat of politics rather than a political leader. His main concern, when he became federal chancellor, was to give his country effective government in pursuit of the objectives that he himself considered right.

Adenauer's very success in achieving this aim had its disadvantages from the point of view of democratic education. He was like a dominant parent who weakened the personalities of his offspring; the offspring in this case being his ministers, his supporters in the Bundestag, and even some of the more politically minded Germans, who, at a very difficult time, were content to leave things in the hands of a man who so clearly knew what he was doing. After twelve years of National Socialism and six years of war the younger generation was disillusioned and politically apathetic. Adenauer's success, as well as his methods, sometimes won their approval and less often aroused their disapproval, but it did not on the whole increase their inclination to play an active part in politics. In every branch of his administration Adenauer established a "style," as it came to be called, which did not encourage healthy democratic development.

The advantages of chancellor-democracy for the prestige of democratic government in Germany were, as has been seen, considerable. Nevertheless, had he had a better understanding of the nature of democracy and been more sensitive to the need for educating the German people in democratic habits, Adenauer could have produced a similar result without establishing so many unfortunate precedents and without leaving behind an apparatus of government which was, in some ways, more suited to an autocratic than a democratic system.

The modern growth in the scope of governmental authority and the increasingly complex and technical character of political administration have led inevitably in most countries to a strengthening of the executive at the expense of the legislature. The framers of the Basic Law were therefore justified in providing that the chancellor should determine "the guiding principles of policy." But Adenauer could have exercised his authority very differently from the way in which he chose to. He could have interpreted his relationship to his ministers in a much more democratic spirit without strengthening his position still further by the rules of procedure. In fact, had he set out to be chairman of a really strong team, his reputation and his moral authority would have been increased and certain weaknesses in his internal policy would have been avoided.

To aid him in the exceptionally heavy task that he chose to undertake Adenauer provided himself with a large personal staff. It soon developed into a government department in itself, known as the Federal Chancellor's Office, and became more important than any single ministry. For the greater part of Adenauer's chancellorship its head was State-Secretary Hans Globke. By 1961 it consisted altogether of thirty-seven senior civil servants. It performed the functions of the British Cabinet Office, and one of Globke's chief duties was the careful preparation of cabinet meetings. But its main task was to serve the chancellor personally, and it alone made possible the smooth working of chancellor-democracy. Without its help Adenauer could not have exercised supervision over every ministry, in accordance with his own interpretation of the Basic Law, nor could he have paid the detailed attention to problems of personnel on which his great authority over the government and the CDU partly rested.

A Chancellor's Office of some kind was needed. But the scale on which it was built up and the way in which it developed were unfortunate. Globke came to be considered the second most powerful man in the country. The vice-chancellor remained little more than a figurehead, and, when Adenauer was away from Bonn, it was Globke who kept in continuous touch with him and to whom everyone turned when the chancellor's decision was needed. The state-secretary was far too good a servant of his master and far too prudent an official to overreach himself in his outward behaviour. But when Adenauer resigned, his conception of the chancellorship had been institutionalized.

A second buttress for the chancellor's authority was the Federal Press and Information Office, which was itself under the control of the Chancellor's Office. It was set up in 1949 with a staff of twelve, and within ten years the number had risen to over five hundred. Its total budget in 1961 amounted to 78 million marks. State-Secretary Felix von Eckhardt, who with one short break was head of the office from 1951 to 1961, was amongst Adenauer's most trusted advisers. A Federal Information Office was undoubtedly necessary, and the Office did in fact perform such essential functions as issuing news and information bulletins and looking after foreign journalists. On the other hand, it has also justifiably been described as the publicity bureau of the government and the chancellor. It would have been difficult in any case to make a clear distinction between serving the interests of the Federal Republic and furthering the prestige of Adenauer and the parties supporting the government. One of its official duties was "to inform the German people about the political objectives and the work of the federal government," and this statement itself could have been interpreted in either sense.[28] Adenauer, being the man he was, had no real interest in keeping the distinction clear and made wide use of the Office in his capacity as chairman of the CDU. Herr von Eckhardt accompanied him in his special train during the 1957 election campaign, and suitable publications of the office were available in large quantities for the CDU's use.[29]

From time to time the opposition took strong exception to the large sums of money for which provision was made under various headings of the budget but which were not subject to normal parliamentary control. For example, in 1960 there were in this category a sum of over 43 million marks, which was allocated to an organization known as the Federal News Service, 13 million marks in the budget of the Federal Press and Information Office which were "at the disposal of the federal chancellor for the furtherance of the information service" (the so-called "reptile fund"), and smaller sums in the budgets of the Foreign Ministry, the Defence Ministry, and other government departments. It was generally agreed that the Foreign and Defence Ministries might need to incur expenditure which was not subject to public control, and the practice of using part of the funds allotted to News and Information services in thinly disguised support of party interests and points of view was common to the federal government and to governments in the Länder which the SPD sometimes controlled. On the whole, however, the SPD criticisms were justified and performed a useful service to the democratic cause. In 1956 Adenauer agreed that the funds of the Federal News Service should be controlled by a small parliamentary committee, and the "reptile fund" was at least subject to the scrutiny of the President of the Federal Court of Audit.

Adenauer also strengthened his personal position at the expense of sound democratic practice by the personal contacts he

[28] It is taken from an introductory note to a section of the 1961 budget.
[29] See U. Kitzinger, German Electoral Politics, p. 108.

established with the more powerful interest groups. These groups have come to play a very powerful role in West German public life, and the responsibility for this development rested very largely on the chancellor himself. He had two main motives. The first was his sensitivity to electoral considerations. If the industrialists, the trade unionists, and the farmers' associations could all be made to feel that he had a personal concern for their interests, it would pay off handsomely. Furthermore, certain wealthy industrial organizations, for example, the Industrial Association of the Iron and Steel Industry, made very substantial contributions to the CDU's election expenses. Secondly, it satisfied his patriarchal urge to establish personal relations with the representatives of large and influential sections of the community. The Rules of Procedure of the federal government laid down that deputations should "as a rule" be received by the minister who was particularly concerned and "only in special cases" by the federal chancellor. But the most important interest groups were usually received by Adenauer himself often without reference to the relevant minister, and it came to be known that an adverse decision at a lower level might be reversed by going direct to the chancellor. Thus Adenauer sometimes overrode and, by normal democratic standards, humiliated his cabinet colleagues. Uwe Kitzinger has described a particularly bad case when Theodor Blank, the Minister for Labour and Social Affairs, had obtained the unanimous consent of the cabinet to a reform of the health insurance system, and the bill incorporating the reform had already gone into the committee stage in the Bundestag. As a result of interventions in the chancellery, however, by representatives of the medical profession, Blank and the Bundestag had to accept Adenauer's reversal of the cabinet's decision.[30]

As regards Adenauer's attitude to the cabinet, it is true that,

[30] "Western Germany: a Pre-Election Survey" in *The World Today*, March 1961.

owing to the religious question, the federal form of government, and the fact that he was dependent for most of his chancellorship on a coalition, he had not the same freedom as, say, the British prime minister to choose its members according to their qualifications and ability. But the fact remains that he acquiesced too readily in rather mediocre standards. His dislike of independent personalities really implied the negation of democracy and contributed to the difficulty of deciding on a successor to himself as chancellor. He appears to have had an instinctive distrust of men who were natural leaders and had the power to attract the allegiance of others. Thus he made little serious effort to include in his cabinet either the able and attractive Kurt-Georg Kiesinger, chairman of the Bundestag Committee on Foreign Affairs, or the highly respected and successful Karl Arnold of North Rhine-Westphalia, who was the leading personality of the CDU's Left wing.

The ineffectiveness of the cabinet as a policy-making body was very largely Adenauer's responsibility. He could have kept it down to a more manageable size and, even assuming his own authoritative interpretation of the Basic Law, he could and should have set out to turn it at least into a trusted body of advisers, in which a valuable interplay of minds and a useful exchange of ideas took place. One writer on the West German system of government goes so far as to say: "In the Federal Republic there is no political discussion," and adds that in its place there is a far-reaching readiness for compromise, which however leads to a decision as to the point on which people can agree, but as a result not usually of a true exchange of ideas but rather of a process of bargaining.[31] Adenauer in fact reduced the real importance of the cabinet quite deliberately until its meetings took on a predominantly formal character with himself as a consummate master of ceremonies. The important

[31] T. Ellwein, *Das Regierungssystem der Bundesrepublik Deutschland*, pp. 304–5.

decisions were made in advance either in the inner circle of his close advisers, or in the meetings of the parliamentary parties supporting the government, or in informal or semi-informal committees set up to deal with special subjects such as defence, economic co-ordination, or social affairs. These committees reported to Adenauer personally and therefore strengthened his position with the weight of expert opinion, when he submitted his proposals to the cabinet.

The ministers themselves bore some share of responsibility for the cabinet's weakness, because very few of them were prepared to question the chancellor's procedure even by implication. One of them, Dr. Heinemann, Adenauer's first Minister of the Interior, resigned in the autumn of 1950 over the question of rearmament and gave as his reason that he was not prepared to take responsibility "when the chancellor's task of determining general policy is so interpreted that no genuine discussion takes place for the purpose of arriving at a common point of view and when anyone who does not willingly acquiesce in the policy can only expect reproaches."[32] During the next federal election campaign the new party, which Dr. Heinemann founded, described its leader as "the only German minister of the twentieth century who gave up his office and income for reasons of conscience." At a cabinet meeting, which was attended by one of Adenauer's most influential nonpolitical advisers, a minister asked the visitor in a whisper how he dared say so much. He received the reply: "You should too: why don't you?" And answered: "Because we might be dismissed."[33]

Adenauer's handling of the Bundestag contributed to the smooth running of his government, but it meant that he missed the opportunity of building up the central organ of West German democracy by associating it fully with his own great suc-

---

[32] See E. Plischke, The West German Federal Government, p. 89.
[33] This incident was related to the writer by the adviser himself.

cess. His attitude to it was summed up in his remark that he would like to see the number of its sessions halved and the number and length of the laws passed halved as well.[34] As the total number of sessions dropped from 282, during the four years of the first Bundestag's to 227 for the second Bundestag, and 168 for the third, his wish was to some extent realized, though the reduction was due partly to the exceptional legislative pressure during the Federal Republic's early years. The amount of time allowed for the plenary discussion of important bills also was sometimes absurdly short. In 1955, for example, less than two days were allowed for debating a budget involving the expenditure of 30 milliard marks. The chancellor did not even make the respectful gesture of reporting to the Bundestag after his official visits abroad.

As a general rule the proceedings in the plenary sessions were perfunctory in the extreme. Occasionally the debates rose to an impressive level, especially on foreign affairs, or when some matter arose unexpectedly and had not therefore been carefully stage-managed in advance. The trouble was not so much the lack of able speakers but the fact that the method of conducting the Bundestag's business did not give them adequate opportunities to extend themselves. Whereas in the case of the cabinet almost all important decisions had been taken beforehand, in the case of the Bundestag not only the policies but the details of procedure had been decided upon previously in meetings of the parliamentary parties. Party members would know who was to speak, what their main lines of argument would be, and how much time had been allotted to a given subject. Only very rarely did a true debate take place in which there was a live and spontaneous interchange of ideas.

A leading weekly newspaper published an article after the federal election of 1953, entitled "Bonn Has Two Parlia-

---

[34] This remark was made to the writer during an interview in the summer of 1957.

ments," in which the writer was "tempted to say" that the chairman of the CDU parliamentary party had a more important political function than the president of the Bundestag.[35] Certainly it was in meetings of their parliamentary parties rather than in the plenary sessions of parliament that Bundestag members had some opportunity of following their consciences, as laid down by the Basic Law, and not allowing themselves to be bound by instructions. While having little interest in the Bundestag for its own sake as a vitally important democratic body, Adenauer was well aware of its electoral significance. He therefore concerned himself closely with the preliminary preparations for the plenary sessions, especially on such matters as foreign policy and social legislation in which he knew there was wide public interest. He would not only discuss the preparations with the party executive but in some cases personally brief the members who had been chosen to speak. In doing this, however, he was contributing to the empty formality of so many Bundestag meetings.[36]

The federal government, senior officials on the Bundestag staff, schools, and various public authorities encouraged citizens and especially adolescents to visit the Bundestag and see

[35] *Die Zeit*, October 15, 1953.

[36] The following description of Reichstag proceedings from Max Weber's *Parlament und Regierung im neugeordneten Deutschland*, which was published in the summer of 1918, applies equally well to the Bundestag in the Federal Republic:

Speeches made by a member are to-day no longer personal statements of belief, still less attempts to make opponents change their minds. But they are official party statements, which are made to the nation, so to speak, from the open window of the Reichstag. When representatives of all parties have spoken once or twice in turn, the debate is closed. The speeches are submitted to a meeting of the parliamentary party beforehand or at least agreed upon there in all essential points. In the same way it is decided there who is to speak for the party.

There could be no clearer proof of the strength of the Bismarckian legacy, even in internal affairs, and of the extent to which Adenauer, in his attitude to the Bundestag, was a product of the pre-1914 era.

from the visitors' gallery the democratic process in action. Up
to the end of 1955 alone more than two and a half million
people had visited the Bundestag as a result. But the spectacle
they observed was not particularly edifying. The proceedings
would be supervised by the president or one of the vice-presi-
dents with appropriate dignity. But very rarely would there be
the atmosphere of expectancy or excitement which is not un-
common in the British House of Commons, especially at question time. The assembly on the whole would be fuller than the
House of Commons usually is, but the manner of members
would be more perfunctory, and a fair proportion of them
might be reading newspapers. An important bill might be dealt
with in an hour or so, and, after the chosen party speakers had
made their official statements—in the case of the different government parties often very similar statements—there would be
little time left for any new and unexpected light to be thrown on
the subject. Even a star speaker cast in the role of a party's
opening spokesman would often give the impression of a lion in
chains. Carlo Schmid, a vice-president of the Bundestag, and
one of its best orators, with a gift for speaking German with a
French lightness of touch, has complained that the atmosphere
in the assembly is like that of a church in which one member
after another preaches a sermon, whereas what is needed is
the sense of personal rivalry present in a sporting contest. Alfred Grosser has aptly suggested that the very seating of ministers in the Bundestag is symbolic. Whereas in England they are
on the front bench facing the opposition leaders, and in France
on the front row of the deputies' seats, in the German parliament they are placed on the right of the president, facing the
members and at a higher level with the air, as Grosser writes,
"of observers of a parliamentary game which they domi-
nate."[87]

The Bundestag's most genuinely democratic work was done

[87] A. Grosser, La Démocratic de Bonn, p. 64.

in its standing committees, of which at the beginning of 1962 there were twenty-eight, because in these small specialist bodies the chancellor had the least opportunity to interfere with the natural tendency of politically minded people to hold discussions. The committees carried out most of the legislative spadework and did so with much greater spontaneity and give-and-take in discussion than the plenary sessions ever achieved. This was due partly to the fact that the meetings were not public and members did not feel obliged to adopt a rigidly party standpoint, partly to the fact that each party, including the opposition, provided its share of chairmen and deputy chairmen, and partly to the tendency of a small body of men, working together on a specialized and important task, to establish good personal relations with one another. The first time the Bundestag resisted Adenauer's autocratic methods with success was at the time of German rearmament during the summer of 1955. In his most cavalier fashion Adenauer introduced a Volunteers' Bill, which it was widely agreed had not received sufficient consideration and did not provide enough safeguards against the resurgence of military influence. The success of the opposition to the chancellor was due very largely to the close co-operation between Dr. Richard Jaeger, the chairman of the European Security Committee and Herr Fritz Erler, the vice-chairman. However, even in relation to the committees, the parliamentary parties began to interfere with free democratic procedure. They set up working groups corresponding to the committees, and during the latter years of the Adenauer era these groups tended to become too active and assertive. They would discuss bills both before and after the committees considered them, and as a result a purely party amendment to a committee's draft would too often be introduced during a plenary session.

The president of the Bundestag, his deputies, and the official staff headed by the director, showed a commendable desire to improve the assembly's procedure and, with this end in view, studied parliamentary methods in other countries. The Bundeshaus, in which the Bundestag and the Bundesrat both meet, was originally a teachers' training college and is hardly suited to be a permanent parliament building. President Gerstenmaier has aimed at getting a new or improved building with seating arrangements similar to the House of Commons in order to stimulate discussion. But financial approval has not so far been forthcoming; a fact which is itself indicative of the attitude of the government towards parliament in a very prosperous country.[38] A considerable improvement was, however, achieved in the method of conducting question time. From the first, written inquiries could be submitted to ministers by groups of members, and at the beginning of 1952 at least one hour a month was allotted to verbal questions from individual members. But in 1960 it was laid down that every plenary session should start with an hour for questions, and the proceedings were at least potentially enlivened by making supplementary questions permissible. So much use was made of the innovation that special plenary sessions for questions sometimes had to be arranged during weeks normally occupied by committee work, and it is probable that Franz-Josef Strauss would not have been forced to resign after the *Spiegel* affair in 1962, had it not been for the newly introduced question hour. If by the autumn of 1963 question time in the Bundestag did not yet arouse the same interest amongst members and the general public as its British counterpart, it was due partly to the lack of experience of members and partly to the attitude of the government. Ministers too often left questions to be answered by their state-secretaries, who were allowed to represent them in the Bundestag.

[38] One reason for not putting up too impressive a building was the desire not to appear to be renouncing the hope of Berlin again becoming the capital. But this was no good reason for opposing reasonable improvements.

These experienced officials could overwhelm the questioner with a flood of expert information. But the process was less interesting than a well-known politician publicly accounting for his responsibilities.

Adenauer did no violence to the parliamentary framework for government that had been set up by the Basic Law. By his presence he added dignity to Bundestag meetings, and during plenary sessions his calm and erect figure was normally to be seen on its prominent vantage point, as he sat patiently through proceedings to whose tedium he had done much to contribute. Now that his heavy hand has been removed, German politicians will have opportunities to fill the well-established framework with a more vigorous and interesting content. But it will be an uphill task, owing to the strength of the habits which were developed during the fourteen years of Adenauer's government and were based upon an imperial past.

In spite of his salutary short-term influence on the German party system as a whole, Adenauer's attitude to his own party and to the opposition had dangerous implications for German democracy from a long-term point of view. Just as he had no interest in the Bundestag for its own sake as the central institution of a free system of government, so he looked upon each of the two great political parties of the Federal Republic as an instrument to serve a particular political purpose rather than as a trustee of a great heritage, worthy of respect owing to the principles and ideals for which it stood. Perhaps he was too much influenced by conservative German tradition to take up any other attitude. According to Hegel, "only uneducated people indulge in argument and fault-finding," and Bismarck once announced in the Reichstag: "The German Empire cannot be ruled by a party. . . . For any one who enters a parliamentary party the affairs of the country as a whole become too big to grasp . . . in the parliamentary party the representative of the people loses his eye for the universal. The party spectacles obscure his vision of the general interest."[39]

Adenauer instilled two big ideas into the CDU: European integration and social stability based on the reconciliation of conflicting interests. It will rest with his successors in the CDU leadership as to whether the party can be held together round these two concepts. But he himself by his autocratic example and his cynical and highly pragmatic methods weakened his party's enthusiasm and resilience and made the task much more difficult than it need have been. A good example of the cynicism typical of the Adenauer era, though in this case by no means limited to Adenauer himself, was the question of party finances.

According to Article 21 of the Basic Law the parties "had publicly to account for the sources of their funds," and the article further laid down that the details were to be regulated by a federal law. For two reasons the matter was of considerable importance. In the first place, the sums spent by the parties, especially the government parties, in the election campaigns were very high. In the 1957 federal election the amount spent by the CDU has been estimated as at least five times as much as that spent by the British Conservative Party in any post-war election.[40] Secondly, owing to the relatively small membership of German political parties they were dependent on donations from such sources as industry, interest groups, and the press. Only the SPD, which had much the largest membership and a system of graduated contributions from its members, raised a substantial proportion of its income within its own ranks. Up to 1955 parties obtained a large part of their funds by indirect and concealed means; for example, advertisements in party news-

[39] Both quotations are taken from Waldemar Besson's article, "Regierung und Opposition in der deutschen Politik" in Politische Vierteljahrschrift, September 1962.
[40] U. Kitzinger, German Electoral Politics, p. 202.

papers and tax-free contributions via societies with political interests but ostensibly charitable aims. Towards the end of 1954 the income-tax law was amended making political contributions up to 5 per cent of income exempt from tax. The exemption greatly favoured the government parties in the 1957 elections, and the SPD appealed against it to the Federal Constitutional Court. In 1958 the court with characteristic courage and objectivity, ruled against the exemption on the grounds that it infringed the principle of equality of rights among citizens, and the government provided that parties in future should be financed from the federal budget. In 1960 five million marks were distributed to the four parties represented in the Bundestag, and subsequently the amount was greatly increased.

When Adenauer resigned in 1963, neither of the two provisions in the Basic Law had been carried out. The SPD published incomplete accounts, and no other party published any accounts at all. In spite of half-hearted attempts, the government had not been able to decide on the terms of an acceptable electoral law. The truth was that no parties considered it possible or desirable to give a full account of their sources of income, and an electoral law, which did not have general support, would have been unsatisfactory.

As regards the SPD, although Adenauer did so much indirectly to alter its character he appeared quite incapable of thinking of it seriously as a potential alternative government, which, in the country's interest, ought some day to attain power. If he did not go quite as far as Bismarck in describing the opposition as enemies of the state, he came near to doing so, in his statement during the 1957 election campaign that an SPD victory would mean the country's ruin. In this respect Schumacher's provocative influence was unfortunate. But *noblesse oblige*, and Adenauer could have improved the situation by more frequent personal meetings to discuss foreign policy with Schumacher and later with Ollenhauer. As it was, his attitude to the opposition did not help the uninitiated German people to understand the nature of democracy.

His election technique was not helpful either. As chancellor-democracy was something between cabinet and presidential government, it was inevitable in the circumstances that great emphasis should have been laid on Adenauer's own personality. But other aspects of the election campaigns were less excusable: the very large sums spent by the government party compared with the much smaller amounts available to the opposition; the substantial if indirect assistance given to the CDU by the Press and Information Office; the systematic cultivation of powerful interest groups at the expense, to some extent, of a more rational appeal to German citizens as such; and a number of the methods employed in the CDU's election meetings. In his campaign speeches Adenauer himself used much the same unemotional well-reasoned and somewhat paternal oratorical style as he did in the Bundestag. But nevertheless feelings were deliberately stirred up by vast demonstrations attended by tens of thousands of people, by bringing in brass bands, and organizing processions of banner-holders, which were sometimes reminiscent of Nazi demonstrations and, to be fair, of some of the big election rallies in North America to-day. Question periods at the end of meetings were not usually successful and were not very often attempted: a heckler had to be very persistent to get a hearing at all and, if persistent enough, would soon be suppressed or removed by party stalwarts.

Adenauer also developed the habit of interfering in Land elections. As a result of the way in which Article 84 of the Basic Law was interpreted, nearly half of all bills—those in which the interests of the Länder were involved—required the Bundesrat's approval. Amendments to the Basic Law also needed that body's consent by a two-thirds majority. As members of the Bundesrat were representatives of the Länder governments, the chancellor wanted to ensure that as many Land governments as possible were under CDU control. He therefore threw the weight of his personal prestige into election campaigns in the Länder and deliberately introduced into them such federal party issues as he thought might exert the right influence; for example, questions of foreign policy, although they were no concern of the Land governments. The Länder, it is true, once the main work of post-war reconstruction had been accomplished, had become little more than administrative units, apart from their cultural and educational responsibilities, and as time went by Adenauer became increasingly restive about the federal nature of West German government. But the fact remained that in the Parliamentary Council the CDU had supported a federal solution against the opposition of the SPD; moreover Germany's democratic future would depend a good deal on political interest being sustained and developed at the Land and local government levels without the cramping effect of too much intervention from above.

The position of the civil service provides an important clue to the political system of the Federal Republic. Germany had long been distinguished for the quality of its well-trained and specialist civil service. Furthermore, its origin could be traced back to the pioneer work of Frederick the Great's father in the first half of the eighteenth century. So in contrast to England and the United States the establishment of an efficient administrative system preceded rather than followed the introduction of democracy, and, on the basis of habit and authority, the German civil servants felt that they should control the government, while members of the Bundestag had an ingrained respect for their authority and expertise.

By 1945 the civil service had lost its former impeccable reputation. Under Weimar German officials had suffered from divided allegiance, and they had not always been entirely loyal to the republican constitution. Under Hitler they had been faced with the alternative of taking a personal oath of obedi-

ence to the Führer or resigning, and most of them had chosen
the easier course. In addition, in a complex technical age, bureaucracy was becoming increasingly unpopular, and the German bureaucrats, no longer enjoying the reflected glory of an
ancient and highly successful dynasty, shared in the general
malaise from which their profession was suffering.

Under military government the Allies, especially the British
and the Americans, set out to make certain changes under the
influence of the systems to which they were accustomed in their
own countries. Their first action had made the situation more
complicated. They had dismissed over 50,000 officials and replaced them by politically reliable people who had not always
had the necessary professional qualifications. They then aimed
at bringing about three reforms. First, the civil service was to
be made nonpolitical: the need for this was shown by the fact
that after the first elections in the American zone 28 per cent of
the membership of the *Land* legislatures were either civil servants or local government officials. Secondly, the training and
qualifications required for civil service appointments were to be
broadened: traditionally the Germans had laid a strong emphasis on legal qualifications, whereas the Allies considered that,
under modern conditions, training in economics, finance, political science, or sociology might be more useful. Thirdly, they
wanted to make the whole service more flexible and democratic
in spirit.[41]

Allied efforts were supported by some of the more modern-
minded Germans. The Americans set up personnel offices in
their zone to deal with problems of standards and qualifications, and leading public figures served in them in an honorary
capacity. In Hamburg, the mayor, Max Brauer, who had spent
the war in the United States, introduced methods of appointment new to Germany, such as aptitude tests and thorough and

[41] The whole complex problem of the civil service is dealt with in more
detail in the writer's *Democracy in Western Germany*, Ch. IX.

carefully prepared interviews. In 1960, President Lübke, just a year after taking office, made a speech at the opening of a new building at the Academy of Administration, which had been set up by the French at Speyer, early in 1947. In the following passage from it he expressed an attitude which was fully in harmony with the spirit of the Allied endeavours: "Only when a civil servant, in his personal contacts, behaves not like a superior authority to his inferior but like a citizen in the public service to his fellow citizen can he become the influence for political and social integration which he should be to-day."

The transfer of political responsibility to the German government took place before the Allies had been able to complete their programme. Their work and events since 1918 had exercised some influence on the attitude of the civil service. German officials had begun to take their authority rather less for granted and to show themselves capable of a measure of self-criticism. Furthermore, some at least of them realized that there was a clear distinction between the political power which made the decisions and the officials who carried them out—that is, that they were subject to democratic control. However, Adenauer himself did not fully see the point of the intended reforms. As a former civil servant and a product of the old German administrative system, he was fundamentally well disposed towards the traditions of the official class, and his influence in practice was conservative and even to some extent retrograde. The new Federal Civil Service Act of 1953, which dealt with the appointment and conditions of service of federal officials, was, on the whole, a conservative and unenterprising piece of legislation. A certain flexibility was allowed in qualifications for appointment, but the influence of legal studies in fact remained too strong. Civil servants were not excluded from political activity. They could take part in *Land* and local politics and even stand for election to the Bundestag. Only if they were actually elected to the Bundestag did they have to give up their posts.

In three respects particularly the resulting situation was harmful to democratic development. The presence of a large number of active officials in the *Land* assemblies meant the sacrifice of the principle of political neutrality in the civil service of the *Länder* and made the service as a whole more party conscious: officials, who were also deputies, could oppose or exert pressure on ministers to whom they were professionally responsible, and a minister therefore would tend not to select officials for duties, for which they might be well qualified, if he knew that they represented parties different from his own in the assembly. Secondly, the fact that state-secretaries attended cabinet meetings and represented their ministers in the Bundestag added to the clumsiness of the cabinet as an executive body, reduced the sense of responsibility of ministers towards parliament, and lessened the interest of the Bundestag's proceedings. Finally, the habit developed by which representatives of interest groups, of which more than 400 had their headquarters in Bonn, made their approaches not to members of the Bundestag, which would have been a natural democratic channel, but directly to officials in the relevant ministries. There were two reasons for this procedure: many members of the Bundestag themselves represented interest groups and had their own axes to grind, while the direct approach to a ministry was found in practice to be more effective. The right official would usually have more influence than a member of parliament either through his own minister or through the omnipresent representatives of the Chancellor's Office. Contacts between interest groups and officials became so frequent and so close that towards the end of Adenauer's regime civil servants were quite often tempted away from their ministries into the service of interest groups.

In a technical age a system giving so much influence to the trained administrator and the expert had clear advantages, and it suited both the German character and German traditions. But the very fact that the age favoured the expert made it all the more necessary that he should be controlled as well as used by the people's representatives, if the government was to serve the nation as a whole rather than the sectional interests of wealthy groups, who could employ the most experienced and skilful lobbyists. Before the Empire had fallen, so distinguished a scholar as Max Weber had analysed convincingly its bureaucratic legacy, and after 1949 Theodor Eschenburg, Germany's leading political scientist, had brought the analysis up to date.[42] Perhaps it is too much to expect that so typical a representative of the bureaucratic tradition as Adenauer himself should have drawn the logical conclusion from their criticisms or even have fully understood what they were saying. But there will be no such excuse for the generation that has been growing up since 1949.

The best method of educating a people in democracy is through the day-to-day example of their political leaders. After the foundation of the Federal Republic in 1949 democracy in Germany was on trial, and German politicians were presented with a pedagogic task. What they achieved would not be more important than the way they set about achieving it. From this point of view Adenauer's contribution to German democratic development was, on balance, harmful. Theodor Heuss summed up the situation by saying: "From a formal point of view everything is in order. But whether we have really become democrats remains an open question, if one considers democracy as something more than the mere act of casting a vote."[43] As a public figure Heuss wisely chose to leave the question open, but, judging from his statement, it is likely that his own answer as a private citizen would have been negative.

[42] See their *Bemerkungen zur deutschen Burokratic* and *Der Beamte in Partei und Parlament.*

[43] Quoted by W. E. Süskind in his article, "Reformatoren vorm Bundeshaus," *Süddeutsche Zeitung*, January 2–3, 1960.

In 1954 Karl Jaspers wrote: "The infinitely hard thing is to breathe democratic life into the formal democracy that was forced upon us. What should have been its basic constituent must now belatedly be roused within it."[44] The greatest need is to convince post-war generations that the task is an infinitely hard one. Only then can they acquire the patience to develop democratic standards and habits; above all, the readiness to assume responsibilities which have been traditionally left to higher authorities.

[44] In his article "The Political Vacuum in Germany," *Foreign Affairs,* July 1954.

4
German Society

(a) The Trades Unions

In the process of West German recovery the trades unions played an important role. The rapid industrial expansion, the increase in the labour force, and the rise in the standard of living all involved problems of industrial relations, and it was mainly due to the unions that the workers obtained a fair share in the growing prosperity and a steady improvement in the conditions under which they worked. Economically and socially the unions exercised a stabilizing influence. They attained their objectives, on the whole, with a minimum of strikes. The loss of working days through industrial disputes was much lower than the average in other industrial countries. The highest German figure was in 1951, when 10.9 days were lost for every 100 workers: the average for the twelve years from 1951 to 1962 was 4.9 days; and in the years 1959, 1960 and 1961 the rate dropped to as low as 0.3, 0.2, and 0.3 respectively.[1]

[1] These figures are taken from *Regierung Adenauer 1949–1963*, p. 629. It has not been possible to obtain exactly comparable figures for the United Kingdom from British sources, but according to figures supplied by the I.L.O. the loss of days through strikes for every 100 workers in mining, manufacturing, construction and transport in the United King-

There were three main reasons for this very satisfactory result. First, Germany had a fortunate tradition in industrial relations. Whereas in England trade-unionism was an urgently needed protest against the inhuman conditions resulting from the industrial revolution and it took the greater part of a century for the movement to win its main battles, in Germany, while the revolution was still at its height, Bismarck recognized with considerable insight that drastic action by the government was necessary. During his last seven years in office he passed a series of laws providing comprehensive insurance for workers against sickness, accidents, and old age, thus giving Germany the most advanced system of social legislation in Europe and establishing a salutary precedent for German employers. The legacy of this historical contrast makes itself felt to-day. In England the bitterness created during the nineteenth century lingers on illogically, blurring the main issues confronting workers and management in the twentieth. In Western Germany, on the other hand, workers have become accustomed to being given, rather than having to extort, many of the advantages that are their due. The loyalty of workers to their firms, therefore exceeds in most cases their class consciousness and is one of the country's greatest assets.

Secondly, the German trade-union movement's tragic past turned out eventually in its favour. Under Hitler all the German unions had been merged into the Nazi Labour Front and had ceased to have any independent existence. After 1945 the Allied authorities looked upon the unions as potential centres of democratic influence and supervised their re-creation carefully. Within a month of the setting up of the Republic the German Trade Union Federation, or DGB (*Deutscher Gewerkschaftsbund*) was founded jointly by members of the three main pre-

dom was 13 in 1951; an average of 27.2 during the twelve years from 1951–1962; and 42, 24, and 22, respectively for the years 1959, 1960, and 1961.

war movements: the Free Socialist, the Christian, and the Liberal trades unions. Apart from the churches it had the largest membership of any organized body in Western Germany and included all the main unions except the Civil Servants Federation and the Trade Union of Employees.

The DGB is a federation of sixteen unions. The individual unions deal with negotiations over wages and hours and disputes with employers. The federal organization, with its headquarters in Düsseldorf, handles matters of common interest to all the unions, such as major negotiations with the federal government and social and cultural questions at the national level. Its membership started at 5.4 million, by 1952 it had risen to over 6 million, and for the remainder of Adenauer's chancellorship it remained at about the same level. It is thus a powerful and wealthy body, its membership being about ten times that of the largest political party. The income of the federal organization, which is based on ten per cent of the dues paid to the individual unions, amounted in 1961 to 40.4 million marks. The only split that has occurred in the movement took place in 1955, when a small group founded the "Christian Trade Union Movement of Germany" supported by the Christian Trade Unions International. But the secession was opposed both by Karl Arnold and Jakob Kaiser, the two most influential Christian trade unionists in the country, and it has remained of very limited importance.

The federation and its constituent unions are nonpolitical in character. According to its official programme it is "independent of governments, parties, and confessions" and determined in its support of religious and political tolerance.[2] It depends mainly for its support on workers sympathetic to the SPD and the Left wing of the CDU, and this dual basis for its strength has contributed to the moderation and caution of its policy. Many of its members and officials do belong to the SPD, but

[2] *Grundsatzprogramm des Deutschen Gewerkschaftsbundes*, 1963, p. 5.

there is not the same close relationship as between the Labour Party and the unions in England, and the unions do not make direct contributions to party funds. Some officials at federal headquarters, and still more in such Catholic areas as the Ruhr and the Rhineland, are deliberately chosen from the CDU membership.

Much depends on the fact that the DGB is an efficient and up-to-date organization, and it is in this respect that the complete break with the past which the Nazi era involved turned out in the end to have great advantages. As a rule since the war each industry in Western Germany has had one well-run workers' organization with a modern outlook and no hang-over of class consciousness. The inter-union overlapping and rivalry that have been so harmful in England and also the unofficial strikes have been largely avoided. As one DGB official put it: "In comparison with us, England has had the misfortune not to have suffered a catastrophe." One of the main tasks and achievements of the unions has been to make wage agreements with the employers' associations covering wage rates, wage increases, and conditions of work in general. Between April 1949 and the end of 1962 over 34,000 wage agreements were made. Strikes undertaken in contravention of such agreements or of trade-union decisions were illegal.

Finally, conditions in Germany since 1945 and the industrious nature of the German workers combined to produce the steady rise in living standards with such a low incidence of strikes. Immediately after the war many were without homes and possessions, and to them were added millions of refugees and returned prisoners of war. In these circumstances the main desire of most German workers was to attain a reasonable standard of domestic comfort, and they had no wish to take the risks involved in striking. By the time the most urgent material needs had been met, economic recovery was in full swing, pay and conditions of work were steadily improving, and the workers were on the whole satisfied. When full employment was achieved in 1960, employers were often competing with one another for labour and were even offering wages above the rates fixed in the agreements. It was thus scarcely a time for strikes.

Adenauer's own attitude to the trades unions was respectful for several reasons. In the first place, he appreciated their discipline and had regard for their leadership, particularly from 1949 to 1951, while Hans Böckler was the DGB chairman. Böckler was one of the outstanding members of the SPD to survive the war, and he had a broad and statesmanlike attitude towards trade-union problems. His wage policy was restrained because he was concerned about industrial revival and the avoidance of inflation. Secondly, Adenauer appreciated the DGB's non-party and independent political attitude and was grateful for its timely support of his policy towards the Allies and European integration. Thirdly, electoral considerations being always present in his mind, he was well aware of the importance of maintaining sympathetic contacts with the trade-union leadership.

It was generally believed that Adenauer's relations with the employers' organizations were much closer than with the trades unions, and this impression was strengthened by the statement of Fritz Berg, president of the Federal Association of German Industry, that the chancellor was more likely to follow his advice than the recommendations of his Minister for Economic Affairs. Adenauer was too good a politician to deny such an assertion, as it no doubt gratified influential industrialists on whom the CDU depended financially. But, though he received the representatives of industry cordially and listened to their arguments, Adenauer formed his own judgment as to what action should be taken, knowing well that the government could rely on their support in any case. The trades unions represented a much larger and more fluid body of voters whom it was necessary to propitiate for electoral reasons and from the point of view of the struggle with communism. In fact, therefore, he tended to be more influenced by the trade unionists than by the employers' representatives,[3] and he gained the respect of both Böckler and Walter Freitag, who was chairman of the DGB from 1952 to 1956.

In his main trial of strength with the unions over co-management Adenauer, as has been seen, gave way. The extension of co-management has remained one of the main objectives of the DGB since the original law was passed in 1951, although the results achieved have been disappointing. The formation of holding companies in the iron and steel industries after 1951 meant the large-scale transfer of policy control from the companies affected by the Co-management Law to the new over-all authorities. In June 1956, therefore, a new law was passed extending co-management to the holding companies. But the provisions of the original law were modified in the new legislation and the powers of the workers weakened. The Works Council Law of October 1952, which covered all but the smallest firms, extended co-management to the works councils in questions of personnel and "social" matters; for example, appointments, dismissals, conditions of work, holidays, and problems of health and welfare. In all enterprises also with more than a hundred employees industrial committees (*Wirtschaftsausschüsse*) were set up which were to meet once a month and keep the workers informed about questions of production and marketing which might affect their interests. In joint stock and limited liability companies a third of the board of directors was to consist of employees' representatives. But these measures did not give the workers a real share in the running of industry, and

---

[3] This statement, I am aware, may cause some surprise. It is based on information given to me independently by two of Adenauer's closest associates. I tested it in a conversation with a DGB official, who confirmed its truth and then remarked that the source of my information must have been very close to Adenauer, as the fact was not generally known.

a further aim of the DGB to extend the Co-management Law of 1951 to the chemical and other industries was not realized.

There were two reasons for this failure. The government was opposed to the extension of co-management, and neither the trade-union leaders nor the workers were in the mood to make an issue of it, as Böckler had done in 1951. Most of the workers were too prosperous and satisfied to favour any crusade for industrial democracy, while their leaders feared that the whole trade-union movement might be weakened, if they were to adopt too aggressive and hazardous a policy. In Walter Freitag's words, an appeal to the workers to strike is better avoided, "because it produces a bad atmosphere, and they lose any zest for their work."[4] A time of increasing prosperity was scarcely favourable to the cohesion of a trade-union movement which had just passed through the demoralizing experience of temporary but complete suppression. The fact that the total membership of the DGB remained almost constant during the decade starting in 1952, while the number of employed persons increased from 14,995,000 to 21,097,000, was significant in itself.

Secondly, opinions were divided on the experiment in co-management that had already taken place. On the one hand, co-management in the coal and steel industries was considered to have done much to increase the workers' incentive and improve industrial relations and to have been an important step in the direction of true economic democracy. On the other hand, it was thought by others to be very limited in its actual and potential effectiveness. The law of 1951 gave the employees and owners equal representation, under a neutral chairman, on the board of directors (Aufsichtsrat). But in addition to the board of directors every firm had an executive committee (Vorstand), which was responsible for its day-to-day management. This

---

[4] Words used during an interview with the writer in March 1956.

body consisted usually of a business manager, a production manager, and a labour manager, and was appointed by the board. But only the appointment of the labour manager required the approval of a majority of the employees' representatives on the board. In practice therefore the workers exercised full co-management solely over questions of personnel and social matters, as laid down by the Works Council Law of 1952. Over the technical and the business side of the management they had influence but not genuine joint control. It was further found that labour managers and employees' representatives on the boards tended to grow away from the unions' points of view and identify themselves increasingly with the managements they had joined. This tendency, though probably inevitable, had the effect of damping the enthusiasm of workers for the whole experiment.

As the German trades unions were wealthy and spent relatively little money on strikes, they had plenty to spare for more constructive purposes. Nevertheless their leaders deserve great credit for the steady and imaginative support they have given since the war to educational and cultural activities. Their motives were a mixture of democratic conviction, enlightened self-interest, and cultural far-sightedness.

The twelve-year gap in the unions' existence that coincided with the Hitler period and the heavy German war losses meant that only a small proportion of their membership after the war had previous trade-union experience. Moreover, nearly all their members had been subjected to the anti-democratic and anti-trade union propaganda of the Nazis. A main objective of the unions' educational programme therefore was to teach members the political and social ideals for which their movement stood, and to turn them into responsible and thoughtful democratic citizens. In this part of their work the unions' non-party character was a decided advantage. It facilitated free discussion, largely eliminated political axe-grinding, and encouraged independent educationalists and many of the more thoughtful politicians to take part in the great variety of interesting courses that were arranged.

The German unions took over from the American unions the idea of employing expert economic and industrial consultants. But their leaders also realized the need for giving professional and specialist training to union officials at all levels, so that they could compete on equal terms intellectually with the employers and their advisers. This was another reason why successive DGB chairmen, from Böckler onwards, attached so much importance to educational work.

Many different institutions and a great variety of methods were used to carry out the programme. Support was given to such semi-autonomous academic bodies as the Social Academy in Dortmund, the Academy of Labour in Frankfurt, and the Academy of Communal Economy in Hamburg. More than twenty residential schools were set up by the federal organization of the DGB and by the individual unions, offering courses of varying lengths; at the district and local levels a large number of week-end courses were held; while in the cities the unions collaborated in their educational work with the various adult education organizations. In addition the trades unions strongly advocated the expansion and reform of the universities, easier access to higher education for the children of workers, and the extension of political and social studies.

The most unusual and far-sighted aspect of the unions' cultural and educational programme was their support of the theatre, music, and the fine arts. This side of their work is summed up in the following paragraph from the DGB's official programme for 1963: "Human society needs art for its cultural existence and development. This holds good with special urgency for the industrial society of our time, whose spirit would otherwise be numbed by the technical character of our age or rendered shallow by its materialism." It received unexpected emphasis in the DGB's various publications, which gave the impression that German trade-union leaders, having set out to achieve a progressive reduction in working hours, were already concerning themselves seriously with the problem of the use of leisure. It found concrete expression in the foundation in 1948 of the Ruhr festivals at Recklinghausen, near the heart of the Federal Republic's most densely populated industrial area. The festivals have been held annually ever since and have brought to the Ruhr workers for some weeks each summer music, drama, and art exhibitions of a high quality.

The trades unions claim with some justification to be the most effective guardians of German democracy against Gaullism, neo-nationalism, and any other threats. With their experiences under National Socialism behind them and Communist regimes in two neighbouring states, they have had good reason to appreciate the advantages of a democratic society and to exert their influence in its defence. Their political neutrality has strengthened their hands in doing so. They have not, like the two main political parties, had sometimes to compromise their principles for the sake of power. Rather, they have been free to champion the basic rights of democratic citizens, to emphasize the international ideals of their movement, and to resist any tendency to arbitrary action by authority, wherever it has revealed itself.

(b) Social Legislation

In the immediate post-war years circumstances combined to make a generous system of social legislation inevitable in Germany. Conditions were such that everyone turned naturally to the authorities for help; first to the Allied military government and then to the German governments which, starting at the local and regional levels, progressively assumed responsibility for administration. With a Labour government in England rapidly completing the edifice of a welfare state, whose foundations had been laid during the war, the attitude of the British occupation authorities towards social welfare in Germany was likely to be favourable. In the case of the Americans, common humanity produced a similar result. No German party which had advocated at this time a doctrinaire programme of *laissez-faire* liberalism would have obtained much support. Quite apart from the Social Democrats, therefore, the CDU in the British zone adopted the Ahlener Programme in February 1947, with its strong emphasis on social responsibility. Even Erhard, who was as close to being a liberal as circumstances allowed, adopted his policy of *social* market economy.

National history and Catholic traditions reinforced the prevailing tendency. Bismarck had set the example of paternal social legislation, which succeeding generations had developed and begun to take for granted, while the great social encyclicals of Leo XIII and Pius XI, *Rerum Novarum* and *Quadragesimo Anno*, had determined the policy of the Centre Party and now strongly influenced its heir, the CDU. In 1961 their influence was further strengthened by John XXIII's *Mater et Magistra*.

A third rather paradoxical reason contributed to the same result. The Right wing of the CDU and the smaller parties on the Right were particularly sensitive to the threat of communism and to its challenge in the social sphere. Even these conservative elements, therefore, which might have been expected to oppose generous social measures, were often willing and even eager to support them, so that the Federal Republic should not compare too unfavourably in this respect with the Soviet zone. As Adenauer wrote in 1956:

Thanks to its geographical position and its history Germany bears a responsibility extending far beyond its frontiers, and it does so not least, because the false doctrine of dialectical materialism which originated in its soil can only be overcome through the existence on that same soil of a social order with an exemplary reputation.[5]

Adenauer's numerous legislative measures, which aimed at producing stability, can be accounted for partly by the circumstances just described and partly, as has been seen, by his own social convictions and his sensitivity to electoral considerations. It was thoroughly characteristic of his methods that, when the pension reform was passed shortly before the federal election of 1957, he should have written a letter to every pensioner, and that the booklet explaining the law's provisions should have had his photograph as its frontispiece.[6] Altogether the whole body of social legislation was impressive. The average pension payable to workers and employees under the 1957 law amounted by 1963 to 3,685 marks a year.[7] Provision was made for unemployment insurance, unemployment assistance, insurance against sickness, accident, disability, and age. A wide range of laws covered working conditions and included hours, wage agreements, the employment of women, adolescents, and children, and workers in the home. Children's allowances were normally paid starting with the third child in the family, but in the case of families whose incomes did not exceed 7,200 marks a year they started with the second child. Those disabled in the two wars and surviving dependants of the fallen were naturally covered. Pension schemes also provided for independent artisans and those farmers who chose to contribute to them.

The total burden of the social services on the West German economy was very heavy, and only the country's remarkable recovery made it possible for it to be borne. Payments made by the federal government alone rose from 5.1 milliard marks in 1950 to 14.5 milliard in 1962. The total expenditure for social

[5] "Die deutsche Aufgabe" in the *Rheinische Merkur*, March 16, 1956.
[6] See U. Kitzinger, *op. cit.*, p. 107.
[7] *Regierung Adenauer, 1949–1963*, p. 661.

services by the federal, *Land*, and local governments, and under pension schemes and the Law for the Equalization of Burdens, in the Federal Republic including Berlin, amounted to about 45 milliard marks in 1962, compared with about 12 milliard in 1950. This was the equivalent of 13 per cent of the gross national product and can be compared with the pre-war figure, for 1938, of 6 per cent.[8] The burden per head of population was greater than that in any other of the leading industrial nations of the world.

Nevertheless the social legislation of the Adenauer era did not represent any well thought out plan and has often and justifiably been described as a patchwork. Schemes for comprehensive reforms were from time to time announced, but, with the exception of the Pension Law of 1957, they were repeatedly postponed. In place of them piecemeal legislation was introduced, often under pressure from interest groups. It was on such a scale and the results were so complex that the calculation of pensions, for example, became something of an occult science. There were three main reasons for this hand-to-mouth procedure.

First, the burden on the Federal Republic was so heavy during its first years, as a result of war losses and injuries and the influx of refugees, that the government could not embark upon any additional comprehensive social programme. In 1951 no less than 12 million people, or about a quarter of the total population, were receiving state aid. It was only as the economy revived, the unemployed were absorbed, and war liabilities gradually decreased that more money became available for social purposes. Secondly, there were wide differences of opinion as to what ought to be done between the different elements within the CDU and between the parties making up the government coalition. On the one side, the attitude of the Christian

---

[8] The figures in this paragraph are taken from *Regierung Adenauer, 1949–1963*, pp. 513–14.

trade unionists was close to that of the SPD, while, on the other side, many members of the FDP were for self-help rather than state help. Even Erhard, for all his social market economy, published a book in 1957 called Prosperity for All, one chapter of which reads like a manifesto for laissez-faire liberalism. The chapter is entitled "Welfare State—the Modern Illusion" (Versorgungsstaat—Der Moderne Wahn) and contains the revealing sentence: "The readiness to overcome life's risks freely and on one's own responsibility is the necessary condition for an independent existence in a liberal economic and social order." Finally, Adenauer himself was not sufficiently interested in social problems for their own sake to make the sustained effort necessary to draw up any comprehensive social plan. The furtherance of social justice conformed with his convictions rather than with his inclinations. In the game of politics, of which he was such a master, social legislation was a method of preparing for elections, of "dishing" the SPD—to use Disraeli's word—and of ensuring a firm foundation on which he could pursue his main interest, foreign policy, with a reasonable hope of popular support.

The social order under Adenauer was criticized on a number of grounds. In general terms there was not, as in England or in France, a national system of social security. In 1963 about 85 per cent of the total population were covered by the state health insurance schemes and almost as many by the various pension schemes, if the voluntary participants were included.[9] But the very fact that the federal government and other public authorities spent such vast sums on the social services made it illogical and, from the point of view of those concerned, unsatisfactory that there should be any considerable gaps. Although in principle social insurance was compulsory for all employed persons, white-collared workers were exempt from health insurance, if their incomes exceeded 660 marks a month, and

[9] Regierung Adenauer, 1949–1963, p. 650.

from unemployment insurance and pension schemes, if their incomes exceeded 1,250 marks a month. Pensions schemes for farmers were also voluntary. Towards the end of the Adenauer regime members of the so-called "free" professions, such as lawyers, doctors, and dentists, became increasingly interested in being included in state pension schemes. But, whereas the government and the Bundesrat expressed approval for their aspirations, the necessary legislation was not passed.

The methods of financing the different services varied. In most cases the cost was borne by the insured persons and their employers, the contributions of each towards pensions and unemployment being equal. The state, however, paid substantial subsidies to the pension funds, and the employers defrayed the whole cost of accident insurance. Altogether, in 1963, about 30 per cent of wages and salaries were deducted for social purposes, if the employers' contributions were included in the reckoning, and in the case of miners the proportion was a good deal more. At this very high cost it was widely felt that the government ought to co-ordinate all the social services in a rational and easily understood plan.

The disadvantages of Adenauer's lukewarm attitude to social reform and of the consequent piecemeal approach to the whole problem can be illustrated by two examples. During the lifetimes of the first two Bundestags very generous legislation was passed in favour of certain powerful interest groups; for example, the refugees, who had formed their own political party, and the dismissed and dispossessed former civil servants, who, in spite of their former Nazi associations, enjoyed the prestige of their profession and the advantage of valuable contacts. On the other hand, pensioners and other recipients of public relief, who were not in a position to exert political influence or often even to voice their complaints, were tragically neglected. A couple on the old-age pension, received only 102 marks a month plus rent, while a widow, who was over forty or had at least one child, got between 70 and 90 marks. It is true that the law of 1957 largely put the situation right and the rates were raised by about 50 per cent. But the injustices had already lasted for too long and were rectified by a measure, which was excellent in itself but was timed chiefly in the interests of electioneering. A second example was the failure to reform the health insurance system. Apart from such common faults as the misuse of the services and medicines provided, the system was open to a number of serious criticisms. The hospitals were often seriously understaffed and the nurses sometimes dealt with in a harsh and unimaginative way. The treatment given in the hospitals was divided into three classes and varied too much with the amount patients could afford. Payment of sickness benefit was limited to twenty-six weeks, protection thus not being provided against a long and serious illness. Theodor Blank's valiant attempt at reform was, as has been seen, prevented at the last moment,[10] and the impression left was that doctrinaire differences amongst government supporters were considered more important than a sound system of medical insurance. Adenauer himself was not sufficiently interested to exert his authority, resist outside pressure, and put the reform through.

The need for a comprehensive plan covering all the social services was frequently recognized, and the proposed plan came to be known popularly and even officially as the "social package." As early as 1952 a motion was proposed in the Bundestag for establishing a commission which was to draw up a social insurance plan. It was not carried, but the proposal no doubt contributed to the passing of the Pension Law of 1957. The idea of a more comprehensive plan recurred throughout the remainder of Adenauer's chancellorship, and in his declaration of policy on October 9, 1962, at the beginning of his last year of office, the chancellor himself made the following statement:

[10] See p. 126.

The federal government is determined to continue its progressive social policy even within the framework of its economy budget. The continuation of social reform is urgent. The "social package" with the bills dealing with family allowances, continued wage payments (during sickness), and reform of health insurance will be submitted to you as soon as possible. The bills complement one another to such an extent in the way in which they redistribute the burden and balance out the social improvements that they can only be put into force simultaneously.

However, the "social package" had never been one of Adenauer's primary objectives, and, in this last phase of his chancellorship, failure to attain it was part of the price he paid for the FDP's support. Within one week of his resignation in October 1963 it was announced that the social experts of the government coalition parties had given up their efforts to reach an understanding between the CDU/CSU and the FDP on the content of the "social package."

(c) The Press and Radio

One of the most successful achievements of Allied military government had been its handling of the German press and radio. Realizing that editors and journalists had been amongst the most subservient and dangerous of Hitler's human instruments, they at first forbad the publication of newspapers altogether. They then with great care selected groups of men with anti-Nazi records and the necessary professional qualifications and gave them licences to edit and publish papers. The three Western Allies pursued rather different policies towards the press, but they all placed great emphasis on the political reliability of the licensees: a high proportion of the selected publishers and editors had been in concentration camps or had been arrested during the Nazi period. By the time military government came to an end in 1949 there were altogether about 150 licensed newspapers in the three Western zones.

The licensees, once they had been chosen, were given full support by the Allied authorities both in material terms and in a more professional sense. In view of the conditions under which they started up, most publishers had not had the capital necessary to invest in much equipment. In the American zone, therefore, under military government protection they were usually given mandatory leases of their printing plants for three or five years. In some cases they had done sufficiently well by 1949 to have started buying their own plant. But to ensure their survival the Allied High Commission continued to give them protection after military government ended. As the great majority of the editors appointed had remained in Germany during Hitler's regime, they were out of touch with the rest of the world, while the younger recruits to journalism had often had no experience of any but a totalitarian form of government. Journalists, therefore, were given a high priority in the various Allied exchange programmes and in other schemes to enable Germans to travel abroad. With Allied encouragement also schools and institutes for training journalists were set up in universities or, in at least one case, under the wing of a successful paper.[11]

When the licensing system came to an end in the summer of 1949, many former publishers and editors, who had been associated with the press under Hitler, came back into business, and the number of newspapers jumped within a few weeks from 150 to 900. The licensed proprietors feared for their futures, but they fared better than they had expected. Most of the newly founded papers were small local journals. The new arrivals brought with them not only their old professional techniques but their old attitudes as well. The German people found they

[11] The Munich *Abendzeitung*.

preferred the new methods and points of view of the licensed newspapers. Six years later, in 1955, the licensees still retained about two-thirds of the circulation of dailies, and most of the leading newspapers, such as *Die Welt*, the *Süddeutsche Zeitung*, and *Die Zeit* had all originated under licence. The *Frankfurter Allgemeine* was the immediate successor of a paper started with a French licence in Mainz by the former editors of the *Frankfurter Zeitung*.

Two circumstances have exercised a good deal of influence on the German press during the Adenauer era and must be taken into account, if the part played by the press in the national life is to be understood.

The Federal Republic, unlike any other country of comparable size and importance, lacks a metropolitan capital. This fact alone largely accounts for the absence of any really national newspapers. Bonn remains, and is likely to remain, nothing more than a provincial town masquerading rather unwillingly as a capital city. Owing to the limitations of its social, intellectual, and cultural life, it cannot provide either the competition or the stimulus necessary to further the development of a national press. No newspaper published in Bonn has any pretensions to national stature, and the three daily papers with the best claims to it, *Die Welt*, the *Frankfurter Allgemeine*, and the *Süddeutsche Zeitung*, originating in Hamburg, Frankfurt, and Munich respectively, are not competitive with one another in the same sense as would be three papers published in one metropolitan centre. Furthermore, by a perverse chance, the *Süddeutsche Zeitung*, which is the most intellectually stimulating of the three, is itself the most provincial in character. The republic has acquired in Hamburg rather fortuitously a kind of press capital. For this is a fair description of a city which, in addition to being the headquarters of the German Press Agency, produces *Die Welt*, *Die Zeit*, *Der Spiegel*; Axel Springer's illustrated daily, *Bildzeitung*, with a circulation of 4,480,000; four

other Springer weeklies and a fortnightly with circulations rang-
ing from 490,000 to 3,860,000; the illustrated weekly Stern,
with a circulation of 1,730,000; and six other periodicals with
average sales varying between 460,000 and 1,460,000. But this
does not make Hamburg, in the extreme north of the country
and with the strong local patriotism of a Hanseatic city, into a
national capital. It is merely fortunate that so much journalistic
activity goes on in a city with strong liberal traditions and the
cosmopolitan atmosphere of a great port.

The second important circumstance is the existence of the
powerful press empire of the Hamburg publisher, Axel
Springer, which he built up as a young man after the war in the
space of a few years, having skilfully made himself persona
grata in turn with the British military government, the socialist
mayor of Hamburg, Max Brauer, and the federal government.
Before the end of Adenauer's chancellorship, he had bought
up the powerful publishing house of Ullstein and the Düsseldorf paper Mittag, and won a dominant position in the
newspaper world, controlling nearly 40 per cent of the market in
newspapers and periodicals. Inevitably the growth of such a
vast organization under one man's control was at the expense
of the variety and independence of the German press.

The press under Adenauer had a number of weaknesses,
particularly from a political point of view, and was the target
for a good deal of criticism mostly from journalists themselves.
On some of the most important political issues the attitude of
most newspapers was apathetic, uncritical, and therefore dull.
The reasons were both financial and political.

The majority of the German people, preoccupied with their
material interests and traditionally respectful of authority, were
little interested in political controversy, especially if it involved
criticism of the government. So far as circulation was concerned, therefore, editors had little inducement to put emphasis
on political problems or to adopt an independent political line.

The hundreds of small local papers, which had come into existence since the summer of 1949, were dependent on matrix services, which provided them with editorials, major news items, and feature articles that had already been written and set up by central agencies. For them circulation was often a matter of survival, and they could not afford to alienate sections of their readers and potential readers by expressing independent or unusual views. The big publishing houses and press agencies, which distributed the matrices, were thus obliged to play for safety. The result was a steady flow of nondescript and rather tedious items, to which no one could take exception.

In addition, the federal government and the more powerful interest groups were not above exerting direct or indirect influence on the more important newspapers, if they were too critical of government policy or took up attitudes that were considered harmful to the interest groups concerned.[12] The Chancellor's Office or the Press and Information Office normally acted on Adenauer's behalf, while the easiest method by which the interest groups could exert their influence was a threat to withdraw advertisements. For the sake of a quiet life, therefore, and out of financial considerations, there was a tendency for editors and publishers, with no strong convictions of their own, either to support the government or to settle down to an attitude of unprovocative and benevolent neutrality.

Under military government the British had favoured the establishment of party newspapers on the grounds that they would encourage the development of lively democratic discussion. But before 1949 they had discovered that many Germans were sick of party points of view, and they had granted licences to a number of independent papers. None of the big dailies during the Adenauer era was a party paper, though each had its own political flavour. This was scarcely surprising in view of

[12] Several examples of government intervention are given in Democracy in Western Germany, pp. 126-7.

the fate of the *Morning Post*, the *News Chronicle*, and the *Daily Herald* in Britain, where public interest in politics was much greater. But it made the German press less interesting than it might have been. Such party papers as there were, like the weekly *Rheinische Merkur* (CDU) or the daily *Frankfurter Rundschau* (SPD), did not have national influence comparable to that of the *Manchester Guardian* or the *New Statesman* in Britain at the time.

The most serious weakness of the German press was its failure to combine constructive opposition with convincing the German people that it would be possible and in the national interests desirable at the appropriate moment to form an alternative government, and that democracy rests on the assumption that governments should be changed from time to time. One German journalist has recently suggested that the majority of the German people do not want opposition and simply have not the capacity or perhaps the will to run a democratic system.[13] If this is so, and if the Federal Republic retains its provisional constitution, then the situation presents a great challenge to German politicians and teachers, as well as to German journalists.

There is no reason why the press should bear the sole responsibility for not transforming the German people into convinced and active democrats since the war, and it is a very good sign that German journalists should have been so alert and critical as regards the record of their own profession. The press in many countries today is, with good reason, the subject of considerable criticism: it manifests, in very noticeable ways, some of the worst characteristics of the age; in particular, its materialism and its acquiescence in the lowering of standards for the sake of convenience. But, when a balance is struck, the

[13] See Helmut Lindemann's letter to *Der Spiegel*, May 19, 1965, and also on the broader problem, Peter Grubbe's article, "Freiheit, die ich meine," in *Der Monat*, April 1965.

German press emerges with a better and more positive record than the press in many other countries.

The Allied authorities, as has been seen, gave it a good start in the immediate postwar years. There were not at the time many good journalists available. Many of the ablest members of the profession, who had been active before 1933, had either emigrated, become the victims of Nazi persecution, or been corrupted in varying degrees by National Socialism. Those who survived and the new generation of post-war journalists took advantage of the start they had been given. They cherished the liberal and independent attitudes that had been encouraged by the Allies, and a high proportion of them treated their profession as a vocation. Apart from the top ranks, postwar German journalists compared on the whole favourably with their colleagues in England, both in their standard of education and in the prestige society conceded to them. They were better democrats than the public for whom they wrote and than the majority of active German politicians.

On a number of important issues the majority of German newspapers have given a good lead, maintained steadily a sound attitude, and done much to educate public opinion in the right direction. For example, they have supported European integration, playing down national prejudice on the subject; they have denounced anti-Semitism; and they have given salutary and balanced publicity to the trials of war criminals in the German courts during the latter years of Adenauer's government. On certain specific occasions also the press has taken a valuable initiative or exerted its influence to produce a desirable result. In 1951 a series of articles in the *Frankfurter Rundschau* was largely responsible for the setting up of a committee to inquire into the presence of former Nazis and reactionaries in the Foreign Service. In 1955 the press on the whole was strongly critical of the appointment as Minister of Education of Lower Saxony of Herr Schlüter, who had been responsible for the publication of a number of neo-Nazi books, and contributed as a result to his subsequent enforced resignation. During the summer of 1959 also some very critical articles were published on Adenauer's behaviour in first accepting and then withdrawing from the presidential candidature.

Although the great majority of newspapers gave general support to the government or were timidly non-committal in their attitude, there were a few notable exceptions. The place of honour must be given to the Hamburg weekly, Die Zeit. While maintaining the highest standards of journalistic dignity and integrity, and giving Adenauer full credit for his great achievements it has at the same time maintained over the years an exceptional record of independent, interesting, and responsible criticism, reminiscent of the Manchester Guardian at its best, and made possible by an excellent editorial staff and a distinguished list of occasional contributors. In fact, after the SPD had adopted the Godesberg Programme and started its policy of restraint, a distinguished German scholar remarked to the writer that the only opposition left was Der Spiegel and Die Zeit.

Der Spiegel, a weekly news magazine modelled originally on the American Time, is very different in character from Die Zeit. Founded shortly after the war, it was built up within a few years into a highly successful magazine by its young publisher, Rudolf Augstein, who is a journalistic genius. Its circulation at present exceeds 600,000. In its sheer technical competence it is comparable to Time itself or to the Daily Express. Throughout the whole Adenauer era it occupied a unique position in German journalism and exercised a quite exceptional influence on German politics and public life. On the one hand, Der Spiegel has been accused of indulging in consistently negative criticism, of revelling in scandal for its own sake and for its effect on sales, and of discrediting politics still further amongst a people little inclined in any case to respect the processes of democratic government. On the other hand, it has been admired and highly commended for giving a most convincing example of the influence that can be exercised by a free press, for its ruthless and courageous exposure of abuses, and for making politics interesting to a wide range of previously apathetic citizens. Its most widespread influence has perhaps been exerted in a preventive sense, as politicians have come to fear being mentioned in its columns. But it has also jogged government departments into action by revealing omissions and inadequacies in internal administration, and it has been responsible for the resignation of members of the Bundestag and of ministers at the *Land* and federal levels. Its most far-reaching achievement, which culminated in the autumn of 1962, will be dealt with in more detail later.

Amongst the dull run of politically neutral or nondescript journals two further exceptions are the Munich daily, *Süddeutsche Zeitung*, and the Berlin monthly, *Der Monat*, although a number of periodicals with small circulations and rather special interests have also played collectively an important role. The *Süddeutsche Zeitung* represents a moderate Left-wing point of view and publishes regularly independent, well-informed articles on important current problems, which deserve investigation and publicity but tend to be neglected. *Der Monat* is as much a literary and cultural as a political periodical. It covers a wide range of subjects from different standpoints and has a varied and impressive list of contributors.

Adenauer's personal relationship with the press was contradictory. His attitude to it reflected his personal position as a product of the pre-1914 era, who was in some respects very well informed on the age in which he was living. He was fully aware of the great influence which the press exercised, and he was far too sensitive to electoral considerations to neglect its representatives. Over many years, therefore, he gave on an average at least two press interviews a week. During the interviews he not only impressed journalists in his favour by the dignity and sedate courtesy of his manner but took full advantage of the opportunities to question his visitors on the subjects on which they were informed or, in the case of foreigners, about the countries from which they came. He was, on the whole, well served by his press advisers, and especially by Herr von Eckhardt.

On the other hand, Adenauer had a strong personal prejudice against the press. He had little or no appreciation of its inherent value as a great organ of free expression in a democratic society. He resented its criticisms, and it jarred against his sense of discipline and his authoritarian temperament that any journalist should be free to disapprove of his policies and even endanger their fulfilment. It was a testimony to the political vitality of some sections of the German press that Adenauer should have disliked it so much.

His dislike was most clearly revealed between 1952 and 1954, when a series of measures were proposed in turn for at least partially curbing and controlling the press. First the Ministry of the Interior drew up a draft press law for banning newspapers "hostile to the state." It was followed by an attempt to set up a Ministry of Information for the purpose of "enlightening the public" and preparing it for the government's legislative proposals. Finally, after the 1953 election, a modified proposal was made for setting up a co-ordinating information committee with much the same objectives. All these attempted measures were defeated. The memory of Goebbels' activities was still vivid in many people's memories, and the Basic Law had guaranteed freedom of the press[14] and laid down that there should be no censorship. Opposition was widespread especially from the SPD and the FDP, and the press was almost unanimously unfavourable. The chancellor himself was

[14] An exception was made in Article 18, in the case of those abusing the freedom "in order to attack the free democratic basic order."

probably most impressed by the strong disapproval of foreign journalists at a time when he was particularly anxious to win the trust of the Western Allies.

Adenauer's basically negative attitude towards the press did some good by the reaction which it provoked. It made German newspapers and periodicals very conscious of their rights and of the need to defend them. In October 1962, when Der Spiegel's office was raided by the police and its publisher imprisoned, almost the whole German press sided strongly with the victim, because they realized that a great principle was involved.

The attitudes towards the radio of the Allied authorities under military government and of Adenauer after he became chancellor were, as might be expected, similar to their attitudes towards the press.

The Allies were concerned to ensure that the radio stations were democratically controlled, and that they became channels for the expression of different democratic points of view. They wanted also to prevent them from coming under direct government control, as, quite apart from the National Socialist record, German broadcasting, even under Weimar, was considered to have been too strongly influenced by the government. After a period of close Allied control, therefore, each station was placed under the supervision of a broadcasting council made up of representative citizens. The day-to-day administration and control were put in the hands of a director general (Intendant), who was responsible to a small administrative committee, which appointed him, subject to confirmation by the council.

Two main systems were used for selecting the councils and they continued to be employed after military government ended. The British, in the north, put the matter in the hands of the legislatures in the Länder, who chose their representatives in accordance with the principle of proportional representation. In the American zone various political, economic, educational, and cultural groups had the right to choose representatives. In Bavaria, for example, the groups included the government, the legislative assembly, the senate (a second chamber unique to Bavaria), the trades unions, the farmers' union, industrial organizations, the refugees, the churches, religious associations, the universities, the teachers, organizations for adult education, and various cultural bodies. Under both systems members of the councils were pledged to serve the general public's interest regardless of their political and personal connections, and they were not bound by orders or instructions. For example, the North German Radio, with its headquarters in Hamburg, is committed to "promote international understanding, serve the cause of peace and social justice. It must defend democracy and freedom and it is bound only to the truth. It must not serve the prejudices of any one political party, pressure group, philosophy or creed."[15] It might be expected that under the American system there would be less likelihood of political influence being exerted. But this is not necessarily true. Under the alternative system the parties take care to choose their representatives from different social groups, and any political influence that is exercised is open and obvious, whereas, when members are not actually chosen by the parties, such political influence as is exerted tends to be disguised, or at least indirect, and is therefore more sinister and difficult to restrain.

The Allies selected the original staffs of the radio stations with the same great care as they used in choosing the licensees for the first post-war newspapers. When control over the radio was transferred to the Germans, therefore, those responsible for selecting the broadcasting councils and new officials made it a point of honour to maintain the recently established tradition of appointing to key posts men with democratic and liberal convictions. As a result, the radio in Western Germany soon ac-

[15] The quotation is taken from the brochure issued by the North German Radio, entitled "N.D.R."

quired a reputation for its objectivity, its independence, and the variety of views it expressed. Each broadcasting station was much more influential than any one newspaper, and great care was taken to maintain standards. Moreover, the broadly representational character of the supervisory councils was a guarantee against any station deteriorating to the level of one of the more timid and nondescript newspapers. If the press was more democratic than the public that it served, the radio, on the whole was more democratic and lively than the press.

To mention a few outstanding examples. Walter von Cube, a political commentator and later talks director of the Bavarian Radio, gave a series of original and surprisingly frank commentaries on internal and external politics between 1946 and 1952, which were later published under the appropriate title, *I Beg to be Contradicted.* The political commentaries from Hamburg were often stimulating and imaginative, while school broadcasts from a number of stations were impressive and did much to give the younger generation a sound attitude towards such important problems as democracy, National Socialism, anti-Semitism, and European integration. Towards the end of Adenauer's chancellorship the West German Radio in Cologne collaborated with one or two other stations to produce a long series of television films, entitled "The Third Reich," which dealt with every aspect of the Hitler era with admirable objectivity, from a broadly democratic point of view, and showed no signs of the inhibited and apologetic attitude towards the subject which has been characteristic of many members of the older generations of Germans since the war. The station also collaborated with Poles and Czechs in making films, and the director exchanged visits with a senior radio official in Poland. Finally, Herr Neven-Dumont, a courageous and highly gifted member of the North German Radio's staff, produced a film called "Poles in Breslau," which came to grips with the problem of the younger generation of Poles growing up in Lower

Silesia. In contrast to the way in which the Polish-administered territories had often been treated by German journalists, Neven-Dumont's film was scrupulously fair and showed great sensitivity to the Polish point of view. It was a human and most moving document, and one of the not too frequent examples of the liberal and imaginative treatment of a long-standing international problem, of which the twentieth century has from time to time proved itself capable.[16]

Although the federal and *Land* governments could approve the liberal and democratic views expressed over the radio on such subjects as European integration and anti-Semitism, some of the criticisms of the more independent commentators and programme directors were naturally at the governments' expense. Adenauer and the CDU were therefore just as touchy about freedom of expression on the radio as in the press, and their irritation was sometimes shared by other parties and by interest groups. The radio stations were all autonomous public corporations and were, in theory, not subject to government control. But nevertheless the federal and the *Land* governments did in fact exercise indirectly a good deal of influence over them through political parties and the membership of the broadcasting councils and the administrative committees. The influence could take effect in two ways. Either it led to the dismissal of members of staff or it curbed the independence of producers and commentators, especially those on short-term contracts, who would become less bold and critical for the sake of their jobs or of a quiet life. By this second means even directors general could be induced to be less enterprising and more compliant. In general, therefore, the independence and democratic vitality of the German radio tended to decline. At the end of the Adenauer era those most closely concerned with

[16] When Neven-Dumont was taking photographs shortly afterwards at a demonstration organized by Silesian refugees, he had to be protected by the police from the anger of the crowd.

preserving these two characteristics, on the whole, agreed that they still had a good deal of freedom and real autonomy but that both privileges had to be fought for all the time.

The Basic Law conferred administrative and legislative powers on the Länder except insofar as it granted them in certain specified matters to the federal government. Since broadcasting was not included in the list of powers allocated to the federal government, it came under the control of the Länder, which indeed were responsible for all cultural affairs. Adenauer, with his keen sense of the importance of publicity, was dissatisfied with this arrangement from the beginning, and, as radio and television became more and more popular, he became increasingly impatient. By 1963 there were about 8 million registered television sets, and with an average of at least 2½ people using each set, this meant that there were altogether about 20 million viewers. Adenauer made a number of attempts to pass a federal radio law, but they were strongly opposed both by the SPD and by the Länder, who jealously guarded their rights. The attempts culminated in September 1957, when a draft law drawn up by Dr. Gerhard Schröder, who was then Minister of the Interior, was approved by the cabinet. The draft was prepared and introduced with extraordinary tactlessness. Dr. Schröder had not even consulted the directors of the radio stations, and Adenauer had not had the discussion with representatives of the Länder which he had promised to hold before any draft was made public.[17] Even such loyal supporters of Adenauer as the minister-presidents of Bavaria and Rhineland-Palatinate objected to the bill, and it was decisively rejected by the Bundesrat.

The events that followed were typical of Adenauer at his most arbitrary and undemocratic. He decided to form a private company with the federal government as the sole shareholder for the purpose of providing a second television programme under federal control. Its legality was challenged, and the mat-

[17]See the article by Walter Panofsky, "Bonn und der Rundfunk," in the Süddeutsche Zeitung, October 2, 1959.

ter was referred to the Federal Constitutional Court. The court gave its ruling in February 1961 and decided that radio and television were a "cultural phenomenon" and thus within the competence of the *Länder*, insofar as the state should take any part in such activities. It pointed out, however, that according to Article 5 of the Basic Law, which guaranteed "freedom of reporting by radio," the state was excluded from direct control over any institution or company which organized radio broadcasts. "Telecommunication services," which Article 73 placed under federal control, covered only the technical aspect of broadcasting. Eight days after the court had delivered its judgment Adenauer spoke as follows in the Bundestag:

As soon as we were in possession of the judgment and our special experts had worked through it, the cabinet met for a session, in order to express its view on this judgment and on this television dispute. The decisions, which the cabinet has taken, were taken unanimously. The cabinet was agreed that the judgment of the Federal Constitutional Court was wrong, Ladies and Gentlemen.

But, Ladies and Gentlemen, the judgment of the Federal Constitutional Court must, according to law, be heeded.

In consequence the cabinet has resolved, likewise unanimously, not to concern itself with any further matters connected with television.[18]

Thus the first minister of a democratic state and his cabinet, having called in question the judgment of the highest court in the land, agreed to respect the rule of law. Yet Adenauer himself with a characteristically stubborn persistence made private inquiries as to whether there was any chance of the court changing its opinion on television.[19]

The Federal Constitutional Court was set up in 1951 in

[18] *Verhandlungen des Deutschen Bundestages,* 3 *Wahlperiode,* Bonn, 1961, 147 Sitzung, 8 März 1961.

[19] The writer was told this on excellent authority, though it is not possible to disclose the source.

accordance with Articles 93 and 94 of the Basic Law. Its main duties are to decide on the interpretation of the Basic Law in the event of a dispute and to settle differences of opinion over the rights and duties of the federal government and the *Länder*. But it has other important functions as well and is the real guardian of the constitution. It has, on the whole, proved itself to be the most satisfactory democratic institution in postwar Germany and has won wide respect. Whereas Adenauer has established a predominantly tactical relationship with most federal institutions and has tended to manipulate them to his own advantage, the court being responsible for its own development and integrity, has set itself and attained a very high standard. The two "senates" into which the court was divided were for a time thought to be susceptible to different forms of political influence. But the court has lived this suspicion down, and it is now realized that its members are independent and highly responsible jurists with a broad sense of their duties towards the state.[20] It has delivered its judgments with complete impartiality. Its decision in 1958 against income-tax exemption for political contributions and its decision in the television case were both very unpopular with the federal government, and the second was accompanied by strong criticism of the federal government's lack of the moderation appropriate to a federal system in its relations with the governments of the *Länder*. If the influence of lawyers on the civil service has been too strong for the best interests of German democracy, it has been offset by the influence of the lawyers in the Federal Constitutional Court, whose integrity and courage have strengthened the democratic principles upon which the state rests.

Up to 1962 there was only one television system in the Federal Republic, which was managed by a joint organization in which all the radio stations participated. It was generally

---

[20] Only when important religious issues are involved do the personal loyalties of the judges sometimes reveal themselves.

agreed that a second television programme was needed, and, after the Constitutional Court had declared Adenauer's plan illegal, a second television organization was set up in Mainz, by an arrangement between the Länder, which was to be financed by 30 per cent of all television fees received by the existing stations. The officers and members of the controlling bodies were selected from the political parties according to their strength in the Länder. As the CDU and the CSU controlled the governments in the majority of Länder, their influence in the new organization was predominant and was supported by the fact that Mainz was in the strongly Catholic Rhineland-Palatinate. However, the new system was better than the federal government's alternative, and the relative influence exerted by the different political parties will in the long run be dependent upon the electorate.

(d) Education

Education has presented the Federal Republic with one of its biggest and most deep-seated problems, and the progress made towards its solution has on the whole been inadequate. Towards the end of the Adenauer era those who had been giving the subject their serious attention had even greater cause for concern than in 1949. The problem assumed different forms as the years went by, and for the sake of clarity it will be convenient to consider three aspects, or stages, of it separately. The three overlapped, so there is an element of artificiality in the division, but each had a character of its own.

Immediately after the war the Allies suspended the German educational system altogether. Schools and universities were closed down with the object of making a completely fresh start. Teachers, like journalists, were subjected to a particularly careful "denazification." When, after a few months, first the schools and later the universities were reopened, the main difficulties, which the occupation authorities faced, were lack of buildings, equipment, and suitable staff. In its first stage, therefore, the educational problem was how to overcome the consequences of Nazi indoctrination and the war.

In many of the larger towns a high proportion of the school buildings had been either destroyed or seriously damaged. For example, in Hanover 95 per cent of all class-rooms had been destroyed; in Cologne, 88 per cent; and in Bremen, 84 per cent. To make use of such buildings as were available children had to be taught in two or three shifts a day. Schools were sometimes housed in inns, cellars, and air-raid shelters. The University of Kiel was for a time accommodated in some ships that were lying in the harbour. As there was so much other urgent re-building to be done, the problem took a long time to solve. At the beginning of 1956 the shift system was still being employed, classes were usually too large, and in the whole country there was a shortage of about 30,000 class-rooms.

The lack of sufficient suitable teachers was a still more diffi-cult problem. The high standards at first adopted by the Allies soon had to be dropped, and many teachers were reinstated who had been members of the Nazi party or associated organi-zations. They were often very competent professionally. But they were not fitted to educate young Germans in the principles and the spirit of democracy. Even those who had been demo-crats by conviction had sometimes been involved in one way or another in Nazi activities and were therefore timid and inhib-ited. Human beings proved even more difficult to rebuild than class-rooms. There was thus no real alternative to waiting for a new generation to grow up, and this was a still longer process than material reconstruction.

The textbooks at first available in history and the social sciences were usually old-fashioned and unenterprising. Their authors were as little inclined as the general run of teachers to treat recent events in any detail or to face the challenge of the National Socialist era. Here also it was necessary to wait until the implicated generation had been succeeded by writers who could handle the recent past without inhibitions, though, so far as national prejudices were concerned, the process was hastened in 1951 by an imaginative foundation in Brunswick known as the International School Book Institute.[21]

Before the specifically postwar and post-Hitler aspect of German's educational problem had been fully solved, it was superseded in the attention of educationists by the problem in its second stage. This concerned the deep-lying deficiencies in the educational system, most of which could be traced back well before the Hitler era, and which aroused increasing concern as the immediate postwar difficulties were gradually surmounted. German education had been so good for so long that nearly everyone assumed that, apart from temporary problems, every thing about it was fundamentally sound. By the middle of the twentieth century, however, this was no longer the case.

In the first place, the educational system was based on the assumption of social inequality. Whereas primary education had for long been both compulsory and free, as late as 1956 secondary education in most *Länder* and university education in every *Land*, except Hesse, was not free. This meant that of the 20 per cent of elementary school children who passed on to the secondary schools only a very few came from the working classes and that only 5.5 per cent of university students were the children of workers.[22] While in the Federal Republic out of a total of 130,000 students more than 85,000 received no financial assistance, in England over 70 per cent of the students received state assistance and about 25 percent had working-

---

[21] The institute is described briefly in *Democracy in Western Germany*.

[22] This last figure may be rather too low owing to the fact that some students do not like admitting that their fathers are workers and therefore tend to describe them by any titles that they may have acquired within the hierarchy of their firms.

class parents. In 1953 nearly half of the male students in Western Germany and nearly a quarter of the female students supported themselves by their own work during their studies. Yet a University Commission set up by military government in the British zone had reported in 1949 that "the universities are for the gifted, not for the moneyed" and had recommended that "every effort should be made to abolish fees and finally to achieve free university tuition."

This state of affairs was all the more serious, because it contrasted very unfavourably with the situation in the Soviet zone. There the number of students admitted to institutions of higher learning almost quadrupled between 1946 and 1954. This gave the zone a relatively higher rate of enrolment than the federal republic, 0.32 per cent of the population attending universities and technical colleges as against 0.24 per cent in the Federal Republic. In 1953, 65 per cent of all university and college students in the zone were drawn from a working-class or peasant background, and the following year, under a generous scholarship scheme, over 96 per cent of all students received from 130 to 180 marks a month, which meant that the average student in the zone had better living conditions and greater financial security that his counterpart in Western Germany. The Humboldt University in East Berlin alone reported in 1957 an expenditure on scholarships of 96 million marks during the previous four years.

The 1949 report of the University Commission, referred to above, was a far-sighted document and anticipated many recommendations that were made later by more specialized bodies. This was due largely to the commission's composition. Six of its twelve members were German educationists with varied backgrounds; there were four non-academic representatives of German public life; whilst Lord Lindsay, of Balliol College, Oxford, and Professor von Salis of Zurich Technical University completed the group. Between them they brought an unusually broad approach to the consideration of German university problems, the universities themselves having suffered in general from excessive conservatism and too much inbreeding.[23]

The commission's report also emphasized two other shortcomings of the universities, both of which reflected their ultra-conservatism: they had not kept step with the social changes of the time and they tended to train the specialist intellect rather than the whole man. One example of the first weakness was their acquiescence in remaining institutions for the socially privileged. But the weakness had also revealed itself and continued to reveal itself in other ways. The universities had not risen to the challenge of the Weimar experiment in democracy. The record of professors under Hitler had been weak, very few of them having dared to protest at the persecution of their Jewish and Left-wing colleagues, while after the war few academics appeared to realize the extent of their failure or of their responsibility for what had occurred. Most professors were content to remain in their ivory towers and to make little response to the new challenge of Germany's second democratic experiment. For example, with one or two exceptions, like Hamburg and Göttingen, the German universities saw no need to broaden the scope of their activities by giving a lead in adult education at a time when the need for it was particularly great.

The two shortcomings were, in fact, very closely associated, because graduates with a well-rounded rather than a purely specialist education were more likely to be aware of social change and what it implied for the country's intellectual leaders. The commission therefore recommended that the training of a student should not be limited to giving him the information needed for his future profession, but that he must be made also into a useful human being. In the community life of students

[23] The commission's report was rejected by the universities, though it was welcomed by some of the more progressive academics.

the greatest value ought to be attached to the use of democratic methods. The unity of culture should be emphasized by means of a *studium generale;* that is to say, lectures should be arranged on subjects of general interest, which students could, and in some cases would be required to attend. Technical universities ought to be expanded to include a faculty for the humanities and social sciences.

To carry out such a programme with success, professors and teachers were required who thoroughly understood its purpose, who were themselves conscious of the changing needs of society, and who were prepared to modify their academic habits and traditions to further broad human objectives. It was necessary also that the university authorities should be willing to make the required changes in organization. Unfortunately the country had lost many of its most liberal and progressive professors during the Hitler period, and the rigidity and conservatism of the academic hierarchy presented serious obstacles. For example, one innovation which was widely advocated by the reformers was the establishment of chairs of political science, a subject that had no place as such in the German academic tradition. The social and educational advantages of such a development were obvious in a country with a democratic constitution and very limited experience of democracy in practice. Yet the idea was greeted at first with a good deal of suspicion and hostility, especially by the professors of law and philosophy, who saw in it a possible encroachment on their own extensive territories.[24]

A fourth deep-lying weakness in the educational system was the lack of a unified or co-ordinated system of administration. Traditionally German education, both after and before the foundation of the empire in 1871, had been a matter for the German states. The principle of academic freedom had also

---

[24] In German universities political theory was traditionally included under philosophy and the study of political institutions under law.

ensured considerable variety in the methods of research and teaching, limited mainly by the fact that the universities recognized one another's semesters and degrees and by the old custom by which students and teachers could move from one university to another. Not until Hitler attained power was a central Ministry of Education set up. It was natural therefore, both as a reversion to tradition and as a reaction against the National Socialist system, that the Basic Law should have given control over education to the Länder, although only a minority of the Länder had historical traditions of their own.

For some years the system worked well. Both before and after the Federal Republic was set up, the Land and local governments worked hard to make good, as best they could, the destroyed and damaged schools and universities and to get their own educational systems working. In an uphill fight their strong local patriotism and competitive spirit acted as a much needed stimulus.

But, from a national point of view, the disadvantages of a federal system became increasingly apparent. In the case of schools, there were considerable variations between the different Länder. In some the normal elementary school course lasted for eight years; in others, for nine. In some a child might transfer to a secondary school after four years of primary education; in others, after six. School terms started at different times, and the holiday periods varied. Secondary schools differed in their organization between city and city, as well as between Land and Land. All these variations could cause great inconvenience to families that moved from one part of the country to another. In the case of higher education the situation was somewhat better, owing to the tradition of transferring from one university to another. Nevertheless the lack of a central educational authority made it difficult to plan for the country's needs as a whole, and from a long-term point of view this disadvantage was even more serious than the inconveniences of the school system. In addition, the efficient fulfilment of the country's needs for more specialized research institutes was impossible without national planning. Two or three *Länder* might decide, partly for reasons of prestige, to invest in similar very expensive scientific equipment, without adequate consultation, when the whole country's needs could have been satisfied with only one or two plants.

Opinions differed on the administrative problem, and the views held by politicians often cut across the normal party alignments. Whereas the CDU was theoretically a federalist party, which championed *Land* rights, it became accustomed to wielding federal authority in Bonn, and its members tended therefore to favour increasingly the creation of some federal educational authority, if not an actual ministry. The SPD, on the other hand, had supported in the Parliamentary Council a unitary form of government, but it held office, at least for a time, in most of the *Länder*, and in some *Länder*, for example, Hesse, Hamburg, and Bremen, it had pursued progressive educational policies with such success that its leaders were jealous of their powers and reluctant to hand them over to CDU control in Bonn. The FDP had always advocated a unitary, though decentralized form of government, and in its educational policy it was consistent.

Two main alternative solutions came to be supported. A minority favoured the establishment of a Federal Ministry of Education, while a majority, and probably a substantial one, preferred some compromise between complete autonomy for the *Länder* and federal control. It was the second of these two solutions which was actually adopted. It was generally agreed that, on the one hand, some machinery should be evolved to ensure smooth co-operation between the *Länder*, and that on the other hand, a federal system would only make sense, if responsibility for such an important matter as education could be shared by the *Land* and the federal governments.

A decisive step towards steady co-operation between the Länder was taken as early as 1948 with the foundation of the Permanent Conference of Ministers of Culture. Starting in that year the ministers formed the habit of coming together regularly to discuss common problems. As the Conference finally developed, the meetings took place at least every two months and on an average about eight times a year. Its task, as laid down in its rules of procedure, was to deal with "matters of cultural policy with a more than regional significance with a view to forming a common opinion and purpose and attending to problems of common concern." To assist it in its work, it set up a secretariat and four permanent committees dealing with schools, universities, art, and schools in foreign countries. The secretariat gradually grew in size and experience, giving continuity to the Conference's work, until it finally had a staff of about ninety, including many well-informed experts. Since the Conference as a body had no power to enforce its decisions in the individual *Länder*, they had to be unanimous, if they were to take effect throughout the country. But its prestige and influence increased, as the value of its work became clearer.

The minister-presidents of the *Länder* considered educational problems from time to time at their own conferences, and one of the most important agreements on education was, in fact, reached by the minister-presidents themselves in February 1955. It covered amongst other things: fixing a date for the beginning of the school year; length of holidays; unified nomenclature for different types of school; school organization; recognition of examinations; and a common marking system.

In September 1953 a decree of the federal government set up the German Education Committee (*Deutscher Ausschuss für das Erziehungs- und Bildungswesen*). It resulted from a recommendation in the previous year's report of the Permanent Conference and from a suggestion put forward in the Bundestag, and its special significance lay in the fact that it was the first body in the field of cultural policy to be sponsored jointly by the federal government and the *Länder*. The Committee consisted of twenty members, who served in an honorary capacity and were appointed by the Federal Minister of the Interior and the president of the Permanent Conference. Their task was "to observe and to further through advice and recommendations the development of German education and culture." The selection was made with imagination from varied branches of public life, and the Committee published a series of interesting and valuable "recommendations and assessments." But its work remained theoretical and advisory in character.

Another instrument for the co-ordination of policy, though its influence was confined to higher education, was the Rectors' Conference. It had its origin in two separate organizations of university heads, which were formed in 1945 and 1947 in the British and American zones and which joined together in the spring of 1949 to form a comprehensive organization, including the universities in the French zone. It co-operated regularly with the relevant departments of the *Land* governments and with the Permanent Conference of Ministers of Culture. Of the co-ordinating bodies it has, on the whole, been the least open to new ideas, but every organization that has considered the country's educational problems as a whole has performed a useful function, and under the influence of more enterprising bodies and challenging international tendencies, it has moved a little, though only a little, with the times.

An innovation comparable in importance to the Permanent Conference was the Science Council (*Wissenschaftsrat*).[25] It owed its existence to the simultaneous efforts of a group of scholars and a group of politicians. Like the Committee for

[25] *Wissenschaft* cannot be translated satisfactorily in one word. But the alternatives "Academic Council" or "Arts and Science Council" both have disadvantages, and "Science Council" is perhaps the best way out, provided it is realized that the word "science" is being used in its broadest sense.

Education and Culture its creation was a joint undertaking of the federal and the Land governments, which in the autumn of 1957 reached an agreement providing for its establishment. It was a kind of planning staff for the development of German learning and research. Its main task was officially described as "on the basis of the plans drawn up by the federal government and the Länder . . . to work out a complete plan for the advancement of learning and the sciences and thus to harmonize with one another the plans of the federal government and the Länder. In so doing it is to indicate the principal objectives and to draw up a list of priorities."[26] The Council consisted of thirty-nine members and was divided into an academic and an administrative commission, though the two could meet together in plenary session. The twenty-two members of the academic commission were to be appointed by the federal president; sixteen of them on the joint proposal of the German Research Association, the Max Planck Society,[27] and the Rectors' Conference, and the remaining six of them on the joint proposal of the federal and Land governments. Of the seventeen members of the administrative commission, six were to be chosen by the federal government and one was to represent the government of each Land.

As compared with the Permanent Conference and the Rectors' Conference, the Science Council had the great advantage of being able to reach its decisions by a majority vote. It had no power to issue orders and could only make recommendations, but, as both commissions included representatives or appointees of the federal and Land governments, the recommenda-

[26] Verwaltungsabkommen zwischen Bund und Ländern uber die Errichtung eines Wissenschaftsrates, Artikel 2; September 5, 1957.

[27] The society which has taken the place, since the Second World War, of the old Kaiser William Society for the Advancement of Science, founded in 1911 for the encouragement of research. It is financed largely by government grants, and in 1963 it maintained forty-five research institutes and laboratories. The German Research Association is a co-ordinating body, which does not maintain its own research institutes.

tions carried great weight, and, in the face of growing concern about educational reform, it would have been difficult for the Land governments not to carry them out. During a lecture he gave in January 1963 the president of the Science Council, Professor Ludwig Raiser, said, with becoming modesty, that the attention paid to the Council's recommendations was rather too uncritical than too little.[28] Relations were good between the Council, on the one hand, and the Permanent Conference, the Rectors' Conference, and the Research Association, on the other, partly because the Council's prestige was high and still more because the membership overlapped.

In addition to its collaboration with the Land governments in educational and cultural matters, the federal government took action on its own in one important instance towards the end of Adenauer's chancellorship. In December 1962 the Ministry for Nuclear Power was transformed into a Ministry for Scientific Research (wissenschaftliche Forschung). The new ministry, while retaining its predecessor's responsibility for nuclear and space research, assumed the broader tasks of supporting research projects in all branches of science and learning, when they were beyond the capacity of the individual Länder and required a collective effort, and of maintaining liaison with such existing organizations as the Science Council and the Max Planck Society. It also co-ordinated federal activities in the different fields of research. For example, a number of federal ministries had their own research departments, and the Minister for Scientific Research acted as chairman of an inter-ministerial committee for encouraging scientific research. How the new ministry will in the end develop remains to be seen, but by the end of the Adenauer era there were no signs that its first incumbent, Minister Hans Lenz, had any intention of encroaching on the authority of the Länder. He described the position of his ministry as follows:

[28] L. Raiser, Die Aufgaben des Wissenschaftsrates, p. 7.

The Federal Ministry for Scientific Research stands for the freedom of research and teaching, for strengthening the autonomous scientific organizations that have proved their worth, and for greater and more generous encouragement of scientific and technical developments by the state. In view particularly of the variety and magnitude of the tasks, the federal government and the Länder must co-operate closely with one another. The new distribution of tasks within the federal government will not affect the constitutionally guaranteed rights of the Länder with respect to the encouragement of learning and scientific research. . . .

As the federal minister responsible for scientific research I consider it to be my principal task to give expression in the cabinet and in parliament to the claims of science and learning and to look after and champion the cause of research.[29]

Finally, after the signature of the Franco-German treaty in January 1963, the question arose as to who should handle the negotiations with France on implementing the cultural provisions of the treaty, in view of the fact that the cultural matters were not within the competence of the federal government. A compromise was eventually reached by which a German cultural representative was nominated by the federal government on the recommendation of the Länder, made through the Minister-Presidents Conference, and Minister-President Kiesinger was appointed.

On the whole, the arrangements that were evolved for solving the administrative problem were satisfactory. There was a reasonable degree of co-operation between the Länder without sacrifice of variety and the stimulus of competition. Opportunities were given to the federal government to exercise its influence, provide support, and approach educational matters from a broad and comprehensive point of view. Perhaps most important of all, a large number of the leading personalities and experts in the field became involved themselves in solving the

[29] *Deutsche Politik* 1962, pp. 421–2.

country's educational problems, owing to the very complexity
of the means employed, and this had very great advantages.
The majority of informed people preferred the system, as it
was, to the alternative of a Federal Ministry of Education. As
one outstanding educationalist ironically observed, with reference to the jigsaw puzzle of Adenauer's cabinet-making, had
there been a federal ministry, there would have been a danger
that the man appointed to it would have been a Protestant
member of the FDP from Baden-Württemberg with all sorts of
political qualities except the knowledge and ability really necessary for the post. A federal ministry might, it is true, have facilitated quick decisions, but it might also have resulted in an
unimaginative mind and a dead hand at the helm. In 1960
Minister Schütte of Hesse, one of the ablest ministers of culture
and a member of the SPD, stated that the German system of
education had never been so uniformly moulded and organized
as at that time, "not even during the Nazi period."[30]

The other deep-lying deficiencies of the educational system,
social inequality and excessive conservatism, proved more
intractable. There was some improvement as regards social
inequality. One of the first recommendations of the German
Education Committee, which was made in June 1954, was that
education in secondary schools should be put forward free
throughout the country, and all the Länder took the necessary
action[31] within a few years. In 1955 the federal and Land
governments came to an agreement at Bad Honnef, which gave
its name to the resulting scheme, by which scholarships
awarded to university students should be at the same level
throughout the country and by which the federal government
and the Länder should share the cost. However, the proportion
of working-class children who attended universities and even
secondary schools remained very low. In 1961 only just over

[30] Quoted by T. Ellwein, op. cit., p. 27.
[31] With the exception, in some Länder, of the technical schools.

14 per cent of the students benefited under the Honnef Scheme. The students justifiably complained that the rates were too low, and, when the federal government finally agreed to increase them, protested strongly that the increase was to be dependent on an extension of the unsatisfactory loan element, which had been included in the scheme from the first.

The struggle against conservatism had reached much the same stage. Some of the suggested changes have been made. A series of recommendations regarding political education in universities and schools were put forward by the Permanent Conference of Ministers of Culture, the Rectors' Conference, and the German Education Committee. They took some time to implement owing to opposition from the established university faculties and owing to lack of qualified or suitable teachers both in the universities and schools. But by the end of the Adenauer era there was at least one chair of political science in all but two or three universities and in many cases more than one. The whole attitude towards politics and recent history in schools had improved with the arrival of a new generation of teachers trained since the war, whose attitude was much less inhibited than that of their predecessors. The plan to broaden the programme of studies had also had some limited success. For example, the principle of the *studium generale* was introduced at the Technical University in Berlin, while at the Darmstadt Technical Institute a Faculty for Culture and Political Science was established. On the other hand, the universities and schools were so hidebound by tradition, so overcrowded and understaffed, that fundamental proposals for broadening and humanizing the education they offered were likely to encounter almost insuperable difficulties. A university teacher who was struggling to combine a heavy load of teaching with administration and research was unlikely to give a lead in the field of adult education or to respond kindly to the suggestion that he should keep in closer touch with social change.

The third and most far-reaching aspect of Western Germany's educational problem revealed itself as a result of the measures taken to deal with the second. In the course of their investigations into their country's own educational difficulties, the Permanent Conference, the German Education Committee, and the Science Council became progressively aware that an educational revolution was taking place on an international scale. The expanding role of science and technology in so many fields and the steady rise in living standards in the more industrialized countries increased the need and the desire for a higher standard of education. Furthermore, it was clear that those countries which responded quickly to the need would in the long run have a considerable advantage over those that did not.

Members of the investigating bodies and other educationists and politicians on an increasing scale were chiefly impressed by the figures that were becoming available which facilitated comparisons between different countries. The work of the Organization for Economic co-operation and Development (OECD), in particular, played a large part in bringing home to West Germans the extent and significance of their educational emergency. For example, the OECD published figures for 1958–9 showing the percentages of their gross national product spent on schools and universities by a number of different countries. The percentage in the United States was 4.53, in Sweden 4.14, in the USSR 3.74, in the United Kingdom 3.67, in France 3.50, while Western Germany with 2.79 per cent came in the second half of the list, after Austria and followed immediately by Ireland, Jugoslavia, and Iceland. Whereas in the United Kingdom compulsory education lasted for ten years in 1963 and preparations were being made to extend it to eleven, and in France and the Soviet Union a ten-year period was about to be introduced, in the Federal Republic the city states, Lower Saxony, and Schleswig-Holstein had already adopted a nine-year course, but the majority of Länder still retained the eight-year system. In the OECD's Third Survey estimates were given for the percentage increase between 1959 and 1970 in the number of schoolchildren who would complete their secondary school courses. The figure for France was 154, for Sweden 138, and for the Federal Republic 4. A great impression was made on German educational experts by the publication in the United Kingdom of the comprehensive Robbins Report with its proposals for the development of British higher education up to 1980.

The West German reaction to such revelations was indicated in the publications of educational bodies, in the work and writings of a few enterprising individuals, and in the statements made from time to time by the representatives of industry.

The two most important publications of official bodies were the Science Council's "Recommendations for the Development of Academic and Scientific Institutions" of 1960 and the Permanent Conference's "Assessment of Needs 1961–1970" of 1962. The first part of the Science Council's recommendations dealt with universities. It was a thorough and comprehensive piece of work and included a frank and critical account of the existing state of the universities. Whereas in 1913 under the empire, it pointed out, there had been 79,000 students in twenty-one universities and eleven technical institutes, there were now in the Federal Republic, including West Berlin, 200,000 students in eighteen universities and eight technical institutes. In some faculties there were two or three hundred students per professor, while some so-called seminars or classes might have as many as two or three hundred members. Accommodation was sometimes so limited that there were no more than 150 seats for over 1,000 students. Contact with professors was so difficult and the supply of books and equipment so limited that there was a general tendency for courses to drag on for an unreasonably long time. In chemistry, a subject in which conditions were particularly bad, a course of study, which ought to have taken eight semesters, would as a rule last for twelve or fourteen, and a student who took his doctorate would require eighteen to twenty semesters or nine to ten years. In the universities, on the whole, it was calculated in 1957 that the average age at which a graduate qualified to become a lecturer (*Dozent*) was thirty-four and the average age at which a professor was appointed was forty-five, compared with twenty-six and thirty-five respectively during the first half of the nineteenth century. The Council's recommendations to deal with this state of affairs included the expansion of existing institutions, the foundation of new universities, medical schools, and technical institutes, and considerable increases in staff. They were comparatively modest, in the circumstances. But this was perhaps wise for a start; and they were at once accepted by all the ministries in the *Länder*.

The Permanent Conference's "Assessment of Needs" covered a very wide range, including schools, teacher training, learning (*Wissenschaft*), research, art, and the encouragement of the arts. It brought out very fully the extent and the importance of the cultural and educational problem. "The cultural expenditure of the *Länder* and the municipalities," the Conference stated in the introduction, "must be treated as of equal importance to the expenditure of the federal government for defence and social purposes." "Experience has taught that in no branch of activity do mistakes and omissions have such long-term and persistent effects as in the sphere of cultural policy." The Conference gave in detail its estimates for capital and current expenditure under every heading. It pointed out that a previous assessment made in 1956, which had seemed "frightening and even Utopian" at the time, had been justified by actual developments, the total cultural expenditure of the *Länder*, excluding the municipalities, having risen from 4.76 milliard marks in 1957 to 7.5 milliard in 1962. Its final conclusion was that the total expenditure under all headings of the *Länder* and municipalities would rise from an estimated 9 milliard marks in 1961[32] to an estimated 19.9 milliard in 1970.

Two active and public-spirited educationists, who in different ways furthered the cause of educational reform in the Federal Republic, provide good examples of the small group of enterprising individual reformers.

Herr Hellmut Becker believed that sound educational reform must be based on a scientific appraisal of modern social conditions, more particularly of the implications of technological innovation and of the growing rate of change, and he was deeply concerned about his country's failure to undertake such an appraisal with the necessary thoroughness. Western Germany's existing educational system, he pointed out, was the answer to the intellectual and social challenge of the beginning of the nineteenth century and a reformed educational system must be the answer to the challenge of today. He made his case so convincingly that the decision was taken to set up in 1963 in Berlin an Institute for Educational Research within the framework of the Max Planck Society, and Herr Becker became its director.

Dr. Georg Picht, who had been a member of the German Education Committee,[33] contributed in February 1964 to the weekly, *Christ und Welt*, a series of articles entitled "The German Educational Catastrophe," which were later published in a separate volume. The articles appearing, as they did, just after Adenauer had given up the chancellorship, really described the state of affairs at the end of the Adenauer era. Dr. Picht set the subject in a deliberately dramatic light and contended that the German educational system was heading for failure, unless drastic measures were taken. For example, he stated that the German people spent as much on tobacco as on their whole school system (5.9 milliard marks) and pointed out that in

---

[32] The full statistics for 1961 were not yet available.
[33] This committee had by this time been dissolved.

1963 they spent as much as 7.2 milliard on foreign touring. His most telling point was that the economic and political leaders who had made possible the so-called "German miracle" went to school before the First World War and that the responsible men in German economic and social life in 1964 had received their intellectual training in the schools and universities of the Weimar period. Now, however, the inherited capital was spent, and Germany had lost its leading position in European education. Picht's indictment was based on the belief that no German generation had left to its successor so relatively little intellectual capital as the present one would leave. His main achievement consisted in giving publicity to a matter of vital importance at the right moment and in making more of the German public aware of the urgency of the problem.

The OECD did much to draw attention to the relationship between educational standards and economic efficiency, and it was largely this which caused their reports and publications to make such a big impression on informed German opinion. In October 1961 an OECD conference was held in Washington on the subject of economic growth and education. German politicians, educational experts, and industrialists were not slow to echo the OECD's emphasis on the relationship. They realized also the economic implications for the future of the fact that both the United States and the Soviet Union spent a considerably higher proportion of their gross national products on education than did the Federal Republic. It was particularly sinister that Germany had lost its leadership in science and research at a time when their influence on industrial efficiency and national prosperity were greater than ever before. In the spring of 1964 Dr. Schröder, the Foreign Minister, lamented the fact that recently Western Germany had been paying out about 500 million marks a year in respect of licences and patents, whereas before the war its balance sheet in this field had been level. The president of the German Industrial and Commercial Association went so far as to say that investment in education had come to be of more importance than material investment. Very large sums had been spent by industries on their own research and development projects since 1949. But the relevance of the research done in academic and scientific institutions had been badly neglected. In March 1964 an SPD member pointed out in the Bundestag that nearly three times as much money was made available to research for defence purposes as for the whole university development programme.[34]

The results of these recommendations and criticisms, and of others which accompanied them, can as yet scarcely be summarized. All those who were interested in German education came to realize that the situation was serious, and that their country's position by international standards was dangerously weak. But the responsibility for taking action was divided in varying degrees between the ministries of culture in the Länder, the bodies that co-ordinated their policies, the federal government and its Ministry for Scientific Research, the groups of experts who had been called upon to give advice, and the universities with their jealously guarded traditions of academic freedom and self-government. The limited recommendations of the Science Council were by 1963 already being implemented. But they had been shown to be inadequate by the Permanent Conference's "Assessment of Needs," and even this was called in question by Picht as in some respects not going far enough. Moreover, all the recommendations and opinions were based on estimates, however expert, and the uncertain element in all of them was well illustrated in March 1964 when the Science Council published an estimate of student numbers up to 1980, which revised considerably its findings of 1960, extending up to 1970, and played for safety by giving three separate assess-

[34] G. Picht, Die deutsche Bildungskatastrophe, p. 114. The speaker, Dr. Lohmar, appeared to be referring to the federal government's grants, though from the report of his speech it is not absolutely clear.

ments based on different hypotheses. The revised figures were substantially lower than the previous ones, but, from the point of view of German education as a whole, this was little comfort, as a lower enrolment of students would diminish the pressure on the universities but at the same time reduce the number of graduates available to provide urgently needed additional staff for the schools.

However, a selective summary of the main points made in the various recommendations and criticisms will help to complete the picture of the problems facing German education at the end of the Adenauer era.

According to the Assessment of the Permanent Conference the increase between 1961 and 1970 in the total number of pupils attending school would be just under 2 million. To cope with this increase and to enable overcrowded classes to be reduced to a reasonable size an additional 207,000 teachers would be required.[35] Dr. Picht calculated that to meet this demand it would not be sufficient if all those graduating from the universities in 1970 decided to become teachers, and that in fact not even half the required number of teachers would be available. He pointed out that in one Land during 1962 a third of the mathematics and science classes in the higher grades could not be held owing to shortage of teachers and concluded that, in order to save the situation, the number of pupils completing their secondary school courses must be at least doubled and the number of university students considerably increased.[36]

Conditions under which teaching was carried out were often

[35] Throughout the Assessment two alternative objectives were referred to: the Zielwerte, which are described as pedagogically desirable and not unrealistic as practical aims, and Mittelwerte, which had already been attained in some Länder and ought to be attained in all Länder within the decade under consideration. The latter is a form of compromise and, for this reason and for the sake of simplicity, it is the former that is always referred to in the text.

[36] Die deutsche Bildungskatastrophe, pp. 22, 24, and 28.

very unsatisfactory. According to the Assessment there was in 1961 still a shortage of 27,190 class-rooms and 44,081 "special rooms" for vocational and specialized training. Throughout the country the size of classes in the schools was frequently much too large, the number of children in a class sometimes running as high as 60 to 70. The situation in the rural districts was particularly bad, the outdated system of the one-class or two-class school persisting on a large scale in a number of Länder. Under this system quite small villages would each have their own schools, and one teacher would either teach all the eight grades in an elementary school or share the task with a single colleague. The remedy was to set up larger central schools and provide transport for the children. But a combination of conservatism, village pride, and sheer inertia caused the old system to continue. In 1959 over 70 per cent of the elementary schools in Rhineland-Palatinate were in one of the two categories. In 1964 there were over 1,800 one-class and 1,900 two-class schools in Bavaria and over 800 one-class schools in Hesse and Baden-Württemberg. Dr. Picht maintained that so long as a rural education was not modernized, German agriculture could not become competitive within the Common Market.

The number of children completing secondary school courses compared unfavourably with other West European countries and with the United States,[37] although the German Standards were in some cases higher. Criticisms were also made of the courses offered in the different types of secondary schools, and suggestions were put forward that there should be greater flexibility, as regards timing and method, in determining a child's school career. In view of the growing criticism of British public schools, it is interesting that their equivalent in Western Germany, the private schools, usually received public financial support and have also been treated kindly and respectfully by,

[37] G. Picht, op. cit., p. 33.

for example, the German Education Committee and the SPD government of Berlin. The Committee's Recommendation on the Question of Private Schools of 1954 contained the following passage:

In the present situation of our schools it is important that new pedagogic ideas are tried out under conditions of freedom. Private schools are particularly suited and competent to fulfil their own new educational and pedagogic tasks. By so doing they serve at the same time the progressive development and reform of the whole school system.[38]

The recommendations and criticisms relating to universities were also made from quantitative and qualitative points of view. The Permanent Conference in its Assessment estimated on a conservative basis that the continuing expenditure on universities and other institutes of higher education would rise from 986 million marks in 1961 to 2,655 million marks in 1970, and that non-recurrent capital expenditure which was 393 million in 1961 would amount to 6,805 million for the period 1962 to 1970. The estimates covered the expansion of existing institutions and the foundation of new ones. The new foundations being planned in 1963 included universities in Bochum, Bremen, Konstanz, and Regensburg, technical institutes in Dortmund and Erlangen-Nürnberg, and medical schools or faculties in Aachen, Augsburg, Essen, Hanover, Lübeck and Ulm.

The Science Council recommended that professorial chairs should be increased by 1,200 and posts for senior assistants and assistants by 7,691. It also suggested that a large number of middle-grade posts should be created, whose occupants would mostly concentrate on teaching but in some cases devote

[38] Many critics of British public schools show a short-sighted willingness to throw out a healthy baby (high educational standards and ideals and a readiness to experiment) with the bath water (social exclusiveness).

their attention to long-term research projects. As regards numbers of students the Science Council, as has been seen, found it difficult to reach any firm decision, although the Permanent Conference foresaw an increase of 22,624 between 1961 and 1966. Two things were, however, clear. The universities were already seriously overcrowded and the additional staff that was recommended would be necessary to handle the existing enrolment efficiently. Early in 1964 the Minister of Culture of North Rhine-Westphalia estimated the existing excess of students at 50,000.[39] Secondly, the number of students would nevertheless have to increase in the future, if the universities were to supply all the necessary teachers and fulfil the demands made on them by the learned professions and industry.

The Council took up a positive attitude towards the problem of foreign students. They considered it the duty of German universities to accept foreign students, up to a maximum of 15 per cent of their total numbers, to provide scholarships for their preliminary language courses, and to reserve places for them in student hostels.

If the Science Council's recommendations of 1960 relating to the universities were limited in scope and character, they stimulated a lively and nation-wide discussion on university problems, and were followed in 1962 by another publication of the Council entitled "Suggestions for the Organization of the New Universities." A great variety of questions were discussed in this volume and in the writings and speeches of interested politicians and educationists. One of the most important of them was the excessive time university studies had come to occupy. This matter had been raised rather tentatively by the Council in 1960, but it was given an increasing amount of attention, and early in 1964 the Minister of Culture for Hesse pointed out that, whereas in 1928-9 over 84 per cent of German students completed their normal studies in the course of seven to ten

[39] P. Mikat, *Aufgaben moderner Kulturpolitik*, p. 9.

semesters, in 1958–9 over 70 per cent of them took eleven or more semesters. Two main remedies for this state of affairs were suggested: first, setting a limit to the normal study period for the state examinations, which, as Professor Dahrendorf of Tübingen put it, would imply "renunciation of a certain extreme and manifestly absurd interpretation of academic freedom;"[40] and secondly, making use of the proposed increase in university teachers to give closer supervision and guidance to students especially during their early semesters.

Another problem was significant owing to its bearing on the recommended increase in professorial chairs. Traditionally part of a professor's remuneration took the form of lecture fees which depended on the number of students attending his lectures. Additional chairs therefore meant fewer students for each professor and lower salaries, and, in consequence, some professors opposed urgently needed increases in staff. In 1960 the Science Council supported making some alteration in the system, which indeed had already been suggested by the University Commission of 1949.

Thirdly, a good deal of discussion took place regarding ways in which university administration could be made more efficient and academics relieved from severe administrative burdens. A few favoured the introduction of the American presidential system. But opinion in the universities was, on the whole, against this, owing to the justifiable fear that it would mean the sacrifice of true academic self-government. The majority probably favoured some form of compromise by which rectors would be elected for two-year rather than one-year terms and would be assisted by permanent academic administrators with adequate staffs. There was widespread agreement that in the new foundations the first rector should be elected for a considerably longer

---

[40] Quoted by Dr. E. Schütte in *Was Können die Hochschulen zur Verkürzung des Studiums tun?*, p. 28.

term, and this was, in fact, the plan adopted at the University of Konstanz.

Finally, the jealously guarded German academic principle of the unity of research and teaching was called in question, as being more suitable to conditions in the nineteenth than in the middle of the twentieth century. It was pointed out that ability in teaching and research was not always combined in the same person; that an expert in research might be driven to change his profession or to emigrate by too heavy a burden of teaching; and that a well-qualified teacher might fail to get a university post owing to lack of competence as a creative scholar. But again the balance of opinion seemed to favour a compromise. There was much opposition to any institutional separation of the two main academic activities by setting up exclusively post-graduate schools on the one hand and colleges devoted exclusively to teaching on the other. Universities, it was felt, should continue the tradition of combining research and teaching, but special provision could be made for specialists in research, by establishing closer links with the existing research institutes, and not every teacher or student need be expected to engage in original creative work.

There was thus a good deal of self-criticism and restiveness in German academic and scholastic circles, and the process of expansion and reform had started. And yet the champions of educational reform had good reason to feel disturbed. The remark of one politician, keenly interested in the subject, that there was a history of educational reform in Germany but so far no reform itself, went too far but was to some extent justified. Dr. Picht lamented the fact that during a Bundestag debate on a bill for the encouragement of research only seventy members took the trouble to be present and contrasted it mournfully with a report from Paris that during the most recent debate on the Ministry of Education's budget the assembly had been unusually well attended. Education, in fact, was arousing the interest of experts but not yet of more than a small minority of the general public. Yet it was the public who would be required to pay the greatly increased sums that would eventually have to be found for it.

Amongst politicians and civil servants and even in the universities and schools enthusiasm for reform was less noticeable than lukewarmness and an instinctive resistance to change. In the governments of the Länder, where the main initiative still lay, as well as in Bonn, there was little interest in the complexities of the educational problem, and the feeling amongst officials was widespread that the schools and universities where they had themselves been educated were good enough for the present generation. "No experiments" had been the most effective slogan in Adenauer's most successful election campaign, and its appeal was strong when Germany's revered educational institutions came under attack.

Some reformers pinned their hopes on the new universities in the belief that they would stimulate the old bodies to take over some of the fresh ideas they had adopted, and no doubt the new foundations will in the end exert a salutary influence. But in their formative years a strong force has been operating in the opposite direction, and their founding bodies have feared increasingly that, if they were too different and too original, they would be looked upon as not quite acceptable and not fit to take their place by the great established universities of the country. The fate of the Institute for Social Sciences at Wilhelmshaven, an experiment in higher education which had been full of promise, was not encouraging. It had been founded in 1949 by the government of Lower Saxony on entirely new lines, but, after thirteen years of a struggling though not altogether unsuccessful existence against heavy odds, it came to an end, the victim very largely of academic conservatism and lack of imaginative support.[41] The new foundations therefore tended to avoid radical experiments, and only in the universities of Konstanz and Bremen did it seem likely that important innovations would be made.

The Bonn government cannot be absolved from responsibility for the shortcomings of German education at the end of Adenauer's chancellorship: for the delay in undertaking the necessary expansion and reform, for the reluctance to make bold decisions, and for the Federal Republic's weak position compared to other Western countries. The allocation of education and culture of the Länder was historically justified and had many advantages, giving variety, resilience, and the stimulus of competition to a branch of the national life, in which over-centralization and uniformity could have had a deadening effect. But the essence of federalism is the sharing of authority on a rational basis. It was the clear duty of the federal government to guide, co-ordinate, and stimulate the cultural activities of the Länder in all cases where the national interest was involved. Indeed the creation at the end of 1962 of a Ministry for Scientific Research was a tacit admission by Bonn of what it could and should have done before. The Basic Law had, in fact, been used as a pretext by the chancellor, the cabinet, and the Bundestag to evade their responsibilities in the educational and cultural fields, and neither of the two main political parties at the federal level had begun to give the question the emphasis and the full attention it deserved, until the OECD publications startled them into activity.

One reason for these failures was an unawareness of the problem. Another was the preoccupation of those interested in education with the postwar emergency in the universities and

[41] From 1949 to 1956 it was known as the Institute for Labour, Politics, and Economics. An account of this interesting experiment will be found in Democracy in Western Germany, pp. 254–6.

schools. In assessing the significance of international statistics it must be borne in mind that Sweden, Britain, and the United States had not suffered the same material destruction as Germany. Thirdly, politicians, professors, and school-teachers had all been blinded by the influence of a great tradition. Any suggestion that everything was not as it should be in the country's educational institutions was considered a kind of cultural treason.

Adenauer himself, however, bore a large share of the responsibility. It is true that he was not particularly interested in education and had other great problems to occupy his mind. But one of the penalties for autocratic methods is that faults of omission cannot fairly be repudiated. He neither dealt with the matter himself nor saw to it that someone else did so. From time to time he paid lip service to the national importance of maintaining intellectual standards, and on one occasion in Berlin he admitted with regret that the position of academics was often better in the Soviet zone than in the Federal Republic. But he failed to give the lead he should have given as chancellor, and he did not really understand the nature of the educational emergency. In his declaration of policy on October 9, 1962, at the beginning of his last year of office, when the problem had already been recognized as urgent, no reference was made to it at all.

5
Rearmament

The German Federal Republic has the largest population, the highest steel production, and the strongest economy of any European country apart from the Soviet Union. In view of these facts and of Germany's great military tradition it was not surprising that within eight years of starting to rearm, the Federal Republic should have been making the largest European military contribution to NATO. Nor was it surprising, in the light of recent history, that the Russians, the Poles, and some people in West European countries should have been apprehensive about Western Germany's military revival.

Yet it is the character of the new German forces and the spirit prevailing amongst their officers and men that is more important for the future of the international community than their actual size. They can never rival the forces of the Soviet Union or the United States in strength. But history provides justification for the fear that they might exercise a dangerous influence on their country's political leaders and their attitude towards foreign affairs. Leading personalities in West German military circles and in politics have paid greater attention to this problem than is generally realized outside the Federal Republic.

Under Allied military government the German armed forces

were dissolved, and it became a capital offence to possess weapons. It was instilled into the German people that militarism was an evil thing and that no German rearmament would be allowed for an indefinite period. There was in fact no army for a period of ten years, and there was thus a complete break in the German military tradition, in contrast to the Weimar period, when von Seeckt was able to train the nucleus of a large army and build up a military pressure group, which exerted great political influence.

The Western Allies themselves reduced their armaments considerably, until the breach with the Soviet Union in 1947-8, the Berlin blockade, and the outbreak of the Korean War in June 1950 led to a radical change in their attitude. They then became aware that communism presented a real threat to their security, especially in Europe, and they could no longer rely on the United States' monopoly of nuclear weapons, since the Soviet Union had tested their atomic bomb successfully in 1949. This was the background to the formation of NATO in April 1949 and the decision during the autumn of 1950 to implement its provisions for mutual defence as rapidly as possible. At the NATO Council meeting in September it was decided also, as a result of an American proposal and in the face of serious French misgivings, that the Federal Republic should contribute to the defence of Western Europe.

Adenauer responded to this decision with great tact and courage. As early as December 1949 he stated in an interview with *The Times* correspondent in Bonn that he was on principle opposed to rearmament, but that, if the Allies demanded that the Federal Republic should participate in European defence, he would be in favour, not of an independent German army, but of a German contingent within a European force. During the summer of 1954, a leading radio commentator in Western Germany, a man with an independent and liberal outlook, who nevertheless stood close to Adenauer on foreign policy, gave the writer his views on rearmament in the form of a list. Best of all, he said, would be no army at all; second best, EDC; third best, rearmament within the framework of NATO; and worst of all, a national army. This order of priority also represented Adenauer's viewpoint. His success in handling the question in relation to the Allies was due partly to his diplomatic finesse and partly to the fact that his own attitude was beyond reproach from the Western point of view.

If Adenauer needed tact to deal with rearmament as an aspect of external relations, he needed political and moral courage combined with tact to deal with the opposition to rearmament amongst the German people. The anti-militarist propaganda of the Allies had aroused a much greater response within the Federal Republic than was realized in foreign countries. After twelve years of totalitarian government and six years of total war this was not really surprising. During the twentieth century the Germans themselves have been amongst the hardest hit victims of German militarism, and two disastrous defeats have done a great deal to offset the glamour of military achievements under Bismarck and Frederick the Great. Moreover, there was a good deal of resentment at the quick change in the Allies' attitude and a feeling that the despised German military qualities were now being made use of to help the victors out of their difficulties.

Opposition to rearmament was particularly strong amongst the young. The youthful and disillusioned Germans, who had suffered in the war and under the misery of post-war years, were on the whole most unwilling to become involved in military service. In relation to the rearmament programme they came to be known as the *ohne mich* generation, *ohne mich* meaning literally "without me" or, according to the translation of an ingenious American, "include me out." At the end of 1950 students at Bonn University voted with 335 votes to 150 against rearmament of any kind, and more than 70 per cent of them said that never, in any circumstances, would they put on uniform again. Three years later their attitude was much the same.[1] The SPD, under Schumacher's leadership, steadily opposed rearmament. Schumacher himself "feared that rearmament and the Federal Republic's inclusion in the Western alliance would seriously endanger the cause of reunification." He even made the absurd demand that no German aid should be given to the West until the NATO powers guaranteed that the first battle would be fought and won on the Vistula, that is to say, until German aid was no longer necessary. Early in 1952 the party appealed to the Federal Constitutional Court to declare rearmament unconstitutional. Strong opposition also came from the Evangelical Church, led by Pastor Martin Niemöller, head of the Church in Hesse. Niemöller and other Church representatives demanded that no rearmament should take place until there had been an appeal to the people through new federal elections. Dr. Heinemann, who resigned from the cabinet over rearmament in the autumn of 1950, was himself lay president of the Evangelical synod.

During November 1950 elections took place in two of the Länder, Hesse and Württemberg-Baden. There was a swing in favour of the Social Democrats, which clearly reflected the opposition to rearmament. Had federal elections been held at about this time, the government might well have been defeated.

In face of this very difficult internal situation Adenauer steadily pursued the policy he thought right. He made clear repeatedly that he was not in favour of rearmament for its own sake but that he was convinced that the country should respond to the wishes of the Allies and contribute to Western defence. A telling argument in support of his policy was that a strong paramilitary "people's police" had already been organized in the Soviet zone. Gradually opinion swung round in his favour. More and more Germans came to appreciate the danger to

[1] T. Prittie, *Germany Divided*, p. 175.

which Western Europe was exposed. They realized that the Federal Republic's international standing and its reputation in the West would depend upon its readiness to participate in European defence. The federal election of 1953 provided clear proof of the chancellor's success in winning over his fellow countrymen.

The conditions under which Western Germany became a member of NATO were agreed upon by the negotiating powers but they reflected Adenauer's own attitude towards rearmament. The Bonn government promised never to use force to achieve re-unification or to modify the existing boundaries of the Federal Republic. It undertook not to manufacture within its territory any atomic, biological, or chemical weapons; the so-called ABC weapons. Furthermore, Adenauer's aim to avoid the creation of a national army was realized insofar as all West German troops were placed under NATO's command.

In October 1950 the chancellor appointed the CDU deputy, Theodor Blank, a Catholic trade unionist, as "Commissioner of the Federal Government for all questions connected with the strengthening of the Allied occupying forces." With this euphemistic title Blank set up an office which gradually developed into a shadow ministry of defence, as the need for such an organization grew. He himself was a sincere, competent, and hardworking man, but anyone less militarist by nature or less reminiscent of the Prussian army tradition could scarcely have been imagined. A Bundestag Committee for Questions of European Security was also established.

Apart from the opposition to militarism as such, liberal and democratic Germans, with memories of the past, were greatly concerned to avoid the resurgence of the kind of military caste that had exerted so much influence under the Second Empire and played such a sinister role in the failure of the Weimar Republic. The problem was to ensure democratic political control of any armed forces that were formed and to prevent the reemergence of the state within a state which had proved so disastrous to Weimar.[2]

In contrast to the nineteen-twenties, when the army had survived a world war more successfully than the empire, after the Second World War the state and the army had both been dissolved, and in 1949 the state had been re-established first. So, if a new army were to be created, the necessary action would be taken by parliament, and the new creation would owe its existence to a democratic regime. The federal government was faced with the challenge of determining the character of the forces in such a way that there would be no revival of an arrogant militarist spirit and no danger of the army's leaders playing a political role. And it had the advantage of making a fresh start.

Theodor Blank's office was solely concerned with planning until the Paris treaties went into effect in May 1955. The importance he and his colleagues attached to the character and mental attitude of Germany's new forces was shown by the creation of a special section in the office to deal with *inneres Gefüge* (Internal Structure) or, as it was later and better named, *innere Führung* (Leadership and Character Training).[3] One of the main ideas to emerge from the section, and certainly the idea that became best known, was that of the soldier as a "citizen in uniform." In a broadcast given towards the end of 1952 Blank himself mentioned some of the points implied in this concept. In the new Germany army, he said, drill in the old

---

[2] See pp. 13–14 and, for full treatments of the subject, G. A. Craig, *The Politics of the Prussian Army 1640–1945*, Chs. VI, X, and XI, and F. L. Carsten, *Reichswehr und Politik*.

[3] The literal translation is "internal leadership." An alternative free translation, which has been used officially, is "Leadership and Morale." Count Baudissin, who headed the section in Blank's office, tentatively suggested "psychological warfare in your own sphere—creative, not destructive." But the full meaning the expression has acquired in this context cannot be briefly and accurately translated, and the German expression will therefore be used throughout this chapter.

Prussian style would be reduced to a minimum; troops would be given education in civics and current affairs; and they would be expected to wear mufti, when they were off duty. This description represented a complete change from the former state of affairs, when every German girl was proud to be seen with a man in uniform and when, as Friedrich Meinecke wrote, "the Prussian lieutenant went through the world like a young god, and the civilian lieutenant of the reserve at least like a demigod."[4]

The man, who was mainly responsible for the concept of the "citizen in uniform" and indeed for the whole idea that the shadow ministry should emphasize *Innere Führung*, was Wolf, Count von Baudissin. He was himself a Prussian and a former regular officer. During the last years of the war he had been a prisoner, but he had stood close to some of the conspirators of July 1944 and had a profound respect for their courage and for the motives which had inspired them. He was a Protestant and a man of deep Christian conviction, and he belonged to the true German *élite*, who in the post-war years faced the most unpleasant implications of the Hitler era with boldness and humility, accepting them as a challenge for their own and their country's future. Baudissin had taken an active part in the work of the Evangelical Academies, which were founded soon after the war as conference and study centres and as "places for discussion between the Church and the world." In 1952 he joined Blank's office; he became head of the section dealing with *Innere Führung*; and he remained on, when the shadow ministry became a real ministry, serving under the first two Ministers of Defence, Blank and Franz-Josef Strauss, until 1958, when he was appointed to the command of an armoured brigade.

Baudissin's general principles accorded with the trend of the more liberal military thinking at the time. A group of men in Blank's office worked with him in developing a series of basic

[4] *Op. cit.*, p. 25.

ideas and a detailed programme which were to be used in the training of the new German army. Others, including senior officers and successive Ministers of Defence, adopted the group's ideas and programme as their own. But Baudissin was the intellectual pioneer. His was the strongest and the most original mind in the group. He had the deepest convictions and the greatest powers of persuasion. And for these reasons he more than any other individual became and remained associated with the two concepts of *Innere Führung* and of the soldier as a "citizen in uniform."

The idea of the citizen, that is, the *democratic* citizen in uniform, as expounded by Baudissin, had three main aspects. First, it implied that a soldier should be, and should feel himself to be, a normal member of a democratic state with the same rights and privileges as any other citizen. He should not think of himself as belonging to a separate military caste with a special relationship to the state. He should be aware and jealous of his basic rights under the constitution. His dignity as a human being should be respected by those in authority over him, and he should have the right to complain of any injustice inflicted on him. He should be encouraged to take an interest in politics and to think intelligently and form sound judgments about political questions. Basically the qualities required in the best type of soldier presupposed the qualities possessed by a free man and a good citizen.

Secondly, under modern conditions of warfare and in the existing state of international relations it should not be expected that a soldier would fight when ordered to for any cause with unquestioning obedience. The German army's most likely enemy was communism. The German soldier, therefore, must understand the nature of communism and why it was that he might have to fight against it. But that would not be sufficient: he must know above all what he would be fighting *for*. The concept of the citizen in uniform implies that a soldier is deeply rooted in the community to which he belongs and is consequently ready to stand up for it. "If he is not," said Baudissin in 1954 before the Bundestag Committee for Questions of European Security, "then he knows at best *against* what he has to take protective action; *against* what he must fight; and that is not enough. . . . Only the soldier's full sense of citizenship enables him to experience the values, which he has to defend, and only the possibility of democratic participation stimulates in him a sense of responsibility."[5] In the autumn of the following year, when the new German army was in process of formation, Baudissin wrote: "Experienced soldiers know how critical the spirit of an army is for its efficiency . . . the German soldier must be given the feeling that he is a member of a free nation standing on the side of freedom."[6]

Thirdly, parade-ground training based on heel-clicking and the goose step has little relevance to soldiering to-day. With modern methods of fighting, self-discipline is more important than discipline imposed from above. Every member of the crew of a tank, an aircraft, or a submarine has his own special task to perform, in which he is likely to be more expert than the officer in command. In these circumstances, automatic and unquestioning obedience are of less value than self-reliance and readiness to share responsibility; the very qualities, in fact, which are amongst the highest virtues in a democratic citizen.

In conservative circles there was a tendency to criticize Baudissin and his fellow reformers for pampering the troops and for not making provision for the necessary toughening process which is an essential part of efficient military training. The accusation was not justified, and was really a form of self-

[5] Count von Baudissin, *Portrait of the German Soldier of the Future.* Quoted by E. Waldman, *Soldat im Staat,* p. 66.
[6] From his article, "The New German Army" in *Foreign Affairs,* October 1955.

defence and counter-attack by those who could not grasp or accept the new ideas. The reformers were against achieving discipline by crushing the spirit of troops in the old-fashioned way, because it involved the sacrifice of qualities which are of special value in a modern army. Their own standards, however, were exacting. They believed in hardness without heartlessness and in a progressively severe training, for which the troops could be made to see the necessity.

In order to realize these ideas in practice, it was necessary that the army itself should become a school of democratic citizens. The reformers realized that the average recruit, when the new army was formed, would not bring with him the qualities they were looking for, because neither his family nor his school would be likely to give him the requisite training. It would be necessary, therefore, for the military authorities to provide not only the uniforms but the education needed to produce citizens to put inside them. This gave rise to resentment and complaints amongst the more conservative officers and ministry officials. But Baudissin himself accepted the logic of the situation and proposed the establishment of a military school for *Innere Führung*, which would, in his opinion, cost less in a year than a single jet aircraft. Such a school was opened early in 1957 at Coblence on the basis of Baudissin's plans.

In 1962 Dr. Richard Jaeger, the chairman of the Bundestag Defence Committee,[7] said that conscription certainly aroused no enthusiasm in the younger generation but was looked upon as a duty that must obviously be fulfilled. In bringing about this change in attitude since the early nineteen-fifties no one played a greater part than Baudissin. In the course of his public relations work he addressed hundreds of audiences on rearmament, particularly groups connected with the Evangelical Church, and

[7] It was created by an amendment to the Basic Law in March 1956 and replaced the Committee for Questions of European Security.

he became a popular and highly respected figure amongst German youth.

The spring and summer of 1955 were the critical period in German rearmament. The period of pure planning came to an end. In May the shadow ministry of defence, which had always been discreetly referred to as "Blank's office," was transformed into a real ministry, and Blank himself became Minister of Defence. This was the moment when the surviving militarist elements might have tried to reassert themselves and regain some at least of their old influence in the state. The danger was increased by the fact that, Adenauer's dominant interest being in foreign relations, his chief desire was to prove to the Allies that Germany would be quick to make its long-awaited contribution to Western defence. It was this which led to the hurriedly introduced Volunteers' Bill, consisting of only three paragraphs, which, as has been seen, provoked the Bundestag to a successful protest.

The protest was supported by members of the government parties, as well as by the SPD, and was reinforced by a strong expression of misgiving from the Bundesrat and a memorandum written on their own initiative by two leading political scientists, Professors Theodor Eschenburg and Arnold Bergsträsser. It resulted in a careful redrafting of the Volunteers' Bill, which was only intended to provide for temporary measures, in the presentation of a second bill for setting up a Personnel Committee; and in permanent and more detailed legislation the following year. Altogether four main safeguards were set up to ensure democratic control of the new defence forces and to prevent the emergence of extreme militarist elements.

In the first place, the amendment to the Basic Law in March 1956, which gave the Supreme Command of the armed forces to the Defence Minister in time of peace and the chancellor in time of war, ensured that the forces would be subject to ultimate parliamentary control. Secondly, the Defence Committee of the Bundestag was given the status of a standing committee of investigation and as such was to remain permanently in being, even during the period between the dissolution of one Bundestag and the election of the next.[8] Thirdly, a Defence Commissioner of the Bundestag was to be appointed "to safeguard the basic rights and to assist the Bundestag in exercising parliamentary control."[9] The duties of this office, which was based on Scandinavian models, were defined in detail by a federal law of June 1957. The commissioner was to be elected by the Bundestag and then appointed by the Bundestag president. In carrying out his duties he was subject to the president's supervision. His tasks fell into two main categories. He had to carry out any investigation which the Bundestag or its Defence Committee might require and submit a report on it either separately or in his annual report. It was his duty also on his own initiative to look into any infringement of the basic rights of the troops or of the principles laid down under the heading, *Innere Führung*. On the one hand, the commissioner had the right to visit any units or administrative headquarters in the defence forces without previous notification. On the other hand, every soldier was entitled to appeal directly to the commissioner without prejudice to his personal position. Lastly, a Personnel Committee was set up to investigate the qualifications of all senior officers before their appointment and lay down guiding principles according to which the suitability of all other ranks should be examined.

The establishment of the committee was an admirable measure, and it carried out its task in an impressive manner. The task was of special importance, because during the previous decade the ablest and most broad-minded military men had as a rule settled down happily in civilian life, and, so long as enlistment was on a voluntary basis and no preventive mea-

[8] Basic Law, Article 45a (i).
[9] Basic Law, Article 45b.

sures were taken, there was a danger that it would be the most narrow and fanatical military types who would return to their old profession and exert a sinister influence in the new forces. The danger was lessened with the introduction of conscription in the summer of 1956, but the committee played a vital role during the early stages of rearmament.

It examined individually the personal suitability of all former officers of the rank of colonel and upwards, who volunteered for service, and by the autumn of 1955 it had agreed on principles which were to guide it in its task. They included the following sentences: "Clear understanding of the value of personal liberty and of the meaning of the rule of law and unreserved allegiance to the democratic political order are the first requirements for the military profession. Only a body of men, which believes in freedom and law, is capable of defending them." The committee had a strong and well-chosen membership, which had been approved by all political parties in the Bundestag. For example, it included Frau Annedore Leber, widow of Julius Leber, the SPD politician who was executed after the plot against Hitler of July 20, 1944. Its chairman was Dr. Rombach, a former senior civil servant and a man of courage and complete democratic integrity. He himself described the committee as the most democratic institution he had ever known in any country.[10] Its members were not bound by any instructions and were responsible only to their own consciences. By its very existence the committee frightened off those with bad Nazi records, and it was for this reason that the number of refused applicants remained low. However, it turned down four officers in the Ministry of Defence, to Herr Blank's great annoyance, and he made unsuccessful representations to the chancellor. The CDU parliamentary party also demanded that the committee should change its rules of procedure. But the reply came back that no change would be made.

[10] In an interview with the writer in March 1956.

During the eight years between 1955 and 1963 great progress was made in building up a West German army, although it was only accomplished in the face of considerable difficulties. While the possibility of a military career aroused little enthusiasm amongst the younger generation, many of the officers and noncommissioned officers of the old German army had grown too old for further service during the ten years that had elapsed since the end of the war. Under conditions of growing prosperity and in the end full employment it was also not possible to find the full number of regulars which was really required to form the nucleus for an army of half a million men. In the face of industry's demands it was particularly difficult to retain the services of the well-qualified technicians who play a vital role in every modern military unit. Furthermore German armament factories had either been dismantled or transformed to peaceful purposes under Allied military government. In these circumstances it was due mainly to Adenauer's enthusiasm for the Western alliance and to the ambition and energy of Franz-Josef Strauss, who was Minister of Defence from 1956 to 1962, that so much was actually achieved.

In October 1955 the first hundred officers and NCOs were appointed as volunteers to the new army. The following summer conscription for a period of one year was introduced, and the period of service was increased to eighteen months in 1962. By the late summer of 1963 the total armed forces amounted to 404,000 including an air force of 93,000, and a navy of 28,000, though the number of officers and NCOs was still considerably below the required strength. The total cost to the federal government of Germany's own forces[11] amounted in 1955 to 95 million marks, in 1956 to 3,405 million, and in 1962 to

[11] That is, excluding the government's contributions to the occupation forces up to May 1955 and to the Allied forces stationed in Germany subsequently.

16,786 million.[12] When President Kennedy visited Germany in July 1963, he was able to refer to the Federal Republic's contribution to NATO as the greatest after that of the United States.

In view of the speed of German rearmament, the shortage of officers and NCOs, and the lack of equipment, it was inevitable that the deficiencies of the new army should, from time to time, have come in for a good deal of criticism within Germany. The quality of its NCOs in particular was repeatedly a target for attack. But with American help its equipment soon reached a high standard, and the German tradition of thoroughness and efficiency in training began to make its influence felt. Before the end of the Adenauer era the German forces had won widespread respect amongst their new Western allies.

However, from a long-term point of view the spirit prevailing in the German army would be more important than its size and efficiency. The extent to which the basic principles underlying the programme of *Innere Führung* were recognized and effective would largely determine the army's relationship to the democratic constitution, the Federal Republic's reliability as a member of the Western Alliance, and its role in the international community. A good deal of light is thrown on this subject by the development of the office of the Defence Commissioner of the Bundestag and by the record of the school for *Innere Führung* at Coblence.

The Bundestag was not altogether fortunate in the choice of its first two defence commissioners. The first appointment was made nearly two years after the passing of the relevant legislation, and the man selected was Lieut.-General Helmuth von Grolman. In the summer of 1961 he left office under a cloud and in circumstances that were unfortunate for the prestige of the commissionership. He was succeeded by Vice-Admiral

---

[12] The figures in this paragraph are taken from *Regierung Adenauer 1949–1963*, pp. 336 and 505.

Hellmuth Heye, who, after presenting two moderately worded annual reports, chose to express his deep misgivings about the situation in the forces in the form of journalistic articles in the illustrated magazine, *Quick*, and, as a result of the commotion resulting from this procedure, he also resigned.[13]

Heye gave as his reason for resorting to magazine articles that he had not the right to make a personal statement before the Bundestag at the time of presenting his personal report. But the argument did not carry much weight owing to the contrast between the strong statements in his article and the comparative restraint of the reports. He could have expressed himself more forcefully in his reports, or alternatively he could have pressed with much greater insistence for the right to speak before the Bundestag. Several leading political and military figures behaved with questionable propriety in connection with the defence commissioner's articles. When the case was still being investigated by the Defence Committee of the Bundestag, both the Minister of Defence and the chairman of the committee expressed themselves critically about Heye's action, while the General Inspector of the army, with a surprising nervousness, issued an order calling on his troops to show their loyalty to their oath of service at "this time of challenge." Neverthless Heye himself, for the sake of the cause he represented, was ill-advised to resort to such drastic and unusual action, unless he was prepared to stand up resolutely to the criticism to which it was bound to give rise.

In spite of these misfortunes the office of defence commissioner justified itself. The troops made full use of their right of appeal. Heye himself was tireless in visiting units and investigating the conditions of service and the prevailing spirit in all

[13] The articles were published during the summer following Adenauer's resignation and do not properly therefore fall within the scope of this book. But Heye's tenure of his office cannot fairly be summarized without some reference to the episode.

ranks of the military hierarchy, and the results of his investigations were set out in detail in his annual reports. There was a
series of unfortunate incidents in some of which individual soldiers lost their lives owing to the unreasonable demands made
upon them during training. In the worst of them fifteen recruits
were drowned after being ordered to cross a river wearing full
equipment. In his first annual report Heye attributed most of
the mistakes to the inexperience of young officers and NCOs or
to misdirected idealism, and only in a very few cases to ill-will.
But in his *Quick* articles he was more critical of the leadership
and lamented the inadequate realization of the principles of
Innere Führung. The existence of the defence commissioner
ensured that abuses received full publicity and the articles
themselves, whatever might be thought of their author's wisdom, performed a useful service by attracting public attention
to the army's problems. They were read with a good deal of
sympathy within the services, and the majority of the younger
generation supported Heye in his subsequent controversy with
the authorities.

The school of *Innere Führung* was attended during the first
six years of its existence by over 6,000 officers and NCOs.
Perhaps the best measure of its achievement is provided by the
results of numerous investigations which were carried out to
compare the knowledge and attitudes of members of the armed
forces with those of the general public as a whole. The fears
of the military reformers that the average recruit would not
bring with him the qualities of democratic citizenship necessary
to produce a "citizen in uniform" had proved justified. Yet the
inquiries organized by an institute for public-opinion research
at the request of the Ministry of Defence led to an unambigu-
ous conclusion.[14] In comparison with the population as a
whole, members of the armed services had a markedly greater

[14] Some of the results of these inquiries carried out by the Emnid Institute are to be found in E. Waldman, *op. cit.*, pp. 228–65.

awareness and understanding of some of the key problems in a democratic society as well as a more positive attitude towards democracy. The questions that were covered by the institute included the influence of the individual on political events, the functions of an opposition party, and the resistance movement against Hitler. The difference was perhaps due partly to the public spirit and idealism of some at least of the volunteers in the forces, but the main reason for it was undoubtedly the education in political responsibility which was carried out under the programme for *Innere Führung*.

On the other hand, the Coblence School turned out in fact to be a compromise with Baudissin's original conception of it. Baudissin had intended that in future no officer should hold a command in the forces who had not taken a course at Coblence and that the school itself should be staffed by well-paid teachers of academic status with short-term appointments, who would later return to the universities from which they had come. This would have ensured a high intellectual level and would have at least increased the chances of the teachers adopting a fresh and independent approach to the ethical and political problems that were discussed. Actually the shortage of officers and NCOs resulted in the courses being too short, while the teachers as a rule were of secondary-school level appointed on a long-term basis. In consequence the principles of *Innere Führung* came to be taught on the whole in a routine manner, which was relieved from time to time by the visits of interesting outside lecturers. The difficulties and deficiencies of the school were reflected in the units themselves. Probably about 25 to 30 per cent of those serving really believed in the new ideals; about 20 to 25 percent were opposed to them; while the remaining 50 per cent were only partially convinced of their validity and accepted them out of a sense of obedience. Owing to the army's rapid expansion and the shortage of officers frequent changes in personnel occurred in every unit, and in these circumstances it was difficult for even the most convinced reformer to carry out fully the principles of *Innere Führung* in practice.

The full realization of the new ideals would have necessitated a degree of support for them from three successive Ministers of Defence, which for different reasons was not in fact forthcoming from any of them, although all three paid consistent lip service to *Innere Führung*. Herr Blank was only minister from May 1955 until he gave way to the ambition of Franz-Josef Strauss in October 1956. He believed in the new principles, but he had neither the assertiveness nor the social assurance always to stand up firmly to the conservatives and traditionalists in his Ministry or in the army. Strauss was a much more effective minister and was far too intelligent not to see the value and importance of the reformers' ideas. But he was above all an ambitious politician and put quick and impressive results in building up the new army before any concern he might feel for its democratic character. Herr von Hassel, who succeeded Strauss as minister at the beginning of 1963, was a hard-working, conscientious and respected politician, but he was too much influenced by tradition and combined a personal prejudice against Baudissin with an intellectual incapacity to appreciate the full implications of his ideas.

Baudissin's theories had a purist and intellectual character that sometimes left the impression of not taking the frailty of human nature sufficiently into account. The American high commissioner, McCloy, and General Clay both expressed the fear that the idea of the "citizen in uniform" was being carried too far, while the military expert of the *Daily Telegraph* wrote in November 1961 that he could not imagine a more drastic break with the Prussian military tradition than was to be found in the German army of to-day, that there had already been some swing away from "the democratic ideal," and that he foresaw a further swing.[15] It was an unintended tribute to the insight and courage of the military reformers that these Anglo-Saxon observers should have been less concerned with the problem of German militarism than were the more enlightened German officers.

However, the attitude of the German public towards the forces, though unenthusiastic, became increasingly positive between 1956 and 1963, and there was a growing feeling amongst the military and political authorities that some concession to the professional pride of the troops was necessary in a society in which the competitive attractions of the armed services were limited. An outward change was therefore agreed upon, which had some symbolic significance. In accordance with the reformers' ideas, the uniforms chosen for the new forces had been modern and utilitarian and had represented a deliberate break with the past, but in the summer of 1962 approval was given for the introduction of more traditional walking-out uniforms and of silver or golden aiglets and embroidered caps for all officers in the army, navy and air force.

This concession can be criticized in detail but was to some extent justified. A more serious indication of the ministry's lukewarm attitude to the new ideals was the treatment accorded to Baudissin himself and to one of the ablest and most senior of the military reformers, Lieut.-General Count von Kielmansegg. When he was appointed to a command in 1958 Baudissin was given to understand that he would return later to the Ministry of Defence to continue his work for military reform. Actually in 1960 he was promoted to major-general and appointed a Deputy Chief of Staff at the NATO headquarters in Fontaine-

[15] See the quotation in E. Waldman, op. cit., pp. 204–5. But in writing in Die Welt that the units of the German army were forbidden to consider themselves as heirs of an earlier military tradition the expert, Brigadier Thomson, was exaggerating: a discriminating sense of tradition was encouraged.

bleau, subsequently receiving two further NATO appointments, which kept him out of Germany for more than five vital years in the development of the new German army. General von Kiel-mansegg was appointed in 1963 to succeed General Speidel as Commander of the NATO Land Forces in Central Europe and took up his post the following year. Both generals served as an excellent if somewhat misleading advertisement of the broad-minded liberalism of some of the new German military leaders, and the authorities in Bonn disavowed the suggestion that they were being deliberately kept out of Germany. But there is no doubt that both Strauss and von Hassell found it convenient not to have these strong reforming personalities in the key positions that would have been their due, had they received appointments at home. In 1964 Major-General de Maizière was made Inspec-tor of the Army. He himself belonged to the reformers' group and had been commander of the school for *Innere Führung*, but he had not the strength of personality of either Baudissin or Kielmansegg.

More sinister than these internal tendencies within the new German forces, so far as foreign countries were concerned, were the suggestions and claims, put forward from 1961 on-wards by the Americans and Germans respectively, that the German army should be equipped with weapons which could be used to fire nuclear war-heads, though the war-heads might remain under American control. In view of Germany's increas-ing contribution to NATO and with so powerful a person as Strauss as Minister of Defence, it was inevitable that Bonn should claim equal status with all of its NATO allies except the United States. The extent to which the claim proves dangerous will depend on the spirit prevailing within the German govern-ment and its armed forces. It is for this reason that the work of the military reformers has been in the past and will be in the future of greater importance than the more widely publicized statements on atomic weapons that have been made from time to time by military and political leaders.

Adenauer himself always paid lip service to the new military ideals. His attitude to the Personnel Committee was correct and positive, and he took a personal interest during its early stages in the school for *Innere Führung*. But, although he was in no sense a militarist at heart, his temperamental conservatism and respect for authority caused him to have more sympathy with the attitude of the old-fashioned and traditional type of officer than with the new and rather disturbing proposals of the reformers. While he accepted the idea of the citizen in uniform as good and even obvious, he had no more appreciation of the finer points of Baudissin's programme than he had of the more radical ideas of the civilian educational reformers, or of the need to cultivate sound democratic procedure as an end in itself. The chancellor therefore did nothing to correct the shortcomings of his Ministers of Defence.

However, the achievements of the reformers, of the Bundestag in 1955, and of Adenauer himself in his negotiations with the Allies should not be underrated. To carry out in full the radical programme of reform would have been extremely difficult in any country, and in Germany with its strong military tradition and social conservatism it was perhaps an impossible undertaking. The creation of the Defence Committee of the Bundestag and of the defence commissioner did much to ensure the primacy of civil over military authority. The incorporation of all Western Germany's defence forces within the NATO framework, the stationing of Allied troops on German territory, and the practice of sending German soldiers to other NATO countries for training has eliminated for the time the possibility of the German army re-emerging as a state within the state. Yet this last source of reassurance will depend on NATO's survival; a point which does not seem to have been appreciated by the venerated anachronism known as de Gaulle.

6
The Seamy Side

Adenauer exerted such a strong influence on the Federal Republic throughout his chancellorship that his deficiencies as a democratic statesman and as a man inevitably had a harmful effect upon the tone of German public life. His autocratic attitude, his cynicism, and his ruthlessness, together with his insensitivity to the finer points of democratic government, gave rise to a series of events, decisions, and faults of omission, which at least were unattractive blemishes on his record as a statesman and, in the most serious cases, will detract permanently from his place in German history.

In the first place, his attitude towards the Nazi legacy laid him open to much justifiable criticism, although there was a contradictory quality about his record in this respect, as there was in other aspects of his policy and character.

The chancellor's policy of tolerance and moderation towards ex-Nazis helped to prevent, as has been seen, the emergence of a strongly nationalist Right-wing party, and it led also to the absorption of many members of the Refugee and German Parties into the CDU. But these were not its only good results. The Nuremberg trials of Nazi war criminals and the Allied attempts at denazification had aroused a good deal of resentment, even amongst those who had always been opposed to

National Socialism. The fact that no Germans or neutrals were represented amongst the judges at Nuremberg meant that the trials took on the character of an action by the victors against the vanquished, while the Allied denazification programme was clumsy and inconsistent and ended in the minor offenders being treated with relatively greater severity than the more serious cases. In consequence, there arose a measure of sympathy for former Nazis, which was based on a mixture of patriotism and humanity and had no necessary connection with political opinions. Adenauer's policy of studied moderation and the exaggerated fairness of civil service law of May 1951[1] made it possible for this sympathy to die a natural death. As the years went by the German people realized increasingly that it was they alone who were responsible for taking action against unpunished Nazi criminals, and they were by now well aware of the nature and extent of the atrocities that had been committed. In 1958 the Ministers of Justice of the Länder set up in Ludwigsburg a centre for the investigation of National Socialist crimes, which had been committed against civilians outside the territory of the Federal Republic and had not therefore been the subject of action by West German public prosecutors. After the centre had had time to assemble evidence both in Germany and abroad a series of trials took place, the most famous of which was the Auschwitz trial at Frankfurt, which was initiated shortly before Adenauer left office. These proceedings, partly owing to the influence of the Eichmann case in Israel, attracted greater attention than any since the Nuremberg trials and were in the nature of a process of national self-purification. That public opinion had developed so far as to make such a process possible was largely due to Adenauer.

Yet, in spite of the wisdom of his general policy towards former Nazis and refugees, he was responsible for a number of

[1] See p. 49.

decisions which were the reverse of wise and had a damaging effect on the reputation of West German democracy both at home and abroad.

Dr. Hans Globke, the state-secretary in charge of the Chancellor's office, had written the legal commentaries to the anti-Semitic racial laws, which were approved by the Nazi Party conference at Nuremberg in 1935. It is true that Globke was never a member of the Nazi Party; he is known to have helped and saved the lives of many Jews and others during the National Socialist regime; his interpretations of the Nuremberg laws were as mild as he could make them; and in May 1951 Adenauer assured the Bundestag, with some convincing illustrations, that he had investigated his past record very carefully before appointing him. Globke was also a highly conscientious and efficient civil servant with an extraordinary memory, whom the chancellor considered indispensable. Yet he had been associated, even if fortuitously, with one of the worst aspects of a criminal regime, and it was therefore wrong that he should have been appointed to such a key post and that he should have been allowed to acquire great influence.

A comparable case was that of Professor Theodor Oberländer, who was Minister of Refugees from 1953 to 1960, although Oberländer lacked some of Globke's more human qualities. Adenauer made him a minister for tactical political reasons as part of the price to be paid for the Refugee Party's support and was grateful to him for seceding to the CDU with seven of his Bundestag colleagues. His record under National Socialism was varied and rather obscure, because most of the time he had been in Eastern Europe, partly in Russia and Poland. But for most of the Hitler era also he had been *persona grata* with the regime, and during his ministry his past career was the object of increasing criticism within the Federal Republic and abroad, particularly in Poland. Finally in 1960 he resigned, Adenauer himself referring publicly to his "deep-brown" past.[2]

Apart from these two much-publicized instances, there was a good deal of undue lenience towards former Nazis, while Adenauer was chancellor. In some cases, it was difficult to avoid. For example, during the Nazi regime the great majority of judges had been members of the party. After the war it would scarcely have been possibly to rebuild the judicial system without reappointing many of them, and in fact, during the early years of the Federal Republic, *Land* statistics showed that up to four-fifths or more of the acting judges had been members of the Nazi Party or its affiliated organizations. Nevertheless more care could have been taken to exclude the more seriously implicated persons. In 1961 an appendix to a new law called upon judges and public prosecutors to resign, if their participation in death sentences in the past laid them open to justifiable reproaches, further action being threatened, if they did not do so. It came as a shock to many members of the public that over 150 acknowledged their involvement by responding to this invitation.

In most cases of excessive lenience, however, there had also been laxity or negligence. The civil service law of 1951 had resulted in a situation where the victims of National Socialism often came off worse than collaborators or conformists. Towards the end of the Adenauer's chancellorship a *Land* chief of criminal police was prosecuted for inhumanity in connection with the mass murder of Jews. One of the worst cases of all, owing to its deliberate defiance of democratic procedure, occurred in 1952. The Bundestag committee, that had been set up to investigate the presence of former Nazis in the Foreign Service, recommended certain limitations on future employment in the case of four members of the service. Although Adenauer was himself foreign minister at the time, two of the

[2] The reference is to the brown shirts of Hitler's S.A. men.

recommendations were disregarded, and the men concerned were promoted to positions of responsibility.

Similar to his attitude towards former Nazis was Adenauer's record with regard to the problem of eastern frontiers. He was no more in sympathy with the extremists on this question than he was with National Socialism: his emotional commitment was to Western Europe and to his country's relationship with France, and he had little personal interest in Germany's lost territories in the East. Yet, through his actions and his statements, he managed to produce a misleading and unfortunate impression. Refugee organizations received subsidies from several federal ministries. Adenauer endeavoured to curb Dr. Seebohm's wilder statements but without complete success, and Seebohm's more extreme and foolish utterances were naturally listened to and repeated as coming from a member of the cabinet. Occasionally Adenauer himself, no doubt mainly for electoral reasons, made speeches which were comparable to his minister's for their reckless lack of discretion. For example, in the summer of 1960 he suggested to an audience in Düsseldorf that the German people should have the right of self-determination in East Prussia. There were by then very few Germans left in that area, and he himself knew perfectly well that it would be impossible as well as fruitless to hold a plebiscite amongst East Prussian refugees in the two Germanys and the many foreign countries to which they had emigrated. His remarks naturally caused great annoyance in Poland and the Soviet Union and gave rise to justifiable suspicions about Germany's future intentions.

The fact that the chancellor based his actions on cynicism and expediency, in matters where important principles were involved, discredited his regime, damaged the tone of West German political life, and confused and bewildered the younger generation, who wanted a clear lead to help them make up their minds about National Socialism and the lost Eastern territories.

It discredited also the Federal Republic abroad. Germany's critics in the West considered that their fears were being confirmed, while Poland, Czechoslovakia, and the Soviet Union felt the deepest misgivings about the ultimate aims of Bonn's external policy. By undermining confidence in Western Germany as a neighbour, it also reduced the already slender chances of reunification, because to allow the strengthening of a revisionist Germany would, for Warsaw and Prague, be suicidal. Adenauer, it is true, did not often made revisionist statements, and there was only one Seebohm in his cabinet, but after the experiences of the recent past little evidence was needed to arouse deep suspicion.

Within the Federal Republic much harm was done by a series of incidents which revealed on Adenauer's part an insensitivity to the niceties of political ethics or an openly disrespectful attitude to the courts of law, unbecoming in the head of the government.

In September 1958 Adenauer's personal assistant, Herr Kilb, who had the rank of *Ministerialrat* in the civil service, came under suspicion for having received a bribe in the form of a smart car placed at his disposal by one of the leading automobile markers in the country. Herr Kilb himself was for some months under arrest pending trial, and officials of the firm concerned were also involved in the proceedings. After more than a year of investigations and a good deal of publicity the Bonn provincial court decided that the case should be dropped, and its decision was subsequently confirmed by the higher provincial court in Cologne. The reasons given were that Herr Kilb had used the car in the service of Adenauer only as CDU chairman and not as chancellor and that it had not been possible to establish the precise nature of Kilb's previous activity as an official.[3] Adenauer himself admitted that the Chancellor's Office had informed the public prosecutor's office, "as it was

[3] See *Süddeutsche Zeitung*, June 2, 1960.

entitled to," that proceedings against Kilb were not, in its opinion, necessary.[4] The whole episode left a thoroughly distasteful impression, which could have been avoided had Adenauer made a clear statement about his attitude in such matters, both as chancellor and as CDU chairman.

Another case involved two important public figures who were also two of Adenauer's most trusted associates: Professor Hallstein, who had been state-secretary in the Foreign Ministry before becoming president of the EEC Commission, and Herr Herbert Blankenhorn, who had been one of Adenauer's closest advisers on foreign affairs and later became successively the West German representative at NATO and ambassador in Paris and in London. In the autumn of 1952 an Egyptian press attaché, in a conversation with Herr Blankenhorn, accused Dr. Strack of the German Ministry of Economics of accepting bribes. His imputations were passed on to the Ministry of Economics, in the course of their official duties, by Herr Blankenhorn and his superior in the Ministry of Foreign Affairs, Dr. Hallstein. The following year Dr. Strack started legal proceedings against a person or persons unknown for slander. The case took six years before it came to court. In April 1959 Herr Blankenhorn, then ambassador in Paris, was found guilty of false accusations and slander, given a suspended sentence of four months' imprisonment and fined 3,000 marks, while the charges against Dr. Hallstein were found "not proven." Herr Blankenhorn appealed to the Federal High Court, and the following year his sentence was quashed, the judge explaining that this would also involve the full rehabilitation of Dr. Hallstein.[5]

The case was extremely complex and aroused strong feelings on both sides. The impression left on a number of people was that in Britain or the United States the differences between

[4] *Ibid.*, January 24–25, 1959.
[5] Herr Strack himself emerged unscathed and was appointed ambassador to Chile in 1959.

personalities from which it arose would probably have been settled within the two ministries concerned. But some of the incidents which in fact accompanied it showed up the administration in a very poor light. The long delay in the legal proceedings was inexcusable. It was alleged in the SPD paper Vorwärts, that the Chancellor's Office made it difficult for the legal authorities to obtain evidence,[6] and the foreign minister admitted that Dr. Strack had been offered an embassy on condition that he dropped the case.[7] While court proceedings were still pending, Blankenhorn was appointed ambassador to France, and Adenauer himself stated that "the cabinet had unanimously decided . . . that the actions of Hallstein and Blankenhorn were in the nature of official procedure, in which they had both acted in accordance with their duty." A government spokesman actually reaffirmed this statement the day after Blankenhorn's conviction.

Finally, there was the chancellor's astonishing statement before the Bundestag in 1961 that the cabinet had agreed that the Constitutional Court's judgment in the television case was wrong. Under National Socialism the German courts of law had become the tools of Hitler. Adenauer felt a genuine disgust for Nazi methods, and he was jealous of his country's reputation in the Western world. It was a strange blindness on his part that he quite failed to realize the harm he was doing to the Federal Republic's young democracy and to its good name abroad by his failure to show a proper respect for the independence of the judiciary.

During the last few years of Adenauer's chancellorship three internal developments occurred which led to a progressive decline in his reputation and authority: his presidential candidature in 1959, the long drawn out inter-party negotiations which

---

[6] See the article by G. W. Heinemann, April 24, 1959.
[7] Frankfurter Allgemeine Zeitung, February 18, 1959.

followed the federal elections in 1961, and the *Spiegel* affair of 1962.

In the spring of 1959, as the end of Heuss's second term as president approached, Adenauer had the idea that he might get rid of Dr. Erhard as a candidate for the chancellorship by persuading him to stand for the presidency. Erhard did not accept this suggestion. Whereupon Adenauer in a radio address during April announced that he was a candidate for the presidency himself, that the position and function of the federal president were much greater than was generally believed, and that he proposed to make a careful study of the Basic Law in this connection.[8]

Two years before, a rumour had gone around that Adenauer was thinking of ending his chancellorship by heading for the presidency, and it is possible that, when he paid his first visit to de Gaulle in March 1959, he was impressed by the position the French president had created for himself in the Fifth Republic. The presidency would also have given Adenauer the chance of another four years in high office at an age when it seemed inadvisable that he should lead his party in another federal election. Nevertheless some of his immediate associates in the CDU were always opposed to his candidature. They did not think he would be happy in the office or that it would make a good ending to his career. From a national point of view he would inevitably have been a president representing a party, or at most a coalition, rather than the people as a whole, and this would have meant an unfortunate break with the tradition steadily built up by Heuss.

Within a few weeks Adenauer too had changed his mind. Early in June he renounced his candidature, giving as his rea-

---

[8] As Adenauer was chairman of the Parliamentary Council, which drew up the Basic Law, it might seem strange that he should have had to study its terms. But, as another member of the Council explained to the writer, Adenauer was chairman of the plenary session, while most of the detailed drafting was done by committees.

sons the serious international situation and the recent death of John Foster Dulles. In the circumstances, he told the parliamentary party of the CDU, he could not take the responsibility for leaving his post. But two other reasons no doubt weighed strongly with him also. In the first place, his researches into the Basic Law do not appear to have had very positive results. Secondly, he encountered unexpected opposition to the strange but for him typical assumption that, as presidential candidate, he would be able to choose his successor as chancellor. This second reason was particularly important, because he himself did not favour Dr. Erhard, who had the support of the majority of the CDU.

The sudden reversal of Adenauer's decision astonished the CDU as well as the nation as a whole. At first a majority of the parliamentary party appears to have been opposed to him. He then won their support for remaining in office with the aid of sentiment, the respect felt for his past record and personal authority, and the trump card, which he always played so well, of the communist danger and his experience in dealing with it. But politically informed public opinion had been deeply shocked and was not so easily propitiated. Adenauer personally came in for the strongest and frankest criticism in the press that he had encountered since becoming chancellor; and with good reason.

He had shown disrespect, almost disdain, for the presidential office by using it capriciously to suit his own purposes. The headship of a great state surely deserved what Kant held to be due to every human being, that it should be treated always as an end in itself, never merely as a means to an end. Moreover, by suggesting that much more could be made of the office than had in fact been made of it, he showed little gratitude or respect for Heuss's services as an exemplary president and for his interpretation of the office. By finally supporting Herr Lübke, as an avowedly party candidate, he missed the opportunity of establishing, on the foundations already laid, a tradition that the federal president should be a national figure rather than the nominee of the largest party. Throughout the whole unfortunate episode Adenauer betrayed the vain and autocratic elements in his make-up with maximum publicity and at the same time revealed an indecision on a major issue, which no statesman can allow himself with impunity. The two highest offices in the land were discredited during the process, and Adenauer's personal prestige suffered a decline from which it did not recover.

The decline, which was carried a stage further by the erection of the Berlin Wall in August 1961, was reflected in the results of the federal election a month later. For the first time since he had become chancellor, Adenauer himself was a liability rather than an asset to his party. Although the German Party had disintegrated since the 1957 elections and the majority of its members had joined the CDU/CSU, the two affiliated government parties lost twenty-eight seats and their over-all majority in the Bundestag. Adenauer, therefore, could only form a government in coalition either with the FDP or the SPD. The FDP was the more natural partner, but the situation was complicated by the fact that its leader, Dr. Mende, had announced during the election campaign that he would not enter a coalition with Adenauer as chancellor, and it was with this statement as part of their election platform that the FDP had increased their seats from forty-one to sixty-seven.

Although the elections were held on the 17th of September the negotiations for the formation of a government dragged on until the 7th of November, when Adenauer was re-elected as chancellor. The most natural and correct solution of the problem would have been for Adenauer to have handed over the leadership of his party to Erhard and for the CDU/CSU to have formed a coalition with the FDP under Mende. An alternative possibility was a great coalition between the CDU and the SPD, for which the serious situation in Berlin provided a rational justification. President Lübke used such influence as he possessed to bring about each of these solutions in turn.

Actually the dominant feature of the negotiations turned out to be every party's desire for power. Considerations of principle and concern for the country's interests took second place. The politically minded public and the more responsible press expressed their increasing disgust, as they watched their rulers and would-be rulers haggling to retain or attain power. The SPD wanted a great coalition; the FDP were reluctant to give up the fruits of their success for a mere election pledge; the CSU under its new chairman, Franz-Josef Strauss, asserted its independence of the CDU, to an extent that it had not done before; and the most constant feature of all in a rapidly changing situation was Adenauer's own determination to remain in office at all costs, though he would have been far better advised to have yielded gracefully to Erhard's claims.

In the end a coalition was formed between the CDU/CSU and the FDP, Mende making a thin gesture to principle by refusing office, though the electors had certainly not interpreted his statement about Adenauer as a personal one. The bargaining about cabinet places was very unedifying, and one of Adenauer's most loyal supporters, Herr von Brentano, was sacrificed in the process. When agreement was finally reached, the chancellor and the parties were bound by so many conditions and undertakings that neither the government nor members of the Bundestag had the freedom of action which the Basic Law intended and which is fundamental to democracy. Professor Eschenburg wrote an article with the appropriate title, "Pact against Democracy,"[9] while another writer referred to the "self-destructive traits" which the eighty-six-year-old Adenauer had developed during the negotiations.[10]

[9] In *Die Zeit*, November 10, 1961.
[10] G. Gaus, "Adenauer" in *Süddeutsche Zeitung*, November 4–5, 1961.

The two central figures in the *Spiegel* affair were Rudolf Augstein, the gifted, courageous, and influential publisher of the magazine, and Franz-Josef Strauss, Minister of Defence.

Strauss is without doubt one of the most remarkable personalities that has emerged in Germany since the war and, from a democratic point of view, the most dangerous. Born in Munich in 1915 and of quite humble origin, he had a brilliant career at school and the university. After the war he rose rapidly in both *Land* and federal politics. In Bavaria he became a *Landrat* (highest official in the county), general-secretary of the CSU, and later its chairman. In Bonn he entered the Bundestag in 1949, and between 1953 and 1956 became in quick succession Minister without Portfolio, Minister for Atomic Affairs, and Minister of Defence. In 1961 Adenauer paid tribute to his energy and drive and said of him that, although far from being an easy colleague, he had set to work to build up the new army with outstanding courage and seriousness of purpose.

He has great ambition and combines with it the advantages of considerable intellectual gifts, an exceptional memory, immense resilience and capacity for work, and the ability to make quick decisions. He also has a typically Bavarian geniality and an adaptability that is of particular value to a politician. He can be equally at home with an audience of Bavarian peasants, middle-class citizens, and politically minded students and intellectuals.

On the other hand, these positive qualities are offset by equally pronounced defects. The unscrupulousness of his political methods exceeds even Adenauer's and is not counterbalanced, as with Adenauer, by good judgment and serenity of manner. Above all he is lacking in self-control and knowledge of men, and has the habit of picking weak and sycophantic companions, when his incapacity for self-criticism makes it desirable that he should have candid and strong-minded friends.

His quick decisions therefore have often been the wrong ones. Martin Walser once wrote of him "he can defend us against everything, only not against himself."[11] Strauss indeed has frequently, and with justice, been described as his own worst enemy. Sometimes he revealed weaknesses that were unworthy of anyone in high political office. After the Cardinal Archbishop of Munich had received him coldly, following the Spiegel affair, although a Catholic himself, he boasted to an acquaintance with the crudest form of vanity that he had kept the Cardinal waiting for three hours at an appointment in a small country town. When eighteen distinguished scientists signed a dignified manifesto against equipping the German army with nuclear weapons, he responded to their protest with insulting personal remarks.

Strauss's arrogance, unscrupulousness, and poor judgment were shown on a series of occasions, culminating in the Spiegel affair, to all of which Der Spiegel itself gave a maximum of publicity. As the SPD leaders restrained their criticisms of the government with an eye on the floating voters and the chance of a great coalition, many people looked upon Der Spiegel as the only effective opposition, although they often disapproved of its journalistic methods. Augstein singled out Strauss for special and sustained criticism, because he considered him the most serious threat to West German democracy, and a feud developed between the magazine and the minister, in which neither side pulled their punches. The following three cases were typical, though there were many others.

On one occasion Strauss demanded that a policeman, who had quite correctly stopped his, Strauss's, car, should be reprimanded and no longer employed as a traffic policeman in Bonn. This demand was fortunately rejected by the CDU minister concerned.

A second case was the complex Fibag affair, which received much publicity in 1962 and arouses doubts in a foreigner's

[11] In Die Alternative oder Brauchen wir Eine neue Regierung?, p. 126.

mind as to whether a correct and impartial political investigation can at present be conducted in the Federal Republic. In the summer of 1960 Strauss wrote to an American minister recommending the Munich firm, *Fibag*, for building accommodation for the families of American servicemen. The case began to arouse interest when it became known that a Passau newspaper proprietor, who was a friend of Strauss, was linked with the firm, and when it was alleged in an article in *Der Spiegel* that his friend had undertaken to use his influence with the Defence Minister to obtain the American contracts. An uncorroborated statement was also quoted which indicated that Strauss might have obtained some financial advantage from such a contract. This last point was cleared up in March 1962, when a libel action by Strauss against *Der Speigel* was settled by the proprietors agreeing that the magazine had not maintained nor would it maintain in the future that the minister had sought to obtain financial advantage for himself. An all-party parliamentary committee of inquiry was set up during the same month to investigate the other allegations against Strauss. On October 25, 1962 its majority report was approved by the Bundestag, against the votes of the opposition, that in the *Fibag* affair Strauss had not been guilty of infringement of his duty as a minister. Nevertheless four aspects of the case were revealing. First, Strauss recommended a German firm to an American minister without first satisfying himself about its full technical competence. Secondly, he declared during the parliamentary investigations that forces directed from East Berlin were at work to vilify him and exclude him from political life. Thirdly, during the investigations also the Ministry of Defence made public a declaration of loyalty by German generals, who were said by a ministry spokesman to have asked the minister to remain in office.[12] Finally, the three SPD members in the seven-

[12] See the article by Rolf Zundel in *Die Zeit* of July 27, 1962: the writer added that the Minister thus "threw in the generals as support troops for his own career."

man committee of inquiry did not approve the committee's report. Professor Eschenburg, who is well known for his balanced judgments, wrote in his analysis of the Spiegel affair, that even the most well-disposed person could not assert "that Strauss had become involved in the Fibag affair in complete innocence" and added his opinion that "an English minister would probably have resigned after the Fibag affair, in order to escape dismissal."[13]

Thirdly, at the height of the Cuba crisis, Strauss's behaviour, during one crucial night, was the subject of widespread critical reports. To quote Professor Eschenburg again:

The press—by no means only Der Spiegel—and the radio have reported a number of times that the Commander-in-Chief (Strauss), during the night in which the Cuba crisis approached its climax and the troops were consequently at the alert, was at a late hour very drunk at a reception given by the federal president in Schloss Brühl. One should not prudishly condemn every case of intoxication at once, but all the same one should consider that every private soldier, who is drunk on guard, is imprisoned.[14]

Strauss's own account of this episode was given in a letter to the editor of the illustrated magazine, Stern, in which he explained that at the president's reception in Schloss Brühl on October 24 he had suffered from circulation trouble, which was due to a liver complaint and general overstrain.

The Spiegel affair itself had its origin in a long article which appeared in Der Spiegel on October 8, 1962, dealing with the recent NATO manoeuvres. Most observers had agreed that the state of the German defences had not shown up in a good light during the exercises. NATO had a scale of four marks to describe the fighting strength of an army, and on this occasion the

13 Die Affäre, pp. 10–11.
14 Ibid., p. 11.

German army was given the lowest of the four, *"Bedingt Abwehrbereit"* (Conditionally Prepared for Defence), which was the title given to the article. It was not so much the quality of the troops that was at fault. The author of the article, Conrad Ahlers, the defence expert of *Der Spiegel*, had sharply criticized the Defence Minister's concept of the German army and its armament. Strauss's prejudice in favour of the nuclear deterrent, which the Germans did not possess, Ahlers believed, had caused him to neglect conventional defences to a dangerous degree.

On the evening of October 26, the day after the *Fibag* report had been accepted by the Bundestag, police occupied and searched the *Spiegel* offices in Hamburg and Bonn. They remained in occupation for over a month, carrying out an exhaustive examination and removing thousands of files. The search was extended to the homes of some of the staff, where it was carried out with a somewhat ridiculous thoroughness, a kind of atavism reminiscent of Gestapo practices. The private correspondence of members of the family, the mattresses on the children's beds, their toys, and even a pony's stable and the straw were all given attention. That night and during the following weeks eleven arrests were made, including Augstein himself, who remained in prison for 103 days, Ahlers, several other members of the editorial staff, and two army colonels, who were suspected of providing information. Ahlers, who was on holiday in Spain, was arrested by the Spanish police at the request of the German military attaché, following telephone conversations between Bonn and the German embassy in Madrid.

During the search of the Hamburg office the proofs of the next number of the magazine were packed, sealed, and sent off to the legal authorities for examination; a procedure which was either a waste of time or a case of unconstitutional censorship.

The charge on which the police action was based was "sus-

picion of high treason." But the publication of an article drawing attention to the inadequacy of the national defences was a
strange ground for such a charge. If any military secrets had
really been betrayed, then the fault must have lain with the
officers and officials of the Ministry of Defence rather than with
a magazine which published available information. Moreover,
as the *Spectator* pointed out at the time: "On a number of
occasions the Minister of Defence personally has been called to
order by NATO, because he has used secret material in public
speeches and articles, when it was a matter of supporting his
demand for atomic artillery."

Throughout the affair the problem as to who initiated the
proceedings was never cleared up. It must remain therefore a
matter of surmise, though it is not one that has given rise to
much doubt. On November 8, however, Strauss stated in
the Bundestag that on the day after the article appeared a
senior officer in the Defence Ministry was in touch with the
federal attorney-general's office about the matter and that the
attorney-general either intended to initiate preliminary investigations or had started to do so.[15] Strauss himself at first played
down his own role in the affair with a series of surprisingly
sweeping statements and made much of the fact that he had
been on holiday until October 15. In an interview for the
Frankfurter Abendpost, which was published on October 30,
he said:

That evening [24th October] I had still no idea of the nature,
the extent and the aim of the federal attorney-general's action.

In an interview for the *8-Uhr Blatt*, published on November
3, he said with reference to the action against *Der Spiegel*:

[15] The important discussions in the Bundestag on the *Spiegel* affair are
to be found in the official *Stenographische Berichte* for the 7th, 8th, and
9th of October 1962.

No. It is no act of vengeance on my part. I have nothing to do
with the matter. In the truest sense of the word, nothing to do
with it.

On November 9, he was asked by Herr Erler if, after October
16 and before October 28, he had himself taken part in a discussion in the Ministry of Defence about the further measures
to be taken as a result of the preliminary investigations that had
been initiated. After a good deal of hesitation he replied:

In the period from the 16th of October to the 26th of October
—I say: 26th of October, colleague Erler—I took part in no
discussion. But, of course, it was pointed out to me by the
responsible gentlemen in my ministry that the affair was going
on. More than that I did not know. I did not know what was
going to happen; I did not know when it was going to happen;
I did not know against whom it was going to happen, and so on.

The *Spiegel* affair was thrashed out in some detail, though
not fully, in the question hours of the Bundestag on the 7th,
8th, and 9th of November. The two ministers most involved
were Strauss and the Minister of the Interior, Herr Höcherl,
though Adenauer also took part. For once the plenary sessions
of the Bundestag sprang to life and for a change also the SPD
pressed the government hard, relentlessly, and with success.
The general impressions left by the government spokesmen on
a reader of the verbatim reports are of hesitation, elaborate
evasion, and questionable statements. The speakers took advantage of the heated atmosphere to avoid or delay answering,
and diverted attention from the questions put to them by references to the villainy of high treason.

Adenauer's performance was remarkable, even in the light of
his own unique past. Had it not been for his age and air of
authority, he could scarcely have survived it as chancellor. On
November 7, at an early stage in the question hour he said:

"High treason has been committed—that is very possible." Later he made the unexceptionable statement that "in every constitutional state it is the supreme duty not to interfere in legal proceedings which are pending." Finally in the heat of controversy he added: "We have an abyss of high treason in the country," going on to speak of "a paper, which, with a circulation of half a million, systematically commits high treason in order to earn money."

During the question hour on November 9 Strauss at first took refuge in a cloud of verbiage and generalizations. But under pressure from Erler he finally made the important admission that he had himself been on the telephone to the German embassy in Madrid during the night of the 26th–27th October. He personally therefore had played a vital part in the arrest of Ahlers.

The whole course of events became much clearer as a result of two developments during the following weeks. In the first place on November 13, Adenauer ordered the four ministers concerned, the Ministers of Justice, Foreign Affairs, the Interior, and Defence, to prepare a report on the preliminary investigations in the *Spiegel* case, describing the measures taken by each ministry to assist the federal attorney-general. The resulting *Spiegel* Report was presented on February 4, 1963. The ministries could not reach agreed conclusions, so the report gave the different statements made by each ministry separately. Secondly, when Strauss realized that Adenauer intended to drop him from the government, he spoke much more frankly. During the Bundestag question hours the three main government spokesmen stood firmly together to cover one another's embarrassments. Now, however, Strauss gave some detailed information about the chancellor's involvement in the affair, and Adenauer repaid him in kind. The *Spiegel* Report also refuted some of Strauss's statements in the Bundestag.[16]

[16] The report was published in the *Bulletin* of February 5, 1963.

As a result the following important facts emerged. Whereas Adenauer had stated in the Bundestag that he had not been informed about the proceedings until the last minute, it now became clear that the Defence Minister had in fact informed the chancellor of what was going on on the 18th, the 22nd, and the 23rd of October. The chancellor had asked to be kept in touch and had assured the minister that he supported with his full authority the action being taken and that he could quote him as having said so. Whereas Strauss had stated in the Bundestag that he had taken part in no discussion between the 16th and the 26th of October, he had in fact done so in his ministry at least on the 16th, the 19th, and the 24th of October. One of the worst aspects of the affair from a constitutional point of view was that the action was taken without the knowledge of the Minister of Justice, Dr. Stammberger. On the 24th of October Minister Strauss told State-Secretary Strauss of the Ministry of Justice that the chancellor had ordered that the number of persons, who were to be told about the contemplated action, was to be limited to a necessary minimum and that the Minister of Justice was therefore not to be informed. Adenauer had, in fact, recommended strict secrecy but he denied having made any specific mention of the minister.

The SPD produced its own report, which consisted mainly of numerous carefully collated quotations from the Bundestag's proceedings and extracts from the *Spiegel* Report. It concludes with a summary in which it attributes five false statements to Höcherl; nine to Strauss, six of them before the Bundestag; and one false statement before the Bundestag to Adenauer. In addition there are lists of eight outstanding obscurities and five infringements of the law and correct procedure.

In response to the public's critical attitude, and under pressure from the FDP, Adenauer on the 5th of November ordered the dismissal of State-Secretary Strauss and the suspension of State-Secretary Hopf of the Ministry of Defence. As propitiatory sacrifices they seemed an unfair choice. Hopf had been working closely with his minister throughout the affair, while State-Secretary Strauss, though he failed to keep his minister informed of what was happening, had acted, as he thought, under Adenauer's orders conveyed by Minister Strauss. On November 19, the five FDP members of the cabinet resigned, making their further participation in the government dependent upon the departure of Minister Strauss. As Strauss was reluctant to give up his post, a few days later the CDU and CSU ministers also resigned, in order to facilitate a reconstruction of the government without Strauss. This took place during December after tough negotiations, neither Strauss nor the unfortunate Dr. Stammberger being included in the new administration. Adenauer himself agreed to resign the chancellorship in the autumn of 1963. So Rudolf Augstein, who was still in prison, had the satisfaction of knowing that Strauss had gone and that Adenauer's term was limited.

The most encouraging aspect of the Spiegel affair was the strength of the German people's reaction against the whole proceedings: against the arrest of Augstein and his colleagues, the occupation of the Spiegel offices, and the prevarication and false statements of leading members of the government in the Bundestag. It was reassuring too that the reaction was strongest amongst the younger generation. In most universities demonstrations took place and many resolutions of protest were passed. In Hamburg students gathered in front of the prison where Augstein was detained, and on successive nights seven to eight thousand of them assembled to hear speakers discuss the subject. Twenty-nine professors of political science and law sent a petition to the president of the Bundesrat expressing their deep anxiety about the authenticity and the future of their free and constitutional form of government. The vital nerve and the inner authority of a free state, they wrote, had been grievously wounded by the fact that members of the government had not even informed parliament in good time and truthfully about what had been going on. The confidence of the citizen in parliament and the government had been shaken and could only be restored, if the ministers responsible would draw the consequences.[17] Practically the whole German press joined in, and often led the nation-wide protests.

It seems an exaggeration to suggest, however, as some writers have done, that the affair marked a turning point in the history of German democracy. The self-purification that had been carried out was not sufficiently complete. The public reaction was a very hopeful sign for the future. But the events to which the public reacted revealed weaknesses that went very deep, and the subsequent actions of responsible people and organizations were often disappointingly inadequate. Professor Eschenburg wrote: "If Strauss in relatively quiet times treats the constitution in this way, what will he do with it in a time of emergency?" Too few Germans in positions of authority recognized the danger signal as clearly as did Eschenburg.

During the inter-party negotiations that took place in November and December over the formation of a new government neither the FDP nor the SPD took the strong line based on principle that would have been appropriate to the occasion. Dr. Stammberger was a member of the FDP. He had been the victim of gross constitutional impropriety and had become unpopular with the CDU/CSU because he wanted the procedure of the Defence Ministry to be investigated thoroughly. Whatever personal reasons there may have been for replacing him as Minister of Justice,[18] it would have made a much better impression had his party stood by him staunchly at a time when expediency was exerting far too much influence in government circles. The SPD actually chose this moment to negotiate

---

[17] M. Löffler, Der Verfassungsauftrag der Presse, Modellfall Spiegel, p. 77.

[18] Dr. Stammberger had a bad accident at about this time.

through Herbert Wehner for a great coalition and offered to support Adenauer as chancellor without a time limit. In view of Adenauer's recent record and the fact that the FDP ministers had resigned in order to get rid of Strauss, this was a piece of cynical political expediency that showed the corrupting influence of example and was a sad anticlimax after the party's performance in the Bundestag a few weeks before.

One writer expressed the following opinion in 1963: "The decisions of those who have to decide in the Spiegel affair are still outstanding. It appears to be the main concern of all involved to dispose of the affair as far as possible without attracting much attention."[19] This judgment has proved justified. In the spring of 1965 the Federal High Court quashed all proceedings against Augstein and Ahlers on charges of treasonable publication of military secrets, owing to insufficient evidence of guilt. But the court did not allow those who had been imprisoned, while the case was being investigated, to apply for legal damages against the state, nor did it allow Ahlers to take proceedings against Strauss for alleged abuse of his ministerial powers.

Until the Spiegel affair Strauss was widely considered one of the strongest candidates for the chancellorship, though not as Adenauer's immediate successor. This fact contributed to the sensation which the case caused. In view of his record in the affair, it would have been reasonable to assume, judged by normal democratic standards, that his departure from the cabinet would have meant the end of his political career. That this has not proved to be the case has been partly due to his own resilience and boundless ambition and partly to the political standards of his supporters.

To mark his departure from the Ministry of Defence Strauss

---

[19] Jürgen Seifert, Die "Spiegel"-Affäre in E. Kuby and others, Franz-Josef Strauss, p. 303.

arranged, with astonishing but successful effrontery, a special farewell parade, which included the beating of the retreat. The SPD and the FDP boycotted the ceremony, but Adenauer attended it and in his speech of thanks said that he had had to respect Strauss's wish not to join his fifth cabinet as Defence Minister but that he had not done so with a light heart. State-Secretary Hopf said: "The attacks on you rest on a tragic misunderstanding of facts, consequences, and intentions."

In the Bavarian elections at the end of November 1962 the CSU was returned with an increased majority, a fact that was generally interpreted as Bavaria's riposte to the treatment of their party chairman. The following summer he was re-elected chairman of the CSU without opposition, in spite of the displeasure of the Catholic Church over his behaviour in the *Spiegel* affair. One observer wrote of the meeting, at which he was elected, that the majority of those present sometimes gave him the impression that they wanted to make of the CSU a C-SA, referring to Hitler's *Sturm Abteilungen*. Alfons Goppel, the Minister-President of Bavaria, who refused to stand against Strauss, made the revealing remark regarding Strauss's role in the *Spiegel* affair: "We must take it from him that he did not lie."

Since leaving the federal cabinet, Strauss has played his political cards with great skill, making full use of his position as leader of the CSU group in the Bundestag. There is a widespread feeling in more responsible political circles that he ought not to return to the government but an equally widespread and cynical acquiescence in the likelihood that he ultimately will.[20]

For Adenauer the *Spiegel* affair marked the third and last stage in the decline of his prestige. Until he finally agreed in

[20] The influential role played by Strauss in the Federal Republic since the *Spiegel* affair can largely be explained by the lack of a national democratic tradition in Germany. But since 1962 Strauss has received an honorary degree from an American university and an article by him described as an "important contribution" was published by the Royal Institute of

December 1962 that he would resign the following year, a marked feeling developed against him even amongst his own party in the Bundestag. That he survived as chancellor was due partly to his skill in preserving a certain detachment from Strauss and Höcherl, the main figures on the government side, and to the attitude of his supporters, who took the line sentimentally that he should not be allowed to fall over such a case. But it was right that he should have been made to commit himself to going. Apart from his contribution to misleading the Bundestag, it was he who bore the responsibility for what went on in his government, and everyone knew that he did not normally interpret this responsibility lightly. After the additional evidence had become available between November 1962 and February 1963, it was clear that Adenauer had condoned and to some extent shared Strauss's arrogance and poor judgment.

When the Profumo scandal broke in England in June 1963, the BBC broadcast a series of reports from foreign capitals about its effect on British prestige. The news from Paris and Washington was depressing. But there was some relief when a statement came from Bonn. In one respect, said the commentator, Britain's reputation had risen: the Germans were impressed that one lie, like Profumo's, before the House of Commons could mean the end of his political career. In his review of Lord Denning's report on the Profumo case Paul Sethe quoted Denning's statement: "The Prime Minister and his colleagues bore the responsibility and no one else. And they were not equal to it."[21] He went on to point out that the prime

---

International Affairs in the most prominent position in their quarterly, *International Affairs*, in April 1965. Such international recognition has naturally been of great value to Strauss in the circumstances. American and British democrats, therefore, must hesitate before reproaching Germans with their cynical attitude in this case.

[21] *Die Zeit*, June 5, 1964.

minister allowed himself a decent interval after the publication of the report and then resigned. Sethe later added that, until the German people had created a living democratic tradition, they must try, as far as possible, to become infected by the British example.

7

The Limitations of Adenauer's Foreign Policy

Although Adenauer's greatest achievements were in the field of foreign affairs, his foreign policy seen as a whole had two serious limitations. In the first place, he pursued a rigid anti-Communist line based on the military strength of the Western alliance, and his diplomacy towards Moscow showed little flexibility or constructive purpose. Secondly, during his last years in power he partially undid, under de Gaulle's influence, some of his own great work for the integration of Europe.

Immediately after the war anti-communism in Western Germany became, in American terms, a bipartisan policy. Before the split between the Soviet Union and the West, which took place in 1947 and 1948, the Social Democrats in the Western zones under Schumacher's leadership made the vital decision, in contrast to their colleagues in the Soviet zone, that they would not co-operate with the communists. The decision had the support of the great majority of West Germans, many of whom had had personal experience of communism in action, either as soldiers on the Eastern front, prisoners of war, or refugees from Germany's former eastern territories. But, whereas the Social Democrats under Schumacher were not prepared to commit themselves rigidly to the West, Adenauer revealed over the years a fixity of purpose and attitude in his opposition to communism which exceeded that of his Western allies.

In fact, Adenauer found in communism an enemy against which he could gather support for his policies. In a sense it even simplified the process of government for him. Just as Bismarck could rally his fellow countrymen by referring to the French desire for vengeance, William II could point in turn to the jealousy of France or of Britain, and Hitler could exploit the dangers of Bolshevism and the "eternal Jew," so Adenauer referred repeatedly to the aggressive designs of world communism and raised the self-esteem of West Germans by contrasting their own social conditions with those obtaining under Marxist totalitarianism. His Carolingian conception of Europe brought an end to frontier rivalry with France but led at the same time to a revival of the concept of Germany as the frontier land of Western culture. In a declaration of policy in October 1962, at the beginning of his last year as chancellor, he made statements which would have been more appropriate before the death of Stalin, before the twenty-second congress of the Soviet Communist Party, and before Great Britain and the United States, under Macmillan and Kennedy, had begun their efforts to bring about a détente. "The federal government," he said, "observes the tensions and uncertainty which prevail in all parts of the world as a result of the expansionist urge of the Communist system. . . . So long as the Soviet Union insists on the division of Germany and aims at the subjugation of West Berlin and the neutralization of the Federal Republic, most of the initiatives which we are called upon to make would serve no purpose."

Adenauer's visit to Moscow in September 1955 might appear

to belie this negative view of his policy towards communism. It was indeed a positive gesture towards post-Stalinist Russia. But it was undertaken at a critical moment in Soviet-German relations, just after the Federal Republic had joined NATO, and with certain specific and limited objectives on the German side.

On June 7, 1955 the Soviet government invited Adenauer to visit Moscow to discuss the resumption of diplomatic, economic, and cultural relations between the two countries. After some hesitation Adenauer decided to accept, adding that he wished also to discuss the questions of reunification and of the large numbers of German prisoners of war and civilians who had been detained in the Soviet Union since 1945. The visit took place during the second week in September, and Adenauer was accompanied by a number of cabinet colleagues and by members of the Bundestag including several Social Democrats.

He did not go to the Soviet Union intending to resume diplomatic relations. Some of his closest advisers, including Herr von Brentano, his foreign minister, were opposed to his doing so. After several days of very hard bargaining, however, the main results of the negotiations were a Soviet undertaking to repatriate some of the detained Germans and an agreement to resume diplomatic relations, which Adenauer made clear did not imply any recognition of the existing territorial situation or of the "German Democratic Republic." Some 10,000 prisoners of war were in fact freed during the following months, and diplomatic relations were resumed early in 1956. These arrangements were a victory for humanity, which no doubt paid dividends in the elections of 1957 as well. They also led to the opening up of channels of communication, which might prove valuable in an emergency, however bad the day-to-day relations between the two countries remained.

The main purpose of the Soviet government in inviting Adenauer to Moscow was to sow distrust within the Western alliance and, if possible, detach the Federal Republic from its new allegiance as a member of NATO. By skilfully contrived incidents and well-managed publicity the impression was given that relations between the Soviet hosts and their visitors were much more cordial than was actually the case. In the interval at a gala performance of the Bolshoi Ballet one of the Soviet leaders suddenly stretched out both hands towards Adenauer, a gesture which he could hardly refuse, and the cameras were already trained in the right direction. It was also discovered from Globke's passport that he would be celebrating his birthday in Moscow, and Khrushchev insisted on drinking *Brüderschaft* with him, a ceremony associated in Germany with a pledge between intimate friends. Yet Adenauer himself, on the whole, maintained a cool dignity throughout the visit, which reflected much more accurately the lack of progress on the fundamental issue of German reunification. When the Soviet government sent as their first ambassador to Bonn Mr. Zorin, who had been in Prague at the time of the Communist coup d'état in 1948, he was treated with embarrassing coolness by German society.[1]

The SPD repeatedly reproached Adenauer with missing a possible chance of reunification in the spring of 1952. On the 10th of March Stalin sent a note to the three Western powers suggesting that a German peace treaty should be concluded without delay, that the four occupying powers should withdraw their forces within a year of its ratification, that a united Germany should be allowed to have its own national forces for defence purposes, but that it should not be permitted to enter into any coalition or military alliance against any power which had taken part in the war against Germany. In a further note on the 9th of April the Soviet government mentioned the possi-

---

[1] This account of the Moscow visit is based largely on the writer's conversations with Adenauer and three of his closest advisers during the visit.

bility of holding free all-German elections very soon, and Soviet commentaries on the proposals referred repeatedly to the need for establishing Germany as a "united, peace-loving, and democratic state." At the time the Federal Republic and the Western powers were engaged in negotiations for setting up the European Defence Community. A draft treaty had been agreed upon in February and the treaty itself was to be signed on the 27th of May. It was characteristic of Soviet tactics to make a tempting offer to the Federal Republic at a time when its negotiations with the West were prospering. A similar offer was made in February 1955 between the negotiation and the ratification of the Paris treaties. Neither the Western powers nor Adenauer, however, allowed themselves to be deceived or distracted, the powers putting forward a counter-proposal that a UN commission should investigate conditions in both parts of Germany regarding the feasibility of holding free elections, a suggestion which the Soviet government was almost bound to refuse.

It is most unlikely, therefore, that any opportunity for reunification on satisfactory terms was missed in 1952. Theodor Eschenburg has pointed out that as the population of the Federal Republic was three times that of the Soviet zone, the result of "free all-German elections" could be foreseen, and it was a result which Stalin would not have been prepared to accept.[2] Moreover, the expression "united, peace-loving, and democratic state" which the Communists used to describe the proposed liberated Germany was precisely the one they applied to the Soviet zone of Germany and the East European satellite states. On the whole, the SPD itself after viewing the episode retrospectively, modified its reproaches and maintained that it was an opportunity for negotiations and for testing Soviet inten-

[2] See the excerpt from "Die deutsche Frage—Verfassungsprobleme der Wiedervereinigung" in H.-A. Jacobsen and O. Stenzl, *Deutschland und die Welt*, pp. 167–8.

tions rather than an opportunity for a settlement that had been missed.[3]

In fact, no strong or clear case can be made against Adenauer's policy towards communism up to 1955. Until then flexibility on his part might have jeopardized the realization of his main objective, which was Germany's acceptance into the Western alliance. Stalin retained control of Soviet policy until his death in March 1953, and it was not until Khrushchev's visit to Yugoslavia and his apology to Tito in the spring of 1955 that it became clear that a change was taking place in the Soviet leadership's attitude towards other Communist countries. Khrushchev's denunciation of Stalin in his secret speech of February 1956 and Gomulka's successful defiance of the Soviet leaders the following October revealed a further significant alteration in Moscow's attitude, though it was temporarily obscured by a return in November to Stalinist techniques of suppression during the Hungarian revolution. It was from 1956 onwards, therefore, that Adenauer's inflexible and unimaginative anti-Communist line became less and less defensible.

The chancellor appeared to realize that he ought to make some response to the changing situation in Eastern Europe. He told the writer during the summer of 1957 that nothing should be done to increase the difficulty of Gomulka's position. When Dr. Hans Kroll was appointed West German ambassador to Moscow in the spring of 1958, he impressed on him the need to establish a sensible and constructive relationship with Khrushchev.[4] And in August 1959 he replied to a letter from Khrushchev on the subject of German reunification in a conciliatory and imaginative spirit, which unfortunately, in his actual policy towards the Communist bloc, he virtually never revealed. The reply contained the following passage:

[3] See H. Wehner's statement in Tatsachen Argumente 1963, No. 71, p. 7.
[4] H. Kroll, Die Sowjetische Deutschlandpolitik im Zeichen der Entspannungsbemühungen, p. 16.

I hate neither socialism nor the form of socialism that is usually called communism. Also I hate no state because it is socialist and no man because he is a socialist. I will go further: in certain stages of a nation's development socialism may perhaps be a form of economic development which furthers progress.

Yet, when a series of attempts were made between 1955 and 1960 to reduce the tension and start up negotiations between the Communist bloc and the West, Adenauer showed no signs of a sympathetic response. Various proposals were put forward for demilitarization or "disengagement" in central Europe. At the Geneva conference in 1955 Eden suggested a demilitarized area between East and West, his idea being that such a plan, even on a modest scale, might reduce the risks of a collision between the opposing forces and prepare the way for a wider agreement. In 1957 and 1958 came the two plans proposed by the Polish foreign minister, Rapacki. Gomulka's government, in contrast to the Hungarians, had had the wisdom to purchase a measure of internal freedom at the price of diplomatic loyalty to the Soviet Union. But it was negotiating for substantial loans from the United States, and some measure of détente with the West would have accorded with the spirit of the new Polish regime. Rapacki's proposals were a genuine Polish initiative, though they could scarcely have been made without Soviet support. His first plan suggested the creation of a zone in central Europe from which all nuclear weapons and installations for launching them would be removed. The second plan, which was devised to meet British and other objections, proposed that the main aim should be attained in two stages and that in the second stage the reduction of conventional arms was to be carried out at the same time as the removal of nuclear weapons. The proposals received a warm welcome in Scandinavia, and the British government gave them careful consideration before replying with reasoned objections from the

Western point of view. A third attempt to reduce tension was Macmillan's twelve-day visit to the Soviet Union in February 1959 to make a "reconnaissance," as he called it, of the Soviet attitude. At the end of the visit the British and Soviet leaders issued a communique in which they reverted to the idea of disengagement and agreed on the usefulness of studying "some method of limitation of forces and weapons, both conventional and nuclear, in an agreed area of Europe."

To all these attempts Adenauer responded with coldness and deep suspicion. He appeared to believe that any East–West negotiations that did take place could only be at the Federal Republic's expense. The British prime minister's visit to Moscow especially caused him great annoyance. He accused Macmillan of reviving and favouring the Rapacki plan in order to win votes in the British general election the following autumn, a procedure on the chancellor's part very reminiscent of a parson's tendency to preach against sins to which he is himself most susceptible.

Adenauer proclaimed publicly on many occasions that Germany's only hope of reunification was dependent on the Federal Republic's establishing a position of strength as a member of the Western alliance. He also admitted that reunification could only come about as part of a general détente.[5] The logical result of these two assertions was that the West, and the Federal Republic in particular, should work towards negotiations from strength with the Soviet Union in order to bring about a détente. Yet Adenauer not only failed to make the necessary efforts but suspected and disapproved of such efforts as were made in this direction by his allies.

In December 1955 the Western German foreign minister, Herr von Brentano, announced the so-called Hallstein Doctrine, by which Bonn refused to maintain diplomatic relations with any state that formally recognized the "German Democratic

[5] To the writer during the summer of 1957.

Republic." Adenauer adhered steadily to this doctrine throughout the remainder of his chancellorship. It meant that the Federal Republic could establish no official relations with the
Communist states of Eastern Europe, and, when the devia-
tionist Tito recognized the "German Democratic Republic" in
the autumn of 1957, Adenauer at once broke off diplomatic
relations with Yugoslavia. In view of the circumstances in
which the Soviet Union brought its German satellite state into
existence, there was a strict logic in the Hallstein Doctrine. But
the doctrine, together with other aspects of Adenauer's policy
towards the East European Communist states, did more than
anything else to unite the Communist bloc and counteract the
divisive tendencies which by the end of 1956 had already revealed themselves in Yugoslavia, Poland, and Hungary. These
other aspects included, for example, Adenauer's repeated emphasis on the Federal Republic's strength as a member of the
Western alliance, the claims on the 1937 frontiers put forward
by representatives of his government, and his refusal to allow
trade with Eastern Europe except on a cash basis. A well-
known West German journalist expressed the view in 1962
that, if since 1945 such an impenetrable iron curtain had existed between her country and, for example, Norway, France,
and the Benelux countries, as between it and the East European states, then the country's Western neighbours would also
have considered West Germans to be militarists and Nazis.[6]
From a long-term point of view it is very doubtful whether rigid
adherence to the Hallstein Doctrine worked out to Germany's
advantage.

The question of the Oder-Neisse frontier is bound up with
the whole problem of Adenauer's East European policy. After
the Federal Republic's entry into NATO an increasing number
of West Germans came to realize that Soviet strength and their

[6] Marion Gräfin Dönhoff, *Die Bundesrepublik in der Ära Adenauer,*
p. 157.

own government's promise never to use force to modify the existing boundaries[7] made any remaining hopes of regaining the former eastern territories illusory. On one famous occasion in May 1956 even Herr von Brentano, at a lunch in London, gave as his personal opinion that his country might one day have to consider whether to give up the eastern territories in return for reunification with the Soviet zone. For electoral and diplomatic reasons no West German political leader could afford to renounce any claim to the territories publicly. The government's power to do so in the future could best be considered as money in its pocket, or a credit at the bank, which could be used when serious negotiations were started over reunification with the zone. Yet it might have been diplomatically more fruitful had Adenauer been prepared from time to time to jangle the money in his pocket, just to remind his partners in negotiation that it was there, instead of reiterating the contradictory statements that he renounced the use of force and yet looked forward to the eventual return of the eastern territories.

This procedure could only have been used to advantage within the framework of a positive and enterprising policy towards Eastern Europe, which had the aim of penetrating the political, economic, and ideological defences of the Eastern bloc and loosening its coherence. The most distinguished and convincing exponent of such a policy during the early years of the Federal Republic was Ernst Reuter. Reuter approved Adenauer's policy of European integration and the inclusion of Western Germany in the North Atlantic alliance, but he reproached him with not pursuing a more active policy towards communism. Within a few weeks of his death he made the penetrating remark: "The strength of communism lies in the inability of the West to pursue the struggle by political and

[7] See p. 211.

spiritual (*geistige*) means."[8] This is perhaps the most fundamental criticism that can be made of Western policy as a whole
since 1945, and none the less valid because it has exacting
implications. It applied with special force to the Federal Republic, since, so long as Bonn evaded the issue, it meant relinquishing any serious hope of reunification.

Adenauer could clearly not have taken any major political
initiative without full American approval and support. But he
could have been more responsive to the attempts to reduce
tension that have already been mentioned and to the efforts of
his second foreign minister, Dr. Schröder, with a similar purpose; he could have talked less about the strength of the Western alliance and the menace of world communism, at any rate
after Stalin's death; he could have been more circumspect in his
attitude to German revisionism; and, as the Federal Republic
became more prosperous, he could have done more to develop
commercial and financial arrangements with Eastern Europe.
As an example of what might have been done, it has been
suggested that, after Gomulka's return to power, the chancellor
should have proposed a compensation treaty with Poland on
the lines of the treaty with Israel in 1953.

In November 1961 eight respected figures in German public
life signed a joint memorandum, in which they gave their views
on different aspects of government policy at a time when Adenauer's fourth administration was about to take office.[9] The
points they dealt with included foreign policy, defence, social
legislation, and educational reform. With regard to foreign
affairs, they wrote, the government's policy appeared to them to
be too one-sidedly defensive. As the most important examples
of the possibilities of a more active foreign policy they sug-

---

[8] In an interview with the writer during the summer of 1953.

[9] The signatories were: Hellmut Becker, Präses Joachim Beckmann,
Intendant Klaus von Bismarck, Professor Werner Heisenberg, Günter
Howe, Georg Picht, Professor Ludwig Raiser, Professor Carl-Friedrich
Freiherr v. Weizsäcker.

gested "the normalization of political relations with Germany's eastern neighbours," adding that without it a lasting solution of the fundamental problems of German policy was unthinkable. Moreover, the new developments in international politics, which were taking place, offered opportunities for such a normalization. As a start in restoring confidence a number of measures would be necessary, for instance, material compensation, nonaggression pacts, and perhaps a request to Warsaw to permit the return to their homeland of suitable Germans who wished to return. They added that the public recognition of the Oder-Neisse line, within the framework of the comprehensive programme they had outlined, would in their opinion ease relations with Poland to a decided degree, make it easier for the Federal Republic's Western allies to support its other objectives, and deprive the Soviet Union of the possibility of playing off Germany and Poland against each other.[10]

These public-spirited and responsible German citizens were not Left-wing opponents of the government. Politically they stood rather closer to Adenauer than to the opposition. But their country's situation led them to approach its problems in a radical spirit. The world-wide ideological conflict and the problem of relations between communism and the West were more concentrated and less easy to evade in Germany than in Washington, London, Moscow, and Warsaw, because the ideological conflict had divided the inhabitants artificially from their relatives and friends and sometimes from their birthplaces. Thoughtful and courageous Germans therefore had more pressing and personal reasons for taking up the challenge inherent in the situation than citizens of the United States or the Soviet Union. When, in the spring of 1961, Die Zeit initiated discussions with writers and commentators in the Soviet zone, its independent publisher, Dr. Bucerius, who had himself formerly

[10] On this last point the signatories' view was rather optimistic, though the opportunities for playing off would no doubt have been greatly reduced.

been a CDU member of the Bundestag, defended his action by saying: "It is not necessary for us to withdraw behind an intellectual Maginot Line, because our arguments are substantially better than the other side."[11] The tragedy of Adenauer's failure to take up the inherent challenge was due fundamentally to the fact that he thought of the East–West conflict in terms of diplomacy and power, more appropriate to the Second Empire in which he had grown up than to the mid-twentieth century and the age of nuclear armaments. He was not an intellectual nor had he the ability or live democratic convictions to present the better arguments that Dr. Bucerius had in mind. But it is fair to add that most other Western statesmen also failed to take up the challenge, although for different reasons.

Adenauer's policy was reflected in his attitude to the different American administrations. His relations with the Eisenhower–Dulles regime became increasingly cordial until the secretary of state's death in the spring of 1959. In particular he established a close rapport with John Foster Dulles personally. The two men had a common viewpoint on the major diplomatic issue facing them, because they shared a deep-rooted hostility to communism, which sprang largely from their religious convictions. As head of the government Adenauer broke with protocol by meeting Dulles at the airport, when he came to Bonn, and during his last visit to Europe referred to him frequently as "my dear friend." Dulles for his part carried his support of Adenauer so far that at a press conference before the 1957 elections he expressed the opinion that if the German voters failed to retain their chancellor it would be "disastrous" to the prospects for German unity. The confidential relationship that was established between the two men was well illustrated two or three years after Dulles's appointment by the answer given to the director of a West German radio station, when he asked his experienced and very well-informed representative in Wash-

[11] Quoted by M. Dönhoff, op. cit., p. 96.

ington who was responsible for German policy, that is to say, who looked after German affairs in the State Department. The answer he received was: "Adenauer."

The situation underwent a great change when Kennedy succeeded Eisenhower in 1961. The new president was much younger than the chancellor and belonged to a generation which Adenauer did not really understand. Moreover he brought with him an intellectual brains trust that applied to current international problems principles and ideas which the chancellor found disturbing. Relations between the Federal Republic and the United States therefore deteriorated rapidly and reached their lowest point since 1949 when Adenauer heard that Kennedy and his secretary of state, Dean Rusk, had been carrying on conversations with the Soviet foreign minister about Germany. Macmillan's visit to Moscow had already aroused Adenauer's suspicions, and he now appeared to believe that any détente between East and West was likely to be at the Federal Republic's expense. In spite of certain errors of judgment on the American side, his fears were largely unjustified, while Kennedy's meeting with Khrushchev in June 1961 and the building of the Berlin Wall in August destroyed any illusions the president may have had about the Soviet attitude. It was most unfortunate however, that, when the United States government had at last begun to take the initiative in its policy towards Berlin, Germany, and Central Europe and to develop constructive ideas on the problems involved, Adenauer should have responded to its efforts with no more than deprecation and distrust. Moreover, his own government had no alternative policy to suggest other than the discredited one of inactivity based on Western military strength.

Adenauer's whole policy towards the Soviet Union and communism had two serious consequences. It did nothing to further a general détente, and, as a result, it brought no nearer the reunification of Germany, although the chancellor said repeatedly that this was one of his main objectives.

These two failures can be attributed less to lack of diplomatic skill on his part than to lack of will combined with the inherent difficulties of the situation. This lack of will was due first to the fact that Adenauer was anti-Communist by conviction and temperament and had an old-fashioned readiness to accept a state of rivalry in international relations as part of the natural order. He had therefore no real inclination or wish to work for a *rapprochement* with the evil men in the Kremlin. Secondly, as a Carolingian he put the French alliance and West European integration before reunion with mainly Prussian territories that had contained before 1933 a substantial socialist element. He pointed out to the French high commissioner in 1954 that he was the only German chancellor who had preferred the unity of Europe to the unity of his own country. Thirdly, as a staunch Catholic he had much less interest than had German Protestants in reunification with the Soviet zone. Before the war North and East Germany had been predominantly Protestant, while the West and South had been mainly Catholic. Catholic influence, therefore, was greater in the Federal Republic than it had been in pre-war Germany or than it was likely to be after reunification.

In an article he contributed to *Die Zeit* during the summer of 1952 Adenauer expressed his views on reunification frankly.[12] It was entitled "Our Two Peoples" and dealt with the problem of Franco-German relations. In it he compared the urgent need for an alliance with France with the desire for reunification and came to the following conclusion:

It is better, and in any case politically preferable, to do what is possible, instead of dreaming about what is at present impossible and thus failing to do what is at present possible.

[12] In the issue dated June 26.

At the beginning and the end of Adenauer's chancellorship two leading thinkers on international affairs also put forward rational arguments for postponing the reunification issue, although they did not share the chancellor's personal attitude towards the problem. In April 1950 Marion Gräfin Dönhoff, one of the outstanding members of the editorial staff of *Die Zeit*, wrote an article in *Foreign Affairs* entitled "Germany Puts Freedom before Unity." The writer herself came from East Prussia and later became a strong advocate of a more flexible policy towards Eastern Europe. But in this article she wrote:

. . . the majority of people in Western Germany realize by now that they cannot have both unity and freedom. For the time being we must choose either the one or the other. Faced with this alternative it seems more opportune to be content with freedom now, and to work for unity later, rather than to begin by striving for a unity which can be gained only under Russian domination, and to renounce freedom for ever.

In November 1962, during a lecture at the Hebrew University in Jerusalem, the president of the Bundestag, Dr. Gerstenmaier, a leading Protestant politician, whose attitude towards reunification therefore differed a good deal from Adenauer's, pointed out that German foreign policy had been determined by a clearly justified order of priorities. Freedom, and with it solidarity with the free world, came first; peace, and with it the renunciation of any aggressive or revisionist war, second; and national unity, as a logical result, third.

Many thoughtful Germans with an understanding of the international situation accepted on rational grounds the inevitability of postponing reunification. Others acquiesced in the postponement for less praiseworthy reasons: because they were prosperous and contented as things were, because they were not much concerned with the lot of their fellow countrymen in the Soviet zone, or because they feared the economic and social effects of joining up with territories that had been inured to communism. Adenauer's attitude to reunification was echoed by these people, though for reasons of convenience rather than of conviction. A private investigator into West German public opinion in 1953 came to the conclusion that for selfish reasons there was a widespread lack of interest in the Soviet zone and in reunification. To say so openly was "not done." Everybody in the Federal Republic had to be in favour of reunification, "as one has to be against sin." But many were so in a rather luke-warm fashion.

This wide acquiescence in postponing the issue accounted for the fact that Adenauer could win successive elections without doing much more than pay lip service to the cause. But the lip service he paid was reiterated and emphatic. There were many other Germans who were deeply concerned about the subject of reunification and about the fate of their relatives, their friends, and their homelands in the Soviet zone. During the latter years of Adenauer's regime these people became increasingly disillusioned with his policy. The disillusionment came to a head with the building of the Berlin Wall in August 1961, which brought an end to the already restricted communication between the two parts of the city and made it far more difficult for inhabitants of the zone to escape to the West.

Nothing had done so much damage to Adenauer's reputation since his acceptance and rejection of the presidential candidature in 1959. The wall seemed to symbolize the complete failure of his reunification policy. It also made rather ineffectual the human sympathy he had so often expressed for the inhabitants of the Soviet zone. For, of the 3.6 million who had escaped to the West since the beginning of 1949, over a million and a half had come via West Berlin, and this channel was now virtually closed. The disillusionment in West Berlin went particularly deep and was intensified by the chancellor's failure to visit the city in its emergency until nine days after the wall had gone up. He was even two days later than Vice-President, now President Johnson, who made a special journey from the United States to express his country's sympathy and moral support.

Under Adenauer's chancellorship West Berlin received very substantial aid from the federal government: from 1951 until the end of 1962 the subsidies and loans provided exceeded 17 milliard marks in value.[13] In spite of its isolated position it became Germany's greatest industrial city, and its production considerably exceeded the prewar level. It was encouraged also to consider itself the real capital of the country; starting in 1955 the Bundestag met there annually for several years running, and the Bundesrat followed its example a year later, while the Bellevue Palace in West Berlin was rebuilt to serve as a residence for the federal president. Yet, so far as Adenauer was concerned, these measures were the result of political calculation rather than of personal choice or conviction. He did not, like Ernst Reuter, consider Berlin to be a symbol for the freedom of the human spirit. On the contrary, he associated it rather with the Prussian tradition which he disliked, and he preferred the country's capital to be in his own Rhineland, where it served as a window opening onto the West.

The second serious limitation of Adenauer's foreign policy resulted from his relationship with de Gaulle, after the general's return to power in June 1958.

Until the two men met a few months later, Adenauer at a distance had disliked and feared de Gaulle, and he was greatly worried by his return. Not surprisingly de Gaulle had said some harsh things about Germany in the past. Moreover he had worked to bring about developments which Adenauer resented. In his memoirs, he wrote that a decentralized Reich was "the first condition for preventing Germany from reverting to its evil

[13] *Regierung Adenauer 1949–1963*, p. 491.

ways,"[14] and during 1948 and 1949 he had used his influence to ensure the federal character of the new West German state. Even worse in Adenauer's eyes, a few years later he had been largely responsible behind the scenes for the rejection of the European Defence Community.

The wish for a meeting originated with de Gaulle. Adenauer himself was at first reluctant to agree to the suggestion. When in the end a meeting was decided upon through diplomatic channels, Adenauer gave way in consenting to go to France, and de Gaulle in allowing his guest to visit his own house rather than going to Paris. In view of the developments to which the meeting finally led there was some irony in the fact that Macmillan played a part, perhaps a decisive part in persuading Adenauer to make the journey.

Lord Avon remarks in his memoirs that de Gaulle is at his best as a host. When Adenauer visited Colombey-les-deux-Eglises in September 1958, de Gaulle certainly exerted all his charm to win him over, and with complete success. Adenauer was impressed and captivated by de Gaulle himself, by the reticence of Madame de Gaulle, by the old house, the family retainers, and the atmosphere of solid tradition that pervaded the place. Those who knew Adenauer well and met him soon afterwards are agreed that the visit transformed him. It made him a happy man, who had found someone he could understand and talk to; Ulysses after he had heard the siren's voice, as one diplomatist told him. To Adenauer it was a source of special satisfaction that the friend he had found and the contact he had established would further the cause of Franco-German understanding which was so close to his heart.

Although the two men were in some ways very different they had certain qualities in common: they were patriots; they were Catholics; they had a strong sense of European tradition; and they were authoritarian by temperament. In the first volume

[14] Vol. III, p. 50.

of his memoirs de Gaulle relates how he set up a National Committee for Fighting France in September 1941. He then describes its working as follows:

No important step was ever taken without the committee having deliberated on it first.

I always received valuable assistance and loyal support from the National Committee as a collective organ, as also from each of its members. . . . In the last resort, indeed, after he had given me his views, no National Commissioner disputed my final word.

If this passage does not quite describe the working of Adenauer's cabinet, when he was at the height of his authority as chancellor, it at least indicates a method of working which Adenauer would have found very congenial. It no doubt contributed to his sense of affinity with de Gaulle that the general had this simple and soldierly conception of committee procedure.

Adenauer's final surrender to de Gaulle in January 1963 cannot, however, be attributed solely to their personal relationship. There were a number of other circumstances which contributed to this retrograde and tragic result.

In the first place, Adenauer did not really understand the Anglo-Saxon countries,[15] and a fundamental suspicion of their leaders' motives, though allayed by American generosity, admiration for Dulles, and Eden's diplomacy in 1954, was never far beneath the surface of his mind. In particular he could not grasp the concern of British statesmen for public opinion and tended to attribute the resulting uncertainties to sheer unreliability. Personally it is probable that he never quite forgave the British for his dismissal from Cologne in 1945, in spite of its

[15] It is not strictly correct to describe the United States as an Anglo-Saxon country; but the Germans usually do, and the best known names in American federal politics, on the whole, justify the somewhat misleading generalization.

unintended influence on his future career. As a European he resented the fact that the ultimate decision on peace or war lay with the United States, and that Britain, as America's closest friend, exerted a corresponding influence on its policy.[16] He was particularly sensitive on this point after the Camp David discussions between Eisenhower and Macmillan early in 1960 and made the remark that was much quoted in Germany at the time: "These Britons should learn that they can no longer run the continent. Germany and France are the leaders of the continent."[17] Adenauer's misunderstanding and distrust were accentuated, as has been seen, by his dislike of the new course pursued by Kennedy and his advisers and by his fear that the efforts of Macmillan and Kennedy to bring about a détente might result in a sacrifice of German interests.

De Gaulle shared Adenauer's feelings as a European, though for a different combination of reasons. He also distrusted the Anglo-Saxon countries and resented the extent of American influence. But, in addition, he had never quite reconciled himself psychologically to France's collapse in 1940, and the dominant influence on his attitude was an over-sensitive patriotism, from which Adenauer was relatively free. He combined a magnanimous recognition of British and American achievement in the war with bitter memories of his own experiences with the Allied leaders. As a traditionalist with a strong sense of history his feeling of rivalry with Britain was rooted deeply in the past—as one perceptive German suggested, if the English had not burnt Joan of Arc, Britain might have been a member of the Common Market in 1963.

Secondly, after his presidential candidature in 1959 Adenauer became increasingly conscious of his declining position at

[16] Adenauer described the Anglo-American relationship to the writer in these terms during the summer of 1964.

[17] Quoted by M. Dönhoff in Die Bundesrepublik in der Ära Adenauer, p. 134.

home; the death of John Foster Dulles and the election of Kennedy caused him to be out of harmony with the American administration; and the weakened position of Christian Democracy in Italy deprived him of a source of moral support which he had enjoyed during his early years as chancellor. As has been seen, the *Spiegel* affair in October 1962 brought his reputation in the Federal Republic to its lowest ebb, and, when he re-formed his government in December, the FDP made it a condition of their participation that he should resign the chancellorship the following autumn. Under these conditions he felt more and more that the one man he could understand and trust was de Gaulle, and he came to believe that the best way of setting the seal on his career was through a formal confirmation of the Franco-German alliance. He distrusted, in some respects, the attitude of his own new foreign minister, Dr. Schroeder. The one way, therefore, of making the Franco-German *rapprochement* definite was to take the necessary action while he was himself still in office.

Thirdly, in a series of meetings between Adenauer and de Gaulle between the summer of 1958 and the end of 1962, the two statesmen strengthened their personal ties and sought to establish common points of view on European and North Atlantic problems. Subsequent events have shown that in their discussions Adenauer was more sincere and also more naive than his partner. De Gaulle, however, exploited to the full his great skill as a diplomatist and the personal influence he had recently established over Adenauer.

The first meeting took place at Bad Kreuznach in the Palatinate. Its main significance was as a gesture on the part of de Gaulle in choosing Germany for his first visit abroad after the referendum approving the Fifth Republic. On subsequent occasions the differences in attitude of the two men became clear, particularly in July 1960 at the Château de Rambouillet. There de Gaulle made clear that he was dissatisfied with certain aspects of the Common Market and NATO and objected to the important part being played by the United States in the defence of Europe. Adenauer appears to have played down his misgivings, defended the American role, and pleaded for a united Western front in face of the Soviet Union. He did not, however, prevent his host from expressing his views on these controversial subjects at a press conference a few weeks later. De Gaulle's technique with Adenauer was, while adhering to his own convictions, to soothe him with general assurances and overhwelm him with hospitality and impressive ceremonial.

In June 1961 President Lübke paid a state visit to France, and he was followed by his chancellor in July 1962. During his own visit Adenauer was first received in Paris. He and de Gaulle then witnessed a joint parade of French and German troops in the battle area of the two world wars and attended high mass together in Reims cathedral, which had been rebuilt after destruction by the Germans in the First World War. The whole programme was a symbol of reconciliation conceived in the grand manner. Two months later de Gaulle paid a state visit to Germany, and was received wherever he went with the greatest enthusiasm, the visit giving Germans an opportunity to indulge their propensity for hero worship and demonstrate their desire for reconciliation with France at the same time. In October Adenauer paid another visit to Paris.

By the end of 1962, therefore, in spite of the differences in attitude of the two national leaders, the moment was diplomatically ripe for a formalization of the understanding between France and Western Germany. Adenauer, in addition to his knowledge that time was running out, had the old man's tendency to simplify issues and the tired man's tendency to follow inclination rather than reason. Compared with the complex problem of European integration a Franco-German treaty was simple to grasp and emotionally satisfying. Moreover, it would be a gesture of independence and a form of national insurance in face of the disturbing experiments of Kennedy and his advisers. For de Gaulle it would be a method of capitalizing his personal ascendancy over Adenauer and strengthening France's position in relation to the United States and the Soviet Union.

Adenauer arranged to go to Paris in January 1963 to sign such a treaty. But a few days before he arrived a development occurred which completely altered the character of the proposed alliance from the points of view of the two countries involved, if not from the personal viewpoint of de Gaulle, who knew his own mind on such matters, if no one else did.

The previous summer a substantial majority of the French National Assembly had signed a declaration expressing their wish "to see France commit herself to the path of European unity," and proposing that the various organizations of the European community should be strengthened and that a European Assembly should be elected by universal suffrage. De Gaulle disapproved of their attitude, and he decided as a test of popular support for himself to hold a referendum on a proposal that the president of the republic should in future be elected by universal suffrage. He won the referendum in October and the parliamentary elections which followed in November. Buoyed up by these successes, by the ending of the Algerian war the previous spring, and by his reception in Germany, he decided to take a strong line on the question of European integration.

At a press conference on the 14th of January he announced what amounted to his veto on Great Britain's entry into the Common Market. Three days later the French government demanded the indefinite postponement of the negotiations with Britain and persisted in its attitude at the end of the month in spite of protests and attempts at conciliation by the other five members. De Gaulle's negative attitude towards further progress in European integration was already well known.

This meant that, if Adenauer now signed a bilateral treaty

with France without making conditions, he would be repudiating the progressive concept of European integration which, in spite of periodic doubts about Britain's role, he had, on the whole, supported steadily, since his first welcome of Robert Schuman's Plan in May 1950.[18] He would in fact, be replacing the concept by a new emphasis on the Franco-German relationship, in face of protests from the four other EEC members and the disapproval of most West Germans.[19] Nevertheless, Adenauer signed the treaty on January 22, 1963. He even embraced the statuesque figure, who, from a lingering feeling of nationalist frustration and a romantic sense of history, was endeavouring with great skill and finesse to lead Europe, as well as his own country, backwards.[20] The seal was thus set on a great process of reconciliation in circumstances ominous for Europe's immediate future and for the future of the reconciliation itself.

The treaty, which went into force the following July, provided for co-operation between the two countries on all important questions of foreign policy, defence, education, and youth. It made arrangements for meetings between "the heads of state and government," "whenever necessary, and in principle at least twice a year"; for quarterly meetings between the Ministers of Defence; and for more frequent periodic meetings between the Chiefs of Staff, the ministers and officials responsible

[18] In spite of his doubts about Britain, in his declaration of policy before the Bundestag on October 9, 1962, after referring to the desire of Britain, Ireland, Norway and Denmark to join EEC and the negotiations regarding their entry, he said: "I welcome the fact that these countries are turning towards Europe, and I wish success to all these negotiations."
[19] The SPD, as well as many of Adenauer's own supporters, favoured the strengthening and extension of the European community.
[20] The real tragedy of de Gaulle's career is that this subconscious frustration has survived the logical justification for it, de Gaulle's own achievements having brought an end to the justification. In the first chapter of his memoirs de Gaulle admits his sentimental approach to his country's history and destiny.

for education and youth, and the senior officials in the Foreign Offices dealing with political, economic, and cultural affairs.

A number of Adenauer's closest advisers were disillusioned and deeply disappointed by his policy and course of action in January 1963. This was scarcely surprising, because his close advisers had, on the whole, been supporters of his policy. They felt now that he was being false to his own vision of an integrated Western Europe that might include Britain and remain in close alliance with the United States. M. Spaak, whose appreciation of Adenauer has already been quoted, wrote in an article published the following summer, with reference to de Gaulle's press conference on the 14th of January:

What occurred that day was something much more significant than the mere dooming of negotiations between Great Britain and the European Community. It was, in plain fact, an attack on the Atlantic Alliance and the European Community—an attack, that is, on the two most significant achievements of the free world since the end of the Second World War.[21]

Yet efforts after the 14th of January to persuade Adenauer to postpone his visit to Paris or to make conditions for signing the treaty both failed.

Adenauer, with his strange susceptibility to de Gaulle's spell, does not seem to have tried to impose any conditions, although he very probably could have done so, had he wished. During his visit to Germany in September 1963 de Gaulle was seriously disturbed when President Lübke told him that the German people were in favour of an integrated Europe that would include Britain and remarked that he might have to change his whole policy.[22] Yet Adenauer made no attempt to follow up on this point. He merely obtained de Gaulle's agreement to put

[21] From the article "Hold Fast" in *Foreign Affairs*, July 1963.
[22] The writer was told this by a member of de Gaulle's party during the visit.

forward fresh proposals for Britain's entry after an interval. The conditions were left indefinite, and de Gaulle in the end refused to act.

The chancellor shared the president's doubts about Britain's readiness to join the Common Market, though for rather different reasons. More concerned as he was with the success of integration he feared more than de Gaulle the fresh difficulties to which Britain's entry might give rise. But they both failed to appreciate the importance of the difficult decision Macmillan had taken. Moreover, de Gaulle's veto was in conflict with a clause in the Rome treaties providing for the entry into the European communities of other countries which wished to join. De Gaulle's real attitude was revealed when he proceeded to make further difficulties within the Common Market, even without the additional complication of Britain's presence.

As regards the Franco-German treaty, de Gaulle's interpretation of some of its main provisions must have been bitter pills for Adenauer to swallow, even when administered by so fascinating a physician and accompanied by soothing drafts of elegantly phrased assurances. On a number of major diplomatic and military matters the consultations provided for in the treaty did not take place; for example, when France decided to recognize Communist China or to withdraw its naval officers from NATO. The contrast between the terms of the treaty and subsequent French policy and between de Gaulle's statements on European co-operation and his own actions[23] recall the contrast between some of his references to Algeria in 1958, at the time of his return to power, and the policy he actually adopted a few years later.

From the point of view of Adenauer's record and reputation as a statesman the tragedy of his surrender to de Gaulle

[23] Adenauer was no doubt reassured by his statement at a press conference on May 15, 1962, that Western Europe must "organize itself politically" in order to ensure the survival of the economic community.

was that it partly undid the greatest achievement of his early years as chancellor. As he himself had said, he had put the unity of Western Europe before the unity of his own country. And now he had sacrificed progress in European integration to his friendship for de Gaulle and a bilateral treaty with France, although, as a German journalist wrote, an agreement with France in 1963 was of no more importance than a treaty between Bavaria and Prussia in 1913.[24]

Nevertheless Adenauer could not entirely undo all that he had previously achieved: it was the superstructure of the building which he damaged, not its foundations. The extent of the harm that he did cannot yet be assessed. But there is irony in the fact that Erhard and Schröder, who, as chancellor and foreign minister, took over the main burden in foreign affairs, were colleagues of whom Adenauer did not much approve. This was fitting and not too severe retribution for an octogenarian's mistake, for his successors may still avert some of its more serious potential results.

[24] M. Dönhoff, Die Bundesrepublik in der Ära Adenauer, p. 128.

8
Looking to the Future

It would have been better for Adenauer's reputation had he resigned the chancellorship some time between his great electoral victory in 1957 and the spring of 1959, when he made his ill-starred venture as a presidential candidate. He would have thus avoided his last rather painful years in office, when he was losing his grip as a statesman and when his political skill was exerted in order to remain in power rather than to further great purposes. The limitations of his foreign policy would have been less apparent, and he would, above all, have avoided submission to de Gaulle.

When he finally gave up office, it would have been better also had he made, like Churchill, a clean break with politics. The last phase of his political career, when he no longer led the government but retained the chairmanship of the CDU, was unworthy of his great period as chancellor. He made difficulties for his successor and, at the same time, by dividing its councils, reduced the influence of the West German government in international affairs. The magic of his rose garden proved insufficient to counteract the spell cast over him by long years of political power, with consequences harmful to his country as well as tragic for himself.

Bismarck and Adenauer, Germany's two greatest statesmen

of the last hundred years, were both unable to reconcile themselves to loss of power gracefully. Neither of them could tolerate really able and independent politicians in their immediate environment, and neither did anything to train and pave the way for an acceptable successor. Bismarck overrated the ability of his mediocre and boorish son. Adenauer seems to have had in mind as a suitable heir the wise and conciliatory but strictly limited Heinrich Krone or the able and respected but politically inexperienced Franz Etzel, who was brought back in 1957 from the High Authority of the ECSC to become finance minister and then given little encouragement or opportunity to develop the public stature necessary for a future chancellor. Both statesmen, after relinquishing the chancellorship, criticized their successors with a lack of magnanimity surprising in view of their past achievements; Adenauer from his own platform as the government party's chairman, and Bismarck, in a more Olympian and often constructive manner, from his country estate.

On balance, Adenauer achieved much for Germany, for Europe, and for the Western world. In his foreign policy he restored his country's links with some of its best traditions as well as winning for it recognition and, owing to its recent past, somewhat grudging admiration from the international community. Mazzini considered a cosmopolitan who talked of duty to humanity and neglected the nation comparable to one who tells a man to climb a ladder and takes away the rungs. Western Germany's allies saw in Adenauer a statesman who thought in national terms but recognized that he had supra-national aspirations appropriate to the age. He played a major part in setting up the organizations that have contributed most to European integration and in so doing gave a new ideal to the younger generation of Germans: through his own partial defection from the European cause he weakened but did not destroy this achievement. By associating his country with the Atlantic

Alliance, he increased the economic and military strength of the West and helped to set a limit to communist encroachment.

By his internal policy he created the conditions necessary for economic recovery and was thus largely responsible for the country's subsequent prosperity. He convinced the West German people that a democratic constitution can be made to work effectively, and his own shortcomings as a democratic leader have provoked a positive and hopeful reaction within his own party as well as in the opposition. Even the tarnishing of his name during his last years in office had its advantages, because it made clear some of the disadvantages of chancellor-democracy.

In an article in Der Spiegel, when Adenauer resigned, Rudolf Augstein generously concluded:

Whoever condemns Chancellor Adenauer's methods in internal policy, whoever considers his foreign policy to have failed in what it aimed at, and to have been sterile, where it lacked aims, can nevertheless, in view of the transience of human endeavour, take off his hat to him, because 'In magnis et voluisse sat est.'[1]

Adenauer's place in history cannot yet be assessed. It will largely depend on developments during the next half century or so; on whether German and European statesmen can rescue European integration from the set-backs it has recently suffered, and on whether the West German people and its leaders are able, in Karl Jaspers' words, "to breathe democratic life" into "the formal democracy" that the country was given in 1949.

There is a strong accidental element in all political developments and in the process by which a statesman's historical

[1] "On the great issues it is enough to have desired the right ends." See the article, Konrad Adenauer und seine Epoche, in the issue of October 9, 1963.

achievement comes to be determined. For nearly fifty years Bismarck was regarded as the founder of a new German Empire with great promise for the future. Now he stands out in the history of his country and his continent as a titanic but myopic and rather tragic figure; the symbol of an age that has passed rather than an architect who built for the future. If the Emperor Frederick had not died of cancer in 1888, if his heir had not been William II, and if German statesmen during the next forty years had been men of different quality and character, it is probable that the positive aspects of Bismarck's policy would not have become the victims of its weaknesses.[2] In the case of Adenauer, much will depend on the record of his successors and on the response of the German people to the challenge of his legacy; on whether they set out with determination to correct its weaknesses and develop its constructive aspects. They have one great advantage over their forbears, because, while Bismarck, like Napoleon, cultivated his legend during retirement, Adenauer destroyed a legend in the making, before he retired.

Yet evidence is already available which gives some indication of the trends in postwar German society and of the probable social and political attitudes of certain sections of it in the future. In conclusion, therefore, it is perhaps appropriate to consider some of these trends; the reactions, especially of the younger generation, to Adenauer's methods and policies; and the developments which are in consequence likely in the future.

As has been seen, Adenauer's attitude to foreign affairs had two different aspects. It was based on the traditional loyalties and sympathies of a Catholic Rhinelander with a strong sense of history. Yet it was strongly influenced also by the sensitivity of a European to the plight of the continent after two catastrophic wars, and the views on European integration to which this sensitivity gave rise came close to those of the new genera-

[2] See p. 10.

tion who were less concerned with the past than with the clear requirements of the age in which they lived.

It was due much more to the French president than to the German chancellor himself that Adenauer's foreign policy culminated in a bilateral Franco-German treaty at the expense of his own broader concept of European integration. The fact that he was himself a product of the pre-1914 age made this development more acceptable to him than to the German people as a whole, whom he had done so much to educate in a European point of view. But they did not allow themselves to be led astray by their teacher's lapse. There is plenty of evidence to suggest that the idea of an integrated Europe makes a deeper emotional appeal to most young Germans than does a narrower loyalty to their own country, just as a greater attraction is exerted on many young Englishmen by an international than by a purely patriotic cause.

It is highly probable therefore that the generation of Germans for whom 1945 was really a beginning, rather than the start of a sad and perplexing epilogue to their lives, will do their best to build on the foundations Adenauer laid. Their success or failure will not rest upon their efforts alone. Progress in European integration will depend largely upon the attitude and the exertions of other European countries, especially France and Great Britain. Progress towards German reunification will depend primarily on the policies of the United States and the Soviet Union and the resulting development of relations between the two main power blocs. But it is unlikely that the younger generation of Germans will follow the example of Adenauer's foreign policy in its two weaker aspects. On the contrary, it is probable that the more enterprising of them will react against it, difficult and challenging as a more constructive attitude in each case will be.[3]

[3] The less enterprising of them will, I think, tend to do and say nothing, rather than to follow Adenauer's discredited course of combining an inflexible anti-Communist policy with the expression of vain hopes of reunification.

As regards internal affairs political apathy, for a number of reasons, was common in the Federal Republic from 1945 until 1963. It was due, in the first place, to a reaction against the Nazi era: to disillusionment with a false political creed; to a desire to make good personal losses by concentrating on work; and to a wish to avoid committing oneself a second time to the wrong cause. For some years after the war the most frequently quoted saying in Germany was, "A burnt child shuns the fire." Throughout Adenauer's chancellorship the pursuit of material prosperity was the main aim of most West Germans, at first as a matter of necessity, and later because it proved rewarding or as an end in itself. Basic necessities having been acquired, wealth was sought after as a means of acquiring amenities, luxuries, and, not least, social status. The *ohne mich* attitude was applicable not only to service in the new army but to political and social responsibilities of all kinds. Most citizens expected more from the state than they were prepared to give it in return.

Adenauer's rather indifferent and sometimes negative attitude towards democracy itself, the rule of law, freedom of expression, and the educational problem, which have been dealt with in previous chapters, reflected the indifference of the majority of West Germans towards these questions. They were naturally matters of concern to the more politically minded citizens and to certain specific social categories, for example, lawyers, journalists, teachers, and students. From time to time also a gathering subconscious interest in such problems amongst broader sections of the community rose to the surface, under the right leadership, and revealed itself on an impressive scale, for example, during the *Spiegel* affair. Yet, on the whole, although old loyalties, such as belief in Hitler or a narrow and assertive nationalism, were progressively discarded, they were not usually replaced by convictions of comparable strength. A democratic constitution and membership of the Western alliance were widely recognized as desirable, but the majority of those who accepted them did so without any deep emotional commitment. It is true that the majority of citizens in other democracies are also non-political. But, whereas in the United States, for example, these people often have fundamentally democratic attitudes and a deep-lying belief in political liberty, the same apathy in Germany, with its non-democratic traditions, has more serious implications.

The chancellor himself made little effort to counteract this apathy. He did a good deal to prevent the revival of the negative attitude to democracy which had been widespread during the Weimar Republic by giving his fellow countrymen efficient government and, for example, by setting up a generously subsidized organization known as the Federal Office for Political Education.[4] But Adenauer and most members of his government made little contribution, either by precept or example, to stimulating in citizens an urge to contribute personally to the democratic vitality of society.[5] So the Federal Republic remained, so far as most people were concerned, in Professor Eschenburg's words "a sleeping democracy."[6]

The real struggle for democracy in Western Germany, therefore, lies in the future, and, in spite of present shortcomings, there are grounds for a measured optimism as to its outcome. In the first place, political stability and prosperity, in spite of the materialism which has accompanied them, provide a firmer foundation for democratic progress than the political and economic uncertainty that prevailed during the greater part of the Weimar period. The Germans have traditionally described themselves as "a people of poets and thinkers." They are more,

[4] It was first called the Federal Office for Service to the Homeland (*Bundeszentrale für Heimatdienst*).

[5] The apathy of young people was illustrated by the following answer given by a youth who was questioned about dictatorship during the summer of 1961: "Dictator? Is that a kind of typewriter?" Walter Jaide, *Dar Verhältnis der Jugend zur Politik*, p. 113.

[6] Eschenburg used the expression in 1952: *Der Beamte in Partei und Parlament*, p. 195.

rather than less susceptible to idealism than other nations, and it is unlikely that they will be content to concentrate indefinitely on the pursuit of greater prosperity. Their main problem is to adjust themselves to the combination of idealism and readiness for compromise which is the key to successful democratic government. Secondly, Adenauer's own example, even from a strictly democratic point of view, was by no means entirely harmful. It reflected his own complex character. If in many ways he was cynical and failed to give a positive lead, there was no cynicism about his absolute rejection of totalitarianism both of the Left and of the Right; and in his attitude towards Israel and towards the whole Nazi legacy he showed dignity and moral courage. He therefore cleared the way for the development of an enlightened minority, which, by combining patience with persistence and self-criticism with self-respect, will have the best chance of leading Germany towards a more vital conception of democracy.

Such an enlightened minority had begun to form even before 1949. It constituted one of the more positive and promising aspects of Adenauer's regime that throughout the period such a minority was able to work on a limited scale and to develop its influence and the variety of its interests. Its membership was to be found rather in academic, intellectual, and ecclesiastical circles than amongst top-level politicians, but it included also politicians, social workers, and educationists, who worked with initiative and imagination in comparatively humble and restricted fields. For the future of German democracy a great deal will depend upon what this minority can accomplish both through their own work and through the force of their example. They will have to deal not only with the problems facing West German society but with the challenges presented by the twentieth century to democracy throughout the world. The following passages from the last speech Friedrich Meinecke delivered might be interpreted as having been specially intended for this minority:[7]

So I ask myself: can our age be called a great age? I venture to say: yes, because today the highest and most sacred values of humanity are at stake: freedom, honour, justice, and the dignity of human personality . . . it is perhaps for many a terrible burden to be living today. But it is also worthwhile to be living today and to be able to fight for the highest human values.

The work done by the enlightened minority in certain fields has already been referred to; for example, in the trade-union movement, in journalism and broadcasting, and in connection with educational reform. In addition to these achievements a great deal was accomplished as a result of individual initiative through a wide variety of voluntary or semi-voluntary moments and organizations, large and small, good examples of which are the religious academies, the adult education movement, and the students' organizations.[8]

In the immediate post-war years the first of the Evangelical Academies were founded. They resulted from the awareness of Protestant leaders of the unequal record of their Church during the Hitler regime and from their frank avowal of the Church's failure to prepare all its members adequately for the National Socialist challenge. The academies were intended as conference centres where, in addition to religious activities, discussions could take place on political, social, or cultural problems of current significance between the social groups most concerned with them. The link between the academies and the military reform movement through Count Baudissin has already been

[7] The speech entitled *Ein Ernstes Wort* is reproduced by F. Meinecke, *Politische Schriften*, pp. 496–7. It was delivered in the Historical Seminar of the Free University of Berlin on Oct. 1, 1951, the day when the Seminar was renamed "The Friedrich Meinecke Institute."

[8] The activities of some of the voluntary organizations are dealt with in more detail in *Democracy in Western Germany*, Ch. XII.

referred to. They were so successful in making Protestants more conscious of their political and social responsibilities[9] that the Catholic Church followed the Evangelical example, though on a smaller scale. The Catholic Academy in Munich particularly became a live discussion centre and exercised a stimulating and liberalizing influence on the traditionally conservative Catholic Church of Bavaria.

After the war the West German adult education movement linked up with the traditions established in Germany before 1933 and was stimulated by Scandinavian and British examples. One of the most encouraging tendencies within the movement was the interest shown in current political and international problems, which grew stronger as the fears and inhibitions that were associated with the Nazi era decreased.

The national union of students and the students' committees in the different universities not only organized numerous activities on democratic lines and so provided practical experience in democratic procedure. They also took a special interest in international relations, arranged exchange visits with other countries, and exerted their influence to combat anti-Semitism, apartheid, and racial prejudice of all kinds.

During the summer of 1958 a voluntary movement was started which revealed unusual enterprise and imagination on the part of the founders. It was called *Aktion Gemeinsinn*, (Campaign to Develop Public Spirit), and its purpose was to stimulate a sense of civic responsibility amongst West German citizens. It set out to organize campaigns from time to time, each of which aimed at increasing the public spirit of citizens in some particular way; for example, by encouraging them to work voluntarily in hospitals; to entertain students from the developing countries at Christmas; to make old people feel

[9] By 1955 there were altogether eighteen Evangelical Academies, including one in West Berlin and four in the Soviet zone, where the Evangelical Church was administratively connected with the Church in Western Germany.

more at home in society; to offer help and first-aid when there was a traffic accident; and to co-operate with the local government in the town or village where they lived. Each campaign was financed entirely by voluntary contributions. The "villain," who was introduced into much of the publicity and who exemplified the wrong reaction to the challenge in each case, was called Herr Ohnemichel (Mr. Include-Me-Out), the sinister survivor of the *ohne mich* generation.

Amongst the intellectual members of the enlightened minority it is reasonable to include writers, composers, and other creative artists. In fact, the cultural standards and developments during the Adenauer era are relevant to an assessment both of the era itself and of the country's future prospects, now that Adenauer has left office.

For a number of reasons the cultural achievements of Western Germany after the Second World War were not comparable to those of the Weimar period. First, owing to Hitler the loss through emigration of great creative figures had very serious consequences, not only in itself but owing to the break in continuity which it involved, the younger generation being deprived of the example and inspiration of the masters. Such names as Thomas Mann, Hindemith, Mies van der Rohe, and Walter Gropius show the extent of the disaster. The almost total loss through emigration or extermination of the Jewish element in the population with its cultural and creative gifts was particularly severe. Secondly, those writers, artists, and musicians who remained were condemned to inaction or frustration owing to Hitler's idiosyncrasies. Thirdly, during the Second World War Germany suffered much greater destruction and dislocation of its national life than during the first. Lastly, the geographical mutilation of the country and the isolation of the Federal Republic from most of Central and Eastern Europe had a limiting and impoverishing effect on its intellectual and artistic life.

There was no cultural miracle during the Adenauer era. Indeed during its early years there was a hard struggle to create the basic conditions for a revival. Before plays and operas could be produced and music performed, the theatres, opera houses, and concert halls had to be restored or rebuilt. Before works of art could be exhibited and museums reopened, the galleries and buildings had to be prepared for them. Before people could afford to buy many books or even modestly priced pictures, their need for clothes, furniture, and dwellings had to be satisfied.

Much was accomplished in a surprisingly short time. But, though the standard of achievement was from one point of view impressive, it was not in the full sense of the word creative. The fine German traditions in singing, playing, acting, and producing reasserted themselves. But the music, operas, and plays that were performed were either classical or, if modern, mostly foreign. The pictures that were shown were mainly art treasures that had been recovered from their wartime storage places or loan exhibitions that had been assembled abroad. The German art of publishing revived, but the books that were sold were either classics or translations. Such modern German plays or books as were produced or published successfully were usually rather thin treatments of topical subjects or themes connected with the war and the Hitler period. German films were banal compared with current standards in France, Italy, Sweden and Britain, and compared with the German film industry itself between the wars.

The long-standing German tradition of having state-subsidized opera houses, theatres, and orchestras together with the wealthy new radio stations were largely responsible for the achievements of German cultural life in its executant aspect. But the shame of the Nazi experience appeared to have destroyed the creative confidence of writers, and they were no longer prepared to deal with important problems in a searching way.

During the latter years of Adenauer's chancellorship, however, a change was already becoming apparent. A few really gifted and original men emerged: amongst them Günter Grass in literature and Hans Werner Henze in music, who were born in 1927 and 1926 respectively. Creative artists in the broadest sense, and in particular writers, began to acquire greater confidence. In more conservative circles they were reproached with having too negative and critical an attitude. Yet the fact remains that they provided the country with an intellectual opposition, and, at a time when the SPD for tactical reasons was exercising a somewhat exaggerated restraint: this in itself was a valuable contribution. Moreover, the weaknesses in German society, which they selected as their targets, were often deserving of criticism; for example, materialism, self-satisfaction, a tendency to forget the troubles of their fellow countrymen in the Soviet zone, and a failure to respond to the intellectual and spiritual challenge presented by communism.

Statesmen are rightly judged not only by the success of their policies but by the achievements, in the broadest sense, of the societies for whose government they have been responsible. Adenauer became chancellor of the German Federal Republic four years after the fall of a regime which, though mercifully short, had morally and spiritually marked the lowest point in German history. It would have been unreasonable to expect a sudden and decisive rise in the cultural level to which Hitler had dragged his country down. From the point of view of culture Adenauer must ultimately be appraised by the soundness of the foundations that he laid and by the quality of the structures that are later built on them. His country's reputation, however, cannot for long be divorced from the intellectual and cultural attainments that form so important a part of its heritage. Not until the German educational system, with its great traditions has faced up to the challenge of the twentieth century, and not until the German creative genius has reasserted itself, will the revival of Germany, as represented by the Federal Republic, be complete.

Bibliography

A. General Reading on the Adenauer Era

Allemann, Fritz René, Bonn ist nicht Weimar, Kiepenheuer and
   Witsch, Cologne, 1956.
Altmann, Rüdiger, Das Erbe Adenauers, Seewald Verlag, Stuttgart-
   Degerloch, 1960.
Bölling, Klaus, Die zweite Republik, Kiepenheuer and Witsch,
   Cologne, 1963.
Dönhoff, Marion Gräfin, Die Bundesrepublik in der Ära Adenauer,
   Rowohlt, Reinbek bei Hamburg, 1963.
Erhard, Ludwig, Wohlstand für Alle, Econ-Verlag GMBH, Düssel-
   dorf, 1957.
Grosser, Alfred, Western Germany from Defeat to Rearmament,
   translated by Richard Rees, Allen and Unwin, London, 1955.
Hiscocks, Richard, Democracy in Western Germany, Oxford Uni-
   versity Press, 1957.
Musulin, Janko, and others, Die Ära Adenauer, Fischer Bücherei,
   Frankfurt, 1964.
Weymar, Paul, Konrad Adenauer, Andre Deutsch, London, 1957.

B. Books and Articles referred to in the Text and Footnotes

Abs, Hermann, "Germany and the London and Paris Agreements," an address given at Chatham House on November 18, 1954, International Affairs, April 1955.

Adenauer, Konrad, "Die deutsche Aufgabe," Rheinische Merkur, March 16, 1956.

Adenauer, Konrad, "Germany and the Problems of Our Time," International Affairs, April 1952.

Adenauer, Konrad, "Unsere beiden Völker," Die Zeit, June 26, 1952.

Alexander, Edward, Adenauer and the New Germany, Farrar, Straus and Cuday, New York, 1957.

Antz, Josef, "Bismarck und seine Wirkung auf das deutsche Volk," Frankfurter Hefte, January 1947.

Augstein, Rudolf, "Konrad Adenauer und seine Epoche," Der Spiegel, October 9, 1963.

Besson, Waldemar, "Regierung und Opposition in der deutschen Politik," Politische Vierteljahrschrift, September 1962.

Bracher, Karl Dietrich, Die Auflösung der Weimarer Republik, Ring Verlag, Stuttgart and Düsseldorf, 1955.

Bulletin. Published by the Press and Information Office of the Federal Republic, Bonn.

Chamberlain, Austen, Down the Years, Cassell, London, 1935.

Coudenhove-Kalergi, Count, "Europe without Europeans," Rheinische Merkur, November 14, 1952.

Craig, Gordon A., The Politics of the Prussian Army 1640–1945, Clarendon Press, Oxford, 1955.

Dönhoff, Marion Gräfin, "Germany Puts Freedom Before Unity," Foreign Affairs, April 1950.

Ellwein, Thomas, Das Regierungssystem der Bundesrepublik Deutschland, Westdeutscher Verlag, Cologne, 1963.

Erhard, Ludwig, Deutsche Wirtschaftspolitik, Econ-Verlag GMBH, Düsseldorf, 1962.

Eschenburg, Theodor, Bemerkungen zur deutschen Burokratie, Institut für Förderung öffentlicher Angelegenheiten e.V., Mannheim, 1955.

Eschenburg, Theodor, Der Beamte in Partei und Parlament, Alfred Metzner Verlag, Frankfurt, 1952.

Eschenburg, Theodor, Die Affäre, Die Zeit, Hamburg, 1962.

Eschenburg, Theodor, Herrschaft der Verbande?, Deutsche Verlags-Anstalt, Stuttgart, 1955.

Eschenburg, Theodor, "Pact against Democracy," Die Zeit, November 10, 1961.

Fecher, Hans and Oberhauser, Alois, Economic Development of Western Germany, District Bank Review, March 1962.

Fischer, Fritz, Griff nach der Weltmacht, Droste Verlag, Düsseldorf, 1964.

Friesenhahn, Ernst, Grundgesetz und Besatzungsstatut. Recht, Staat und Wirtschaft, Vol. II, W. Kohlhammer, Stuttgart and Cologne, 1950.

Gaus, G., "Adenauer," Süddeutsche Zeitung, November 4–5, 1961.

Gooch, G. P., "Bismarck's Legacy," Foreign Affairs, July 1952.

Götz, Hans Herbert, weil alle besser leben wollen, Econ-Verlag, Düsseldorf, 1963.

Grubbe, Peter, "Freiheit, die ich meine," Der Monat, April 1965.

Grundsatzprogramm des Deutschen Gewerkschaftsbundes, 1963, Beschlossen auf dem Ausserordentlichen Bundeskongress des Deutschen Gewerkschaftsbundes am 21 und 22 November 1963 in Düsseldorf.

Jacobsen, Hans-Adolf and Stenzl, Otto, Deutschland und die Welt, Deutscher Taschenbuch Verlag, Munich, 1964.

Jaide, Walter, Das Verhältnis der Jugend zur Politik, Hermann Luchterhand Verlag, Berlin-Spandau, April 1963.

Jaspers, Karl, "The Political Vacuum in Germany," Foreign Affairs, July 1954.

Kitzinger, Uwe, German Electoral Politics, Clarendon Press, Oxford, 1960.

Kitzinger, Uwe, "Western Germany: a Pre-Election Survey," The World Today, March 1961.

Kroll, Hans, Die Sowietische Deutschlandpolitik im Zeichen der Entspannungsbemühungen, Lücke and Lemmermann, Kommanditgesellschaft, Hannover, 1964.

Kuby, Erich and others, Franz-Josef Strauss, Verlag Kurt Desch, Munich, 1963.

Lenz, Hans, Deutsche Politik 1962.

Löffler, Martin, Der Verfassungsauftrag der Presse, Modellfall Spiegel, Verlag C. F. Müller, Karlsruhe, 1963.

Mann, Golo, "Bismarck and Adenauer," Encounter, April 1964.

Meinecke, Friedrich, *Die deutsche Katastrophe*, Eberhard Brockhaus Verlag, Wiesbaden, 1946.

Meinecke, Friedrich, *Politische Schriften und Reden*, herausgegeben von Georg Kotowski, Siegfried Toechte-Mittler, Darmstadt, 1958.

Mikat, Paul, *Aufgaben moderner Kulturpolitik*, A. Henn Verlag und Druckerei, Ratingen, 1964.

Mommsen, Theodor, Letter to Lujo Brentano, January 3, 1902. Kurt Rossmann, *Wissenschaft, Ethik und Politik*, L. Schneider, Heidelberg, 1949.

Oncken, Hermann, *Das Deutsche Reich und die Vorgeschichte des Weltkrieges*, J. A. Barth, Leipzig, 1933.

Opie, R. G., *Western Germany's Economic Miracle*, Three Banks Review, March 1962.

Panofsky, Walter, "Bonn und der Rundfunk," *Süddeutsche Zeitung*, 2nd October 1959.

Picht, Georg, *Die deutsche Bildungskatastrophe*, Walter-Verlag, Freiburg, 1964.

Plischke, Elmer, *The West German Federal Government*, Historical Division, Office of the U.S. High Commissioner for Germany, 1952.

Pounds, N. J. G., *The Economic Pattern in Modern Germany*, John Murray, London, 1963.

Prittie, T., *Germany Divided*, Hutchinson, London, 1961.

Raiser, Ludwig, *Die Aufgaben des Wissenschaftsrates*, Westdeutscher Verlag, Cologne, 1963.

Regierung Adenauer 1949–1963, Franz Steiner Verlag, Wiesbaden, 1963.

Schnabel, Franz, "Das Problem Bismarcks," *Hochland*, October 1949.

Schulz, Klaus-Peter, *Sorge um die Deutsche Linke*, Verlag für Politik und Wirtschaft, 1954.

Schütte, Ernst, *Was Konnen die Hochschulen zur Verkürzung des Studiums tun?*, Mitteilungen des Hochschulverbandes, March 1964, Postverlagsort, Hamburg.

Spaak, M., "Hold Fast," *Foreign Affairs*, July 1963.

Statistisches Jahrbuch für die Bundesrepublik Deutschland, 1964.

Süskind, W. E., "Reformatoren vorm Bundeshaus," *Süddeutsche Zeitung*, January 2–3, 1960.

von Baudissin, Wolf Count, "The New German Army," *Foreign Affairs*, October 1955.

von Cube, Walter, *Ich bitte um Widerspruch* (I Beg to be Contradicted), Verlag der Frankfurter Hefte, 1952.

Waldman, E., *Soldat im Staat*, Harald Boldt Verlag, Boppard/ Rhein, 1964.

Walser, Martin, *Die Alternative oder Brauchen wir Eine neue Regierung?*, Rowohlt Taschenbuch Verlag GMBH, Reinbek bei Hamburg, 1961.

Weber, Max, "Parlament und Regierung im neugeordneten Deutschland (Mai 1918)" and Deutschlands künftige Staatsform," *Gesammelte Politische Schriften*, J. C. B. Mohr (Paul Siebeck), Tübingen, 1958.

Wehner, Herbert, "Es hätte auch schlimmer kommen Können . . .", *Tatsachen-Argumente 1963 Band I* (No. 71, October 1963), Vorstand der SPD, Bonn.

Welchert, H., *Theodor Heuss, Ein Lebensbild*, Athenäum-Verlag, Bonn, 1953.

Wheeler-Bennett, J. W., *The Nemesis of Power*, Macmillan, London, 1953.

White, John, "West German Aid to Developing Countries," *International Affairs*, January 1965.

Index

Abs, Hermann, 32-33, 67
Academics, 13
Adenauer, Dr. Konrad: biographical
details, 2-3, 41, 62-64; chairman
of CDU (British Zone), 2-3;
elected Chancellor, 3, 16, 27;
supporter of Western Alliance
and opponent of Communism, 3;
mixture of human qualities, 17,
42; optimism, 28; principles of
his foreign policy, 29; Petersberg
Agreements, 30-32; attitude to
foreign debts, 32-33; compensation to Jews, 34; first Foreign
Minister, 34; confidence of the
Allies, 35; his tact regarding participation in defence, 35-36, 208;
support for Schuman's Plan and
a European solution for every
major problem, 36; establishment
of relations with Western Alliance, 36; visits abroad, 36-37;
seat in NATO Council, 39; his
personality an asset, 41; interest
in wages, prices, and stabilization
of currency, 44-45; and co-management, 45-46; his policies appealed to electorate, 48-49; his
Carolingian conception, 65, 257,
270; and European economic
integration, 65-68; and European
Defence Community, 70; his
achievements by May, 1955, 72;
little interested in "developing
countries," 74-75; his policy re-

garding the Saar, 75-76; Petersberg Agreements debate, 77-78;
his cabinets, 92-94; the Bundestag no challenge to him, 94-95;
rigid discipline imposed on CDU,
96-97, 105; discussion on Adenauer's 'chancellor-democracy' 96-
98; his policy regarding party government, 98-105; his character
and ability, 113-120; his personality, 120; Federal Chancellor's
Office, 123; attitude to Cabinet,
126-127; attitude towards Bundestag proceedings, 128-129; and
party finances, 135-136; election
technique, 137-138; interference
with Land elections, 138; relations with press, 168-170; television, 174-175; responsibility for
shortcomings of German education and in cultural fields, 205-
206; and rearmament, 208-211;
his influence on prevention of
emergence of strongly nationalist
Right-wing party, 229-230; Kilb
case, 234-235; Strack case, 235-
236; his manoeuvres regarding
chancellorship and presidency in
1959, 237-238; his disrespect for
the presidential office, 238-239;
support of Lübke as president,
238; the *Spiegel* affair, 242-254;
limitations of his foreign policy,
256-283; attitude to communism,
257-270; to Oder-Neisse frontier,

The Author

A leading authority on Germany, RICHARD HISCOCKS has lived, studied, and worked in Germany and surrounding countries during the years of greatest turmoil on the Continent. After leaving Oxford he took his doctorate at the University of Berlin during the first years of the Hitler regime, from 1932 to 1935. In 1945 Dr. Hiscocks commanded a military government detachment in Germany, and from 1946 to 1949 he was British Council representative in Austria.

Dr. Hiscocks' work on *The Adenauer Era* was greatly enhanced by his numerous contacts in the Federal Republic: much of his critical analysis comes from two extended conversations with Adenauer, in which the ex-Chancellor patiently answered numerous questions, and from long talks with six of Adenauer's close collaborators.

From 1952 to 1962 Dr. Hiscocks was United Kingdom member of the United Nations Sub-Commission for the Prevention of Discrimination and Protection of Minorities, an assignment which brought him to New York for three or four weeks each year. He is now Professor of International Relations at the University of Sussex.

Dr. Hiscocks' earlier books include *The Rebirth of Austria*, *Democracy in Western Germany*, and *Poland: Bridge for the Abyss?*

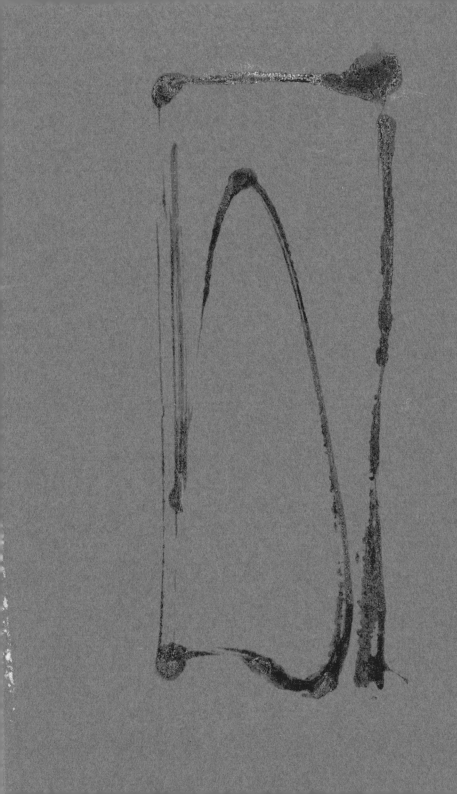